The Facts On File

Dictionary of
Classical,
Biblical
and
Literary
Allusions

The Facts On File

Dictionary of Classical, Biblical and Literary Allusions

Abraham H. Lass
David Kiremidjian
Ruth M. Goldstein

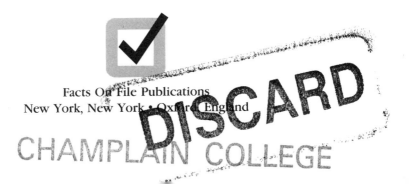

Facts On File Publications
New York, New York • Oxford, England

The Facts On File Dictionary of Classical, Biblical and Literary Allusions

Copyright © 1987 by Abraham H. Lass, David Kiremidjian, and
Ruth M. Goldstein

Library of Congress Cataloging-in-Publication Data

Lass, Abraham Harold, 1907-
      The Facts On File dictionary of classical, Biblical, and literary
allusions.

        1. Allusions—Dictionaries.   I. Kiremidjian, David, 1936- . II. Gold-
stein, Ruth M. III. Title. IV. Title: Dictionary of classical, biblical, and
literary allusions.
PN43.L37   1987   803   86-24366
ISBN 0-8160-1267-9

Composition by Facts On File/Maxwell Photographics
Printed in The United States of America

INTRODUCTION

Not long ago, a *New York Times* drama critic, D.J.R. Bruckner, reviewed a new play, *The Sovereign State of Boogedy Boogedy*. Here are some lines from the opening paragraph of the review:

> Nebuchadnezzar is on trial in "The Sovereign State of Boogedy Boogedy" at the new Federal Theatre; his judges are Shadrach, Meshach, and Abed-Nego and his lawyer is Danielle. But . . . this court room is no place of order and decorum. The judges have all dabbled in petty crime, the angel who rescues the three men from the fiery furnace is a fireman of dubious morals; the king, possibly on the principle that the sins of the sons will be visited on their fathers, is shackled with a charge he threw Danielle into the lion's den and doomed by the handwriting on the wall that spelled the downfall of Belshazzar in the Bible. . . . (July 22, 1986)

What is especially striking about these lines is that they manage to crowd no fewer than eight Biblical allusions into 111 words:

Nebuchadnezzar
Shadrach, Meshach, and Abed-Nego
Danielle
Lion's den
Fiery furnace
Sins of the sons will be visited on their fathers
The handwriting on the wall
Belshazzar

Unless the reader has read his Bible and remembers precisely who these Biblical characters are and what events are being alluded to, he won't be able to make much sense out of this passage. For what he is faced with here, in highly concentrated form, is a set of *allusions*. An *allusion* is a figure of speech that compares aspects or qualities of counterparts in history, mythology, scripture, literature, popular or contemporary culture.

The English language abounds with such allusions. They have, in many instances, become an integral part of the substance and fabric of our language—so much so, that we often use them unaware that they are allusions but fully aware of what they mean in present context.

But the reader who knows neither the original meaning nor contemporary application of the allusion won't understand what he is reading. And he or she will get no help from the writer, who must assume that the reader will have no problem making the necessary connections, and that the original meaning of the allusion, its source, and its specific application in this context are known.

The following sentences are a case in point. Each one contains a fairly common allusion:

If Congress passes this law, it will open up a Pandora's box.

When the Governor recommended that drug traffickers be sentenced to life imprisonment, he said that he did not consider this a draconian law.

In joining the opposition, Farley had crossed his Rubicon.

Horton and James were a modern Damon and Pythias.

Parkinson, all agreed, had a Dr. Jekyll-Mr. Hyde personality.

The prosecutor, pointing to Lily Jones, yelled "You are a Delilah!"

Actually, many modern readers have had little or no firsthand contact with the original events, characters, or ideas being referred to in any given allusion. A limited education may have cut them off from their literary and cultural roots as these are expressed in the allusiveness of our language. Ironically, as writers continue to enrich their writing with these allusions, they simultaneously obscure their message for their uninitiated readers—whose name, to use the Biblical allusion, is legion.

Now back to our *New York Times* drama review. Suppose that our reader has not read or studied the Bible or encountered it as part of his religious experience. He will, of course, be baffled by this passage. And suppose that he wants to find out what these allusions mean. Where can he seek out the original meaning and contemporary point of comparison for each of these allusions? A good desk dictionary? There are several available, but they don't, by any means, list all of these allusions. When they do, they generally tend to provide terse, truncated explanations.

How about an unabridged dictionary? It will usually contain a fuller account than the desk dictionaries. But there is one drawback. Very, very few people own one. Practically every library owns one. But that isn't going to be very helpful to the reader who needs the information quickly and conveniently.

So for the common—and the uncommon—reader, we have put together this dictionary of allusions. It is designed to help him or her track down the source, original meaning, and relevance of more than 1,300 allusions drawn from Greek, Roman, and Norse mythology, Medieval and Arthurian legend, and the Bible. To these sources of allusions central to Western tradition, we have added another: literary characters who have become a part of our language: such as Pecksniff, Falstaff, Faust, Fagin, Macbeth, Hamlet, Tom Sawyer, Huck Finn, Candide, Sydney Carton.

We have confined our list of allusions to the Judaeo-Christian and European literary and cultural traditions because it is simply not possible to read anythng of consequence without encountering them. (Some allusions from Eastern literatures, when such allusions have become "Westernized" and absorbed into our discourse, have also found their way onto the list.)

We have avoided most contemporary allusions except where they clearly have become a part of the fabric of our culture. We have also avoided allusions we felt would be of interest only to scholars and specialists.

In choosing each allusion for this book, we have applied a very simple criterion. If it "rang a bell" with us, if we had encountered it in our reading, we included it. If, after a lifetime of reading, none of us had run across it, we did not include it. We are aware that this method of selection may leave us open to the charges of subjectivity or failure to be inclusive, but since there does not now exist any objective means by which to ascertain how often each allusion occurs in our literature, we have relied upon our cumulative reading experiences to provide you with what we believe is a reliable, workable guide.

A word about the format of the *Dictionary*. It is designed for easy access:

- The entries are alphabetically arranged—as in a dictionary.

- The source and original meaning of each allusion are set down simply and clearly.

- The contemporary meaning in a given context is indicated for each allusion. Where possible, illustrations are supplied.

- Cross-references to variants or related terms are indicated where necessary.

We expect that some readers will tell us, "We like your *Dictionary*. It is very useful. But *why did* you ever include   ,   , and   ?" We also expect that some of our readers are going to tell us, "We like your book. It is very useful. But *why didn't* you include   ,   , and   ?"

To all our readers: We hope you like the book. We hope you find it useful and reader-friendly. And we hope that you will regard this book as an earnest, if imperfect, attempt to do something we felt needed doing in this imperfect world of ours.

                                        A.H.L.
                                        D.K.
                                        R.M.G.

The Facts On File

Dictionary of Classical, Biblical and Literary Allusions

A

Aaron.   Son of Amram the Levite, brother of **Moses** and **Miriam**, and head of the Levite priesthood (Numbers 18:1-7). He was Moses' spokesman and helper during the Ten Plagues; his rod turned into a serpent, in the presence of Pharaoh, and swallowed the Egyptians' rods that had also turned into serpents (Exodus 7:8-12). While Moses was away on Mount Sinai, he made the **Golden Calf**. The Lord refused to allow Aaron and Moses to enter the Promised Land because they had rebelled against His word; on His order, Moses stripped Aaron of his garments and put them on Aaron's son Eleazar. See also: **Plagues of Egypt**. Walt Whitman, in *Democratic Vistas*, indicates the type of reference in modern times: "The magician's serpent in the fable ate up all the other serpents, and money-making is our magician's serpent, remaining sole master of the field."

Abaddon.   Hebrew for "abyss" or "destruction." As "the angel of the bottomless pit," he was king over a swarm of tormenting locusts similar to scorpions (Revelations 9:1, 2, 11).

Abednego.   See **Shadrach, Meshach and Abednego**.

Abel.   See **Cain and Abel**.

Abelard and Heloise.   Pierre Abelard (1079-1142) was a brilliant French philosopher and scholastic theologian, and a very popular lecturer at St. Genevieve and Notre Dame. He emphasized

1

rational inquiry in theology, and espoused Aristotelian logic over Platonic theory. But his popular fame rests in his tragic love affair with Heloise (1101-1164), niece of the Canon Fulbert of Notre Dame and his pupil until he seduced her in 1118. They were secretly married, over Heloise's objections, after the birth of their son Astrolabe. When the affair became known, Heloise became a nun and Abelard a monk—after Fulbert had him castrated. Their correspondence survives. Centuries after, in 1817, the lovers were buried in a single tomb. They are included today in references to immortal, tragic lovers.

Abigail.   The beautiful and understanding wife of Nabal, whose shepherds **David** had protected (I Samuel 25:3). When Nabal refused David supplies, David sought revenge, but was intercepted by Abigail, who thus saved her husband from his fury. After Nabal's death, Abigail became David's wife. She has given her name to any loyal and resourceful handmaiden. In Joseph Heller's *Oh God*, David remembers her more fondly than any of his other wives.

Abraham's bosom.   Paradise, symbolically. Abraham is the first of the great Old Testament patriarchs, the founder of the Hebrew nations, to whom God revealed the tenets of the Jewish religion. When Lazarus the beggar died he "was carried by the angels into Abraham's bosom" (Luke 16:22-23). The contemporary reference is to heavenly rest and peace. See also: **Lazarus and Dives**.

Absalom, o my son.   "And the King (David) said, Is the young man Absalom safe? And Cushi answered, The enemies of my lord the king . . . be as that young man is. And the king . . . wept: and as he wept, thus he said, O my son Absalom, my son, my son Absalom. Would God I had died for thee, O Absalom, my son, my son" (II Samuel 18:24-33). Absalom, the ambitious son of King **David**, rebelled against his father and was killed by Joab. His loss symbolizes the loss to a father of a favorite, handsome, popular but rebellious son.

Aceldama.   The apostle Peter identifies Aceldama as the field in Jerusalem purchased by Judas with the blood money he got for betraying **Christ**: "Now this man purchased a field with the reward of iniquity; and falling headlong, he burst asunder in the midst, and all his bowels gushed out. . . . That field is called . . . Aceldama, that is to say, The field of blood" (Acts 1:18-19). According to Matthew, the chief priests used Judas's blood money to buy a "potter's field, to bury strangers in" (Matthew 27:7-8). Today the word signifies a bloody battlefield. See also: **Judas Iscariot; Matthew, Saint; Peter, Saint.**

Achates.   In Vergil's *Aeneid*, the friend of **Aeneas** whose steadfast loyalty has become a byword for friendship. He is often called *"fidus Achates"*—faithful Achates.

Acheron.   One of the four rivers in **Hades**, the Greek world of the dead. "Acheron" means the river of woe or the river of pain.

Achilles.   Son of Peleus and Thetis; the leading Greek hero in the **Trojan War**, whose story is related in Homer's *Iliad*. His feud with **Agamemnon** and its resolution form the central theme of that epic. He was killed, in the last days of the seige of **Troy**, by an arrow wound in his only vulnerable spot, his heel: in his infancy his mother sought to make him immortal by dipping him in the river Styx, but since she held him by the heel, it was the one part of him vulnerable to death. Hence an "Achilles heel" is any point of particular vulnerability. Violent in his anger, prone to lose his temper, impetuous in his hate, merciless to a foe (**Priam's** sons), Achilles also was capable of tender love (Briseis, **Patroclus**). Though he "sulked in his tent" at one point, he had unquestioned courage and strength—the earliest type of tragic hero, who made a choice from which tragic events followed for himself and for his people.

Actaeon.   A hunter in Greek legend who accidentally saw **Artemis**, the chaste goddess of the hunt, in her bath. The goddess transformed him into a stag and he was then ripped to pieces by his own hounds.

Actium.   The promontory on the western coast of Greece where the navy of Octavian, later the first Roman emperor Augustus, defeated the forces of **Mark Antony** and **Cleopatra**, September 2, 31 B.C. A climactic, decisive defeat.

Adam.   In the Bible, the first man, created by God out of the dust of the earth. Adam and Eve, who was formed from **Adam's rib**

while he slept, lived in innocence in the **Garden of Eden** until the serpent tempted Eve to eat the fruit of the Tree of Knowledge and Eve convinced Adam to eat, too. In punishment, God decreed that henceforth Adam must earn his bread "in the sweat of thy face," and that Eve must bear children in sorrow. He banished them from Eden. Allusions to Adam usually refer to his fall from innocence or to the "original sin" he committed with Eve. See also: **In the Sweat of Thy Face; Tree of Life, Tree of Knowledge**.

Adam's curse.   See **In the sweat of thy face**.

Adam's rib.   "And the Lord caused a deep sleep to fall upon **Adam** and he slept: and He took one of his ribs, and closed up the flesh instead thereof; And the rib which the Lord God had taken from the man, made He a woman, and brought her unto the man. And Adam said, This is now the bone of my bones, and flesh of my flesh: she shall be called Woman, because she was taken out of man" (Genesis 2:21-23). Hebrew: *ishshah*, woman; *ish*, man. This story is the origin of the false notion that men have one rib fewer than women. Today, a lightly ironic term for woman.

Add a cubit to his stature.   "Which of you by taking thought can add one cubit unto his stature?" (Matthew 6:27). The cubit was an ancient measurement, variously given as from 18 to 22 inches. Supposedly the distance from the elbow to the fingertips (from the Latin *cubitus*, "elbow"). By a natural extension and generalization of meaning, to add a cubit to one's stature now means "to go beyond one's natural limitations."

Adonis.   The surpassingly handsome youth, Adonis, was loved by **Aphrodite**, Greek goddess of love, while still quite young, and was killed by a wild boar (perhaps Aphrodite's lover **Ares** in disguise). After his death the anemone flower grew up from his blood. An "Adonis is a young man of godlike beauty.

Aeneas.   Son of Anchises and Aphrodite, a Trojan warrior who appears in Homer's *Iliad* but is better known as the hero of **Vergil**'s epic, the *Aeneid*. As Vergil tells the story, he is destined to escape from burning Troy, and after many years of wandering and hardship, to land in Italy where his descendants will found a new city and an empire that will hold sway over the nations. Aeneas, like

Odysseus, is an archetypal hero. The traits most closely associated with him are piety and faithfulness to family and tradition.

Aeneid. **Vergil**'s epic poem, in Latin hexameter verse. In 12 books, the *Aeneid* recounts the adventures of **Aeneas** from the time he fled the sack of Troy until the fight in which he killed Turnus, the chief warrior of the Latins, in a duel recalling the battle between **Achilles** and **Hector**. Vergil aimed to show the fulfillment of a destiny, that a great empire was eventually to be established by Rome after many hardships were encountered and overcome. Though Aeneas never reaches Rome (founded by his descendants, **Romulus and Remus**) nor even Alba Longa (founded, according to tradition, by his son, Ascanius), he prepared the way. The *Aeneid* furnished Rome and her burgeoning empire with a kind of "national" myth.

Aeolus. A god of the winds, ruler of a floating island, who extends hospitality to **Odysseus** and his men on their long trip home following the **Trojan war**. "Aeolian" refers to storms or winds. An aeolian harp is an instrument that makes music by the action of the wind on stretched strings.

Aeschylus. Earliest (525-456 B.C.) of the three great Greek writers of tragedies (the other two are **Sophocles** and Euripides). Out of approximately 90 plays by Aeschylus, seven have survived, including *The Suppliants, The Persians, Seven Against Thebes,* and *Prometheus Bound*, and the only trilogy that has come down to us, the *Oresteia*, consisting of the *Agamemnon, The Libation Bearers* (*Choephoroe*), and *Eumenides. The Persians* was on the contemporary theme of the Persian War, in which Aeschylus took part; the others dealt with mythological themes. Aeschylus tried to reconcile the ways of the gods with human justice and morality; to teach that excessive pride (*hubris*) brings destruction, and that a criminal taint endures for generations. His style is one of primitive grandeur; he has been likened to the Hebrew prophets.

Aesop. Traditionally the famous writer of fables, mainly about animals. Aesop's fables were not actually written by him: He either collected existing fables or else wrote them in prose. Today Aesopian fables like that of the fox and the sour grapes are referred to in order to illustrate a universal truth.

Agamemnon. Son of **Atreus**, husband of **Clytemnestra**, father of **Orestes**, **Electra** and **Iphigenia**, brother of **Menelaus**. As king of Mycenae, the most powerful city of the Achaeans, Agamemnon was chosen leader of the expedition against Troy (when Helen, the wife of Menelaus, was taken by Paris to that city). At Aulis he was compelled to offer his daughter Iphigenia as a sacrifice to **Artemis**, thereby incurring the hatred of Clytemnestra. Upon returning home, he was murdered in his bath by Clytemnestra and Aegisthus, her lover. His death was avenged by Electra and Orestes. Agamemnon is the subject of the *Agamemnon* by **Aeschylus**, part of the *Oresteia*, and of the *Agamemnon* by Seneca. Today Agamemnon is most remembered for his military prowess and his tragic death. See also: **Trojan War**.

Aglaia. One of the three **graces** or charities.

Aguecheek, Sir Andrew. In Shakespeare's *Twelfth Night* (1599), the silly and cowardly companion of **Sir Toby Belch**, and Olivia's suitor. He is wounded in a duel with Sebastian. One of Shakespeare's memorable comic characters.

Ahab. The king of Israel (I Kings 16-22) who married **Jezebel** and converted to the pagan worship of **Baal**. Later Ahab was killed in battle "and the dogs licked up his blood." In Herman Melville's *Moby Dick* (1851), Ahab is the name of the captain of the whaling ship *Pequod* who obsessively hunts the white whale. Because he betrayed the god of his people and supported the worship of the pagan gods, Ahab's name became a byword for wickedness.

Ahasuerus. See **Esther**.

Ajax (or Aias). Greek warrior in **Trojan War** and described in the *Iliad* as being of colossal stature, second only to **Achilles** in courage and strength. He was, however, comparatively slow-witted and excessively proud. After losing a contest with **Odysseus** for Achilles' armor, he went mad and killed a flock of sheep. After coming to his senses, he killed himself in shame.

Aladdin. The hero of one of the tales of the *Arabian Nights*. Aladdin gets hold of a magic lamp that contains a genie (a spirit in Islamic mythology, also known as a jinn) who will do Aladdin's bidding. Through the genie Aladdin amasses great wealth and in the end marries the sultan's daughter. Aladdin's lamp is symbolic of any vehicle that will bring instant power and fortune.

Alastor.   One of the epithets of **Zeus**, meaning "avenger," or an epithet for any avenging god or spirit.

Alcestis.   The daughter of Pelias and bride of Admetus. **Apollo** offers to allow Admetus to escape death if someone will die for him. Alcestis offers herself as sacrifice, but is rescued from **Hades** by **Heracles** (Hercules). The death and resurrection of Alcestis are the subject of Euripides' tragedy *Alcestis*, produced in 438 B.C. Her name is symbolic of self-sacrifice.

Ali Baba.   Hero of the tale *Ali Baba and the Forty Thieves* in *Arabian Nights*. He overhears the magic words "Open Sesame," which give him entrance to a cave of riches.

Alice.   The heroine of Lewis Carroll's *Alice in Wonderland* (1865), an imaginative and strong-willed little girl who experiences a series of fantastic adventures among strange animals and stranger people. No matter how bizarre her surroundings or the behavior of the characters she encounters, Alice always manages to maintain her composure and insist upon finding the rational explanation, logical solution and literal meaning of the surreal phenomena of Wonderland.

All is vanity.   "Vanity of vanities, saith the Preacher, vanity of vanities; all is vanity . . . and vexation of spirit" (Ecclesiastes 1:2; 2:11,17,26; 4:4,16; 6:9, etc.). "Vanity" in this context does not mean "conceit" so much as "folly" or "emptiness." "I looked on all the works that my hands had wrought, and on the labour that I had laboured to do: and, behold, all was vanity and vexation of spirit" (Ecclesiastes 2:11,26; 4:4,16; 6:9).

All things in common.   The early Christians lived a communal life, sharing wealth and goods as necessary: "And all that believed were together, and had all things in common" (Acts 2:44-45).

All things to all men.   "I am made all things to all men, that I might by all means save some" (I Corinthians 9:22). Paul means that to make converts he approaches Jews as a Jew, Gentiles as a Gentile, and so forth. Today the phrase may suggest a calculating and not wholly admirable adaptability. See also: **Paul, Saint**.

Alpha and Omega. The first and last letters of the Greek alphabet, used metaphorically by Christ to signify He was all things: "I am Alpha and Omega, the beginning and the end, the first and the last" (Revelations 22:13). In modern reference, "the first and the last" of any concept or philosophy.

Alpheus and Arethusa. Arethusa, a young, beautiful and chaste huntress in the service of the virgin goddess **Artemis**, was pursued by the river god Alpheus. When she could no longer escape him, she called to Artemis for help. The goddess changed her into a sacred spring on the island of Ortygia off Sicily. The fountain of Arethusa, noted for its beauty, may still be seen today, and a story is still told, that a wooden cup thrown into the Alpheus River in Greece will reappear in the fountain of Arethusa.

Amazons. A mythical race of women warriors who lived somewhere in Asia Minor or perhaps in Scythia, north of the Black Sea. They customarily removed the right breast so as not to hamper use of the bow, admitted men to their company only for breeding, and exiled or killed male offspring. They appear in various legends: for example, **Achilles** defeated their leader Penthesilea in single combat during the **Trojan War**; **Theseus** fought them successfully and married **Hippolyta** (some sources say Antiope) who bore him **Hippolytus**; **Heracles** succeeded in capturing the girdle worn by the Amazon queen by claiming it as ransom for the captured Melanippe. Generally, an "Amazon" today is a particularly robust, masculine and belligerent woman.

Ambrosia. The nourishment of the Greek gods which conferred immortality upon them. Hence any food especially delicious or fragrant.

Am I my brother's keeper?   See **Cain and Abel**.

Amphitrite. A goddess of the sea; daughter of **Nereus** and Doris, wife of **Poseidon**, and mother of **Triton**. Symbolically, a sea-loving woman.

Ananias. In Acts 5:1-10, Ananias retained for himself part of a sum, from a sale of land, meant for the church; when accused by Peter of lying to God, Ananias dropped down dead, as did his wife Sapphira when she persisted in the deception. Ananias now refers to any liar or deceiver. See also: **Peter, Saint**.

Anathema. "If any man love not the Lord Jesus Christ, let him be Anathema Maranatha" (I Corinthians 16:22). Anathema: Originally, "dedicated to God." Since the ancient Hebrews dedicated their defeated enemies to God by sacrificing them (I Samuel 15), the word came to mean something hateful and to be destroyed. In the New Testament, it means "accursed" (Romans 9:3); thence it passed into Christian usage in formulas of imprecation (e.g., in the Athanasian Creed). In English, it is a noun meaning (1) the thing accursed or (2) the act of cursing; also a quasi-adjective used only in the predicate (not the attributive) position. "Maranatha" is actually two Aramaic words meaning "the Lord has come" (cf. Philippians 4:5). It should be read as a separate sentence, which Paul uses in Corinthians 17 as a concluding benediction for his epistle. Most Christians, not knowing any Aramaic, erroneously took Paul's formula as a solemn intensification of "anathema," and read the two words as a double curse.

Anchises. Member of royal family of Troy. The goddess **Aphrodite** was so enamored of Anchises' beauty that she bore him a child, **Aeneas**. In the *Aeneid*, Vergil describes how Aeneas carries the aging Anchises on his shoulders from Troy after its defeat by the Greeks in the **Trojan War**.

Andromache. The wife of the Trojan warrior **Hector**, and mother of Astyanax. The parting of these three in Book VI of the *Iliad* is one of the most moving passages in that epic. After the fall of Troy, her further destiny is told by Euripides in *The Trojan Women* and *Andromache*. See also: **Trojan War**.

Andromeda. Daughter of Cepheus, king of Ethiopia, and Cassiopeia, who boasted that she was more beautiful than the **Nereids**. **Poseidon** promptly retaliated by sending a sea monster to terrorize the countryside. Andromeda was offered as a sacrifice to appease the monster. Chained to a rock, she was rescued by the hero **Perseus**, just returning from his adventure against the

Gorgons. He showed the head of **Medusa** to the monster, who was turned to stone. Perseus then married Andromeda, whose name was given to a constellation after her death.

Anemone.   See **Adonis**.

Anointed of the Lord.   Those who are chosen by God: His prophets, priests and kings. Suspected of wishing to kill King **Saul**, **David** said, "I will not put forth mine hand against my lord; for he is the Lord's anointed" (I Samuel 24:10).

Antaeus.   One of the race of **giants** in Greek myth, the son of the earth goddess **Gaea** and the sea god **Poseidon**. A wrestler who killed those who could not defeat him, he remained invincible as long as he could renew his strength by touching the earth. He was eventually killed by **Heracles** who held him off the earth and strangled him. Today someone who must renew the source of his strength might be compared to Antaeus.

Anthropophagi.   Literally "eaters of human beings"— cannibals. **Odysseus** meets a race of cannibals, the **Laestrygonians**, who destroy all his ships but the one he himself captained.

Antichrist.   "He is antichrist, that denieth the Father and the Son" (I John 2:18, 22; 4:3). The embodiment of the denial of Christ's principles of goodness and love, variously applied to the Roman Empire; Mahomet; the Pope and the Roman Catholic Church (by Luther and after him by the Puritans); Napoleon; Stalin; Hitler, etc.

Antigone.   Daughter of **Oedipus** and **Jocasta**. After her two brothers, Eteocles and Polyneices, had been killed in the struggle for the kingship of Thebes, her uncle, **Creon**, had forbidden, under penalty of death, the burial of the body of Polyneices because he had fought against the city. However, Antigone managed to pour dust over the corpse as a symbol of burial. She was sentenced by Creon to be entombed alive, but she committed suicide in the cave in which she had been enclosed; and Haemon, son of Creon, to whom she was affianced, also committed suicide. The struggle between Antigone and Creon has been interpreted in its simplest terms as a conflict between private conscience and public duty, between sacred obligations (since the dead had to be buried) and the arbitrary punishment of the state. However, as portrayed in the play *Antigone* by **Sophocles**, both Antigone and Creon are uncompromising and unyielding, she all through her life, he only until just before the end of the play. Today Antigone is symbolic of family piety and extreme self-sacrifice.

Antonio.   The merchant of Shakespeare's *The Merchant of Venice* (1596?), Antonio borrows money from the Jewish moneylender **Shylock** and offers as a bond a pound of his flesh. **Portia**, disguised as a lawyer, defends Antonio against Shylock when Antonio cannot repay the loan. See also: **Pound of flesh**.

Antony, Mark.   Protagonist of Shakespeare's tragedy *Antony and Cleopatra* and Roman general and member of the Roman Triumvirate with Octavian and Lepidus (82-30 B.C.). When the Triumvirate divided Rome's territories, Antony took the eastern provinces. He married **Cleopatra** and their combined forces lost to those of Octavian at the Battle of **Actium** (31 B.C.). Shakespeare drew on the events of Antony's final years. In the play, Antony, by pursuing his great love for Cleopatra, causes his worldly fortunes as general and triumvir to deteriorate. He finally commits suicide after his crushing defeat at Actium.

Aphrodite.   Called Venus by the Romans, Aphrodite was the Greek goddess of love, supposedly born from the foam of the sea on the shores of the island of Cythera. She was given by **Zeus** in marriage to **Hephaestus**, the only ugly god, and was many times unfaithful to him. Her son was **Eros** or **Cupid**, the winged, impish god of physical desire. Among her lovers were **Zeus**, **Hermes**, **Ares**, **Dionysos**, and the mortal **Anchises**. Her symbols are the dove, sparrow, and myrtle tree. Her name is the symbol of love and passion.

Apley, George William.   Protagonist of John P. Marquand's *The Late George Apley* (1937), an urbane gentleman for whom family, class and Boston were the way of life.

Apocalypse.   Greek for disclosure or revelation, refers to the Revelation of St. John the Divine, the final book of the Bible that foretells God's ultimate purpose, the final battle of good and evil, and the **Last Judgment**. Apocalypse is also a generic term for a category of religious writings in Judaism, Christianity and Islam that depicts the world on the brink of a final and decisive battle between good and evil. Apocalyptic has come to be an adjective for total destruction or universal disaster. See also: **John of Patmos**.

Apocrypha.   Greek word meaning "obscure" or "hidden," later "unauthoritative." In Biblical literature, those books rejected by the Jews as uninspired, and hence excluded from the Old Testament, although they were later accepted by the Roman Catholic Church (Council of Trent, 1546) and the Greek Orthodox Church (Synod of Constantinople, 1638) as canonical and divinely inspired. Among them are I and II Maccabees, Judith, Tobit, Ecclesiasticus. Hence, by extension, literature of questionable authorship or authenticity.

Apollo.   In Greek and later Roman mythology, among the most important of the gods. Sometimes given the epithet **"Phoebus"** ("Shining") and identified with the sun. Apollo was the god of intelligence and of understanding, of archers, of healing (he both sent plagues and cured them), and god of music and poetry. He was prophetic himself, and seers and **oracles** were under his protection, particularly the oracle at Delphi. Apollo represents the most highly refined of the virtues esteemed by the Greeks. Today, "Apollonian" means serene, disciplined, well balanced. The opposite is Dionysian. In art, Apollo is represented as an ideal type of young man, as in the famous statue called the Apollo Belvedere. See also: **Delphic Oracle; Dionysos**.

Apostle.   Literally "person sent," originally the 12 followers (also known as disciples, or simply "the Twelve") chosen by Jesus to receive and spread His teachings. The list varies, but the 12 most commonly included are **Peter**, James and John (sons of Zebedee), Andrew, Philip, Barholomew, Matthew, Thomas, James (son of Alphaeus), Thaddeus (or Judas the son of James), Simon the Cananaian (or the Zealot) and **Judas Iscariot**. Paul also bore the title "Apostle of the Gentiles" for the missions of conversion he made to the peoples of the Roman world. Later in the history of Christianity the term came to be applied to chief officials of the church and later still to the first or most eminent Christian missionary in a region. Nowadays the term is frequently used in a secular sense for a zealous advocate of a cause or leader in some movement for reform. See also: **John, Saint; Matthew, Saint; Paul, Saint.**

Apple, the forbidden fruit.   Called also the "apple of knowledge," it hung from the Tree of the Knowledge of Good and Evil in the **Garden of Eden. Adam** and Eve were forbidden by God to taste of it, but were tempted by **Satan** to disobey Him (Genesis 2). A piece is supposed to have stuck in Adam's throat; hence, "Adam's apple." See also: **Tree of Life, Tree of Knowledge.**

Apple of discord.   Only Eris, goddess of Discord and Strife, was not invited to the wedding of Peleus and Thetis. Offended, she came without an invitation and threw among the guests a golden apple with the inscription on it, "To the most beautiful." The apple was claimed by three goddesses: **Hera, Athena** and **Aphrodite.** Since no god wished to settle the dispute, **Zeus** sent **Hermes** to Mt. Ida where **Paris,** son of **Priam** and **Hecuba,** was living at the time. Paris was persuaded by Hermes to be the judge. Each goddess offered him a prize if he should decide in her favor. Hera promised power; Athena promised wisdom and success in war; Aphrodite promised the love of Helen, the most beautiful woman in the world, wife of Menelaus, king of Sparta. Aphrodite's offer prevailed; Paris went to Sparta; Helen went off with him to Troy; and the **Trojan War** ensued. Today, the expression "throwing the apple of discord" means setting the forces of strife in motion.

Apple of the eye, the.   Something or somebody very valuable or dear, especially to God: "Keep my commandments, and live; and my law as the apple of thine eye" (Deuteronomy 32:10; Psalms 17:8; Proverbs 7:2).

Apples of the Hesperides.   See **Hesperides.**

Apples of Sodom.   See **Dead Sea fruit.**

Arabian Nights.   A collection of Eastern folk tales that, according to legend, the princess **Sheherazade** told her husband the Emperor Shahriar on one thousand and one successive nights (the tales are also called *The Thousand and One Nights*). Some of the more famous tales tell of **Sinbad the Sailor, Ali Baba** and **Aladdin**.

Arachne.   The most skillful weaver of Lydia in Asia Minor, who dared to challenge **Athena** (Minerva, as told by Ovid in *Metamorphoses*, VI) to a contest. Maintaining her "**hubris**," Arachne wove scenes of the love affairs of the gods. In anger, Athena tore the web and struck Arachne, who then hanged herself. Out of pity, Athena then changed Arachne into a spider. Today her name is the source of "Arachnida," the scientific designation of the class that includes spiders.

Aramis.   See **Athos, Porthos and Aramis**.

Ararat.   The mountain in eastern Turkey, near the Iranian border, upon which **Noah's ark** is said to have come to rest after the flood waters receded (**Genesis** 8:4). Sometimes called the second cradle of the human race.

Arcadia.   A district in the mountainous region of Greece's Pelopennese, supposed to be an ideal place of peace, harmony and rustic happiness. It is the scene of Sir Philip Sidney's prose romance entitled *Arcadia*, published posthumously in 1590. Sometimes used synonymously with Arden or Eden. Today, "Arcadian" carries the suggestion of rustic simplicity and innocence. See also: **Arden, Forest of; Eden, Garden of**.

archy and mehitabel.   The characters of the cockroach, archy, and the cat, mehitabel, were created by Don Marquis for his newspaper column and were published in various popular collections between 1927 and 1940. The stories, often narrating the raffish adventures of mehitabel, were supposed to have been written at night in a deserted office by the cockroach, who jumped from one typewriter key to another, dispensing with keyboard chores beyond his power, like capitalization (thus "archy" and "mehitabel").

Arden, Forest of.   In Shakespeare's *As You Like It*, the forest of Arden is a quasi-pastoral region where the characters liberate themselves from the constraints of the court in Act I. Hence the term is a variant of the Garden of Eden or any paradisiacal setting of relative innocence and freedom. See also: **Arcadia**; **Eden, Garden of.**

Ares.   The Greek god of war, son of **Zeus** and **Hera**; identified with the Roman Mars.

Arethusa.   See **Alpheus and Arethusa.**

Argonauts.   The Argonauts, or sailors of the good ship *Argo*, were brought together by the hero **Jason** to accompany him in quest of the **Golden Fleece** (a fleece of pure gold taken from a winged ram). They were heroes in their own right, men such as **Heracles, Orpheus, Castor and Pollux**, Peleus, Admetus. After a series of adventures they finally came to Colchis, stole the fleece with the help of **Medea** and after more adventures returned home. The story, told by a number of classical writers, is second only to the Homeric epics in the literature of Greece and is a great source of mythical materials. Argonauts are archetypal heroic adventurers.

Argus.   (1) The shipwright who constructed the *Argo*, supposed to have been the first seagoing ship, in which **Jason** went in search of the **Golden Fleece**. (2) The monster of 100 eyes, slain by **Hermes**; **Hera** then put his eyes into the tail of a peacock. (3) **Odysseus'** faithful dog, who recognizes his master on his return after 20 years. The most familiar modern reference is "Argus-eyed," from the second definition, meaning vigilant.

Ariadne.   Daughter of Minos, King of Crete. She gave **Theseus** a spool of thread which helped him escape from the **Labyrinth** after he had killed the **Minotaur**. She accompanied Theseus on his flight but was abandoned by him on the island of Naxos, where **Dionysos** found her and married her. See also: **Cretan bull.**

Ariel.   The sprite of the air who serves **Prospero** in Shakespeare's *The Tempest*, Ariel can become invisible at will. He embodies the lightness, illumination and sprituality which Prospero employs as principles of his good magic against the brutish evil and ignorance of **Caliban**. As Prospero had bound him in his service after freeing him from imprisonment by the witch Sycorax, so also does Prospero free him when renouncing his magic at the end of the play. Synonymous with the spirit of lightness and magic.

Aristophanes. Greek comic playwright and satirist (445-380 B.C.), a sharp critic of Athenian political policy and cultural trends after the beginning of the Peloponnesian War (431 B.C.) and the death of Pericles (429 B.C.). He is known for the biting humor, ribaldry, lyrics, puns and topical satire in such plays as *Lysistrata*, *The Frogs*, *The Birds*, *The Clouds*. He is often referred to today as the father of comedy.

Aristotle. The Greek philosopher (384-322 B.C.), who at 18 came from Stagira, his birthplace, to Athens to study at **Plato**'s Academy, where he became known as the *nous* (mind) of the school. After Plato's death in 348, he was invited by Philip of Macedon to tutor his son, Alexander. Aristotle emphasized logic and rationality and a strict scientific approach to philosophical questions. Plato had maintained that immutable reality was embodied in pure Forms or Ideas, entities existing outside the mind and accessible to the mind alone, particular and material objects being only an imitation of these eternal types. Aristotle departed from this metaphysical outlook, postulating a duality of Spirit and Matter, in which form is inherent in material being and man's knowledge stems from the experience of the senses, out of which the universal is then perceived. Thus he emphasized deduction and the investigation of concrete objects and situations. His works include the *De Anima*, *Physica*, *Metaphysica*, *Politica*, *Nicomachean Ethics*, *Rhetoric*, *Poetics*. Today Aristotelian has the critical connotation of an objective approach, focusing on the work directly under consideration rather than on its social or moral contexts.

Ark of the Covenant. The Ark of the Covenant was a box carried by poles and containing the tablets of the law given by God to Moses. It accompanied the Israelites in their wanderings and was regarded as a **palladium** for protection against their enemies (I Samuel 5). It was so charged with numinous power that to touch it, even accidentally, brought instant death; the walls of **Jericho** fell down before it (Joshua 6:4-12). **Solomon** placed it in the temple at Jerusalem, where it remained until the **Babylonian captivity**; thereafter nothing more is heard of it, and the Holy of Holies of the Second Temple was empty. In modern synagogues, the Ark is a chest or closet facing the congretation and containing the **Torah**. A small coffer representing the Ark is the most sacred feature of the Christian churches of Abyssinia. In proverbial usage, "to lay hands on the Ark" is to treat sacred things irreverently.

Armageddon.   "He gathered them together into a place called in the Hebrew tongue Armageddon . . . and the cities of the nations fell" (Revelation 16:16). According to prophecy, the place where the forces of evil will make their last desperate stand against God. In modern usage, Armageddon is the battleground of good and evil before Judgment Day; also, the final and totally destructive battle, as in "nuclear Armageddon." See also: **Day of judgment.**

Arrowsmith, Martin.   The doctor protagonist of Sinclair Lewis' *Arrowsmith* (1924). Arrowsmith is torn by the conflict between his devotion to research and the practical world of medicine. He undergoes a series of compromises, frustrations and misfortunes, and eventually retires to a secluded laboratory in Vermont. Often imitated in fiction or non-fiction; e.g., A.J. Cronin's Dr. Andrew Manson in *The Citadel*. An Arrowsmith, in contemporary allusion, would be a highly idealistic person forced to struggle with the temptations and compromises of the real world.

Artemis.   Called Diana by the Romans, daughter of **Zeus** and **Leto**, twin sister of **Apollo**, born on the island of Delos. She was a huntress armed with the bow and quiver, and the protectress of the young. Like **Athena** and **Hestia**, she was a virgin goddess. She was associated with **Selene**, the Moon goddess, and with **Hecate** of the underworld. She played a key role in the numerous myths: the sacrifice of **Iphigenia** (see **Agamemnon**); the death of **Actaeon**, whom she changed into a stag because he saw her bathing; the death of **Orion**; the slaying of the children of **Niobe**; the story of **Phaedra** and **Hippolytus** (see **Theseus**). Artemis and Diana are referred to today as symbolic patronesses of the young woman athlete.

Artful Dodger, The.   Pupil of Fagin and expert pickpocket and thief in Dickens' *Oliver Twist* (1838). The term is also used generally for any skillful thief or trickster engaged in illegal action.

Arthur.   Legendary, perhaps historical, ancient English king who, with the help of the magician **Merlin**, succeeded at age 15 to the throne of his father Uther (see **Pendragon**). He presided over the knights of the **Round Table** at **Camelot** and led them in many battles, as chronicled by Geoffrey of Monmouth, the Norman poet Wace, Chretien de Troyes, and Sir Thomas Malory in *Morte d'Arthur*, among others. Among the many legends associated with Arthur are his enchantment by the **Lady of the Lake**, the quests for the Holy **Grail**, his death in battle with his nephew **Mordred** and burial on the mythical island of **Avalon**.

Asclepius.   The son of **Apollo** and Coronis, Asclepius was instructed in the arts of healing by the centaur Chiron, and knew how to return the dead to life. After being slain by **Zeus**, he was proclaimed the god of medicine (he is held to have been the first physician). His symbol is the staff with the serpent wound about it, the familiar symbol of doctors today.

Asgard.   "Dwelling-place of the Aesir"; home of the gods in Scandinavian and Germanic mythology, where each god had his own palace. It was connected with earth by a celestial bridge, Bifröst, the rainbow. **Odin's** palace was called **Valhalla**.

Ashley, Brett.   In Hemingway's *The Sun Also Rises* (1926), a sophisticated, beautiful Englishwoman, in love with Jake Barnes, but compulsively involved in a series of sterile love affairs. Archetypal of the "Lost Generation." See also: **Barnes, Jake**.

Ashtoreth   (Ashtoroth). The Canaanite and Phoenician goddess of love and fertility, called Astarte by the Greeks and corresponding to the Babylonian Ishtar and the Greek love goddess **Aphrodite**. Her rites were connected with those of the male god **Baal**; the sacred prostitution practised in her temples attracted **Solomon** (Judges 2:13; 10:6; I Samuel 7:3-4; I Kings 11:5, 33).

Astarte.   See **Ashtoreth**.

Atalanta.   The daughter of Iasus (perhaps **Zeus**) and Clymene. She was very swift of foot, and refused to marry anyone unless he first defeated her in a race. If the runner lost, he had to die. After a number of suitors had failed, **Aphrodite** gave the apples of the **Hesperides** to Hippomenes (in some versions Milanion) who carried them into the race and dropped them at crucial points,

knowing Atalanta would pause to gather them up. The ruse worked
and she became his bride. Atalanta is also known for having taken
part in the hunt of the Calydonian boar. An "Atalanta's race" refers
to a contest in which a ruse is successful.

At ease in Zion. The prophet Amos attacked the complacent
rich who loved comfort and luxury, saying "woe to them that are at
ease in Zion" (Amos 6:1). Contemporary usage suggests an application to those who may be called "the idle rich."

Athena. Sometimes called **Pallas Athena** and by the Romans
Minerva, Athena was primarily the goddess of wisdom of the city,
and of civilized life. When she plays the role of battle goddess, it is
usually in defense of these values. One of the virgin goddesses, she
was said to have sprung fully grown and clad for battle from the
head of **Zeus**. After besting **Poseidon** in a contest, she was made
the patron goddess of Athens, her shrine being the **Parthenon**. She
was said to have created the olive tree, and her symbol was the owl.
She remains the classic patroness of wisdom in civilized life.

Athos, Porthos and Aramis. The three friends whose adventures are celebrated in Dumas' *The Three Musketeers* (1844). Athos
is gallant and reserved; Porthos large, strong and somewhat
mediocre intellectually; Aramis mysterious, black-garbed and
pious. The three musketeers have become the symbols of any
companions in adventure.

Atlantis. According to **Plato** in the *Timaeus* and the *Critias*, a
continent to the west of the Pillars of Hercules (the Rock of Gi-
braltar) with an advanced civilization reputed to have existed some
9,000 years before the Greeks. It was reported to have been
destroyed by earthquake and flood. The term "Atlantis" is
sometimes applied to a long-cherished fable or myth of a lost
marvel. See also: **Deucalion; Noah**.

Atlas. One of the race of **Titans** of Greek myth, who was said to
bear the burden of the heavens upon his shoulders. **Heracles**, on
one of his adventures, offended that Atlas refused him hospitality,
showed him **Medusa**'s head, thereby changing him into the rocky
mountain range running east-west across northern Africa. The

image of Atlas holding the burden of earth/sky appears frequently in literature. By extension, anyone who supports a weighty burden.

Atreus.   Son of **Pelops** and Hippodamia, brother of Thyestes, and king of Mycenae, inheritor of the curse that fell upon the House of Pelops. "The house of Atreus" is a reference in modern literature to a cursed or doomed family.

Attic salt.   Particularly acute, graceful, biting wit, as embodied in the satirical comedies of **Aristophanes** (445 B.C.-380 B.C.).

Attila the Hun.   Famous for his wars and depredations against parts of Europe which hastened the final disintegration of the Roman Empire. He was called "the scourge of god." His armies overran the Balkans between 447 and 450, and in 451 he invaded Gaul, withdrawing after a series of defeats. His armies were feared for their violence and cruelty; Attila died in 453. He is the hero of Pierre Corneille's tragedy **Attila** (1667). Colloquially applied to anyone of extreme brutality and violence.

Attis.   A fertility god from an early period of Greek mythology. Attis was the beloved of the earth goddess **Cybele**. Jealous of a mortal love of his, Cybele drove Attis mad; in his frenzy he castrated himself. Violets grew from his blood, and Cybele brought about the resurrection of his body. In the cult of Attis, initiates would imitate this dismemberment of the god in orgiastic rituals.

Aucassin and Nicolette.   From late in the 13th century, one of the best and most popular of the medieval romances (*chantefable*), written in alternating verse and prose sections. Aucassin, the son of the Count of Beaucaire, falls in love with a captive Saracen girl, Nicolette. Their difference in station leads to a complex series of misfortunes and separations, as a result of which Nicolette is made aware that she is a king's daughter; she returns to Aucassin disguised as a minstrel and sings their own story to him. The lovers are happily joined at the end. References today stress the romance rather than its vicissitudes.

Augean stables.   Cleaning the Augean stables was one of the **labors of Heracles**. King Augeas of Elis in Greece had an immense herd of oxen whose stables had not been cleaned in 30 years. To accomplish the task, Heracles diverted the waters of the Alpheus River through the stables. Hence, the task of clearing up a gigantic mess is termed "cleaning the Augean stables"; sometimes applied to the efforts of a reform government upon succeeding a corrupt one.

Aurora.   Latin name of **Eos**, goddess of the dawn, whom **Homer** called "rosy-fingered." She loved several handsome young men, **Orion** among them, but her most famous mortal lover was Tithonus, son of Laomedon, king of Troy. Memnon, son of Aurora and Tithonus, became king of the Ethiopians and later fought in the **Trojan War** on the side of the Trojans. He was slain by **Achilles**. Aurora's tears over her son's death were said to glisten in the morning dew on the grass. Contemporary reference to Aurora is usually in terms of an Homeric "rosy-fingered"—that is, a romantic description of dawn. The "aurora borealis" is the northern lights, a luminous meteoric phenomenon caused by solar particles.

Avalon.   An island paradise in the western seas where King **Arthur** and the other heroes of the Arthurian legends went after they died. "The Isle of Apples" to which the dying Arthur was taken.

Avernus.   A lake in Campania in central Italy. Its strongly mephitic vapors led people to believe it was the entrance to the lower world; the name has become identified with hell itself, as in Vergil's line of verse *Facilis descensus Averno*, "easy is the descent to Avernus" (*Aeneid* VI, 126). Hence, "easy is the descent to Avernus" by extension means "easy is the fall to destruction."

B

Baal. The male consort of **Ashtoreth** (or Astarte) and the god of fertility of the Canaanites and Phoenicians, Baal has come to represent the false pagan worship to which the Israelites fell prey.

Babbitt, George F. The hero of Sinclair Lewis' novel *Babbitt* (1922). He is a typical, standardized, middle-class American, holding to all the bourgeois values. A Babbitt is a conformist, content to toe the line and pursue material comfort and success.

Babel. "And the whole earth was of one language, and they said, Go to, let us build us a city and a tower, whose top may reach heaven . . . And the Lord said, Behold, the people is one, and have all one language; and this they begin to do . . . let us go down and there confound their language that they may not understand one another's speech . . . Therefore is the name of it called Babel" (Genesis II:1-9). The story of the tower of Babel in the land of Shinar (Babylonia) preserves confused memories of the Babylonian ziggurats, great towers in the shape of stepped pyramids, used for ancient sanctuaries. Here the tower is a symbol of man's aspiring arrogance, rebuked by God. The name Babel (literally, "the gate of God") is a Hebrew rendering of the name **Babylon**. In modern English, Babel simply means a noisy confusion. See also: **Babylonian captivity**.

Babes and sucklings, Out of the mouths of. "Out of the mouth of babes and sucklings hast thou ordained strength" (Psalms:

8:2). The psalm praises the Lord for the excellence of the things He has created, and the phrase is so used in contemporary allusion.

Babylon. The grand, luxurious and wicked city on the Euphrates River, the place to which the Jews were exiled. References to it occur throughout the Bible. Refers today to grandeur, wickedness and wealth. See also: **Babylonian captivity.**

Babylon, Scarlet whore of. The whore who sits upon a scarlet-colored beast with seven heads and ten horns, a cup of abominations in her hand, and written on her forehead the words "Mystery, Babylon the Great, The Mother of Harlots and Abominations of the Earth" (Revelation 17:1-7). In John's allegory she represented the Roman Empire; some Protestant exegesis interprets her as the Roman Church. See also: **Apocalypse; John of Patmos.**

Babylonian captivity. The period in ancient times during which the Jews served out their exile in **Babylon** (597-538 B.C.). By extension, the phrase was used for the exile of the popes at Avignon in the late Middle Ages (1309-77).

Bacchae. Title of a tragedy by Euripides, in which **Dionysos**, or **Bacchus**, comes to Thebes, which is ruled by his cousin, Pentheus, who objects to the introduction of Bacchic worship. Dionysos instills a frenzy into the women, and, when they discover Pentheus spying upon them, causes them to tear him into pieces as if he were an animal. The play shows the awesome nature of the Bacchic ritual, the effect of occult cabala upon human reason, and the results of the excesses of mystic belief. It is now regarded as one of Euripides' most powerful plays. See also: **Bacchantes.**

Bacchanalia. The feast and celebrations of **Bacchus** (the Greek Dionysus), god of wine. His rites were characterized by drunkenness, disorder and orgies. Hence, any dissolute and riotous celebration.

Bacchantes. Also known as **Bacchae**, **Maenads**, or Thyiades, they are female followers of **Bacchus**, or **Dionysos**. They were also priestesses who took part in the wild celebrations or orgies at the festivals of Bacchus and worked themselves up into an ecstatic frenzy. In modern usage, orgiastic female celebrants. See also: **Bacchanalia**.

Bacchus.   Latin name for **Dionysos**, and a form of another Greek name for the same god.

Balaam's ass.   Balaam, a heathen prophet, refused the command of the king of Moab to curse the Israelites (Numbers 22:1-20). He is remembered now only for his talking ass, who remonstrated with her master in reasonable language when Balaam tried to beat her.

Balder.   Son of the chief Norse god, **Odin**. Beautiful and just, he was the favorite of the gods. Most stories about him concern his death, when a blind god was tricked into striking him with mistletoe, the only thing that could kill him. Some scholars think that his passive, suffering figure was influenced by that of Christ.

Balm in Gilead.   "Is there no balm in Gilead; is there no physician there?" (Jeremiah 8:22). Gilead was known for medicines and aromatic herbs; the phrase "balm of Gilead" is now applied generally to any kind of healing or solace.

Banquo.   A noble man and comrade of Macbeth in Shakespeare's *Macbeth*. He is murdered by **Macbeth**'s henchman, and later his bloody ghost appears at Macbeth's table to presage Macbeth's tragic doom.

Barabbas.   It was the custom in the Holy Land during Roman times that the people could choose to free one condemned man after his trial. At the trial of Jesus, Barabbas the thief (and, according to Luke and Mark, a seditionist and murderer as well) was chosen to be freed instead of Jesus. The case has become one of the popular examples of rank injustice, and a Barabbas is any criminal who escapes unfairly the consequences of his crime.

Bardell, Mrs.   The landlady in Dickens' *Pickwick Papers* (1837) who sues Mr. Pickwick for breach of promise.

Bard of Avon.   Shakespeare, born at Stratford-on-Avon. Also, Sweet Swan of Avon—from Ben Jonson's elegy, "To the Memory of my Beloved, the Author, Mr. William Shakespeare."

Bardolph. Falstaff's volatile companion in Shakespeare's *Henry IV, Parts One and Two*.

Barkis. The carrier in Charles Dickens' *David Copperfield* (1850) who courts and wins Clara Peggotty by having David tell her "Barkis is willin'."

Barkley, Catherine. In Ernest Hemingway's *A Farewell to Arms* (1929), the mistress of Frederic Henry; a beautiful English volunteer nurse on duty in Italy. Serenely selfless, incapable of cynicism, she focuses every facet of her profoundly feminine sensibility on her lover. She escapes with him to Switzerland after becoming pregnant, and dies in childbirth. See also: **Henry, Frederic**.

Barmecide. In the *Arabian Nights* story "The Barber's Sixth Brother," a rich Barmecide prince sets a wholly illusory feast before a poor Schacabac, who eats and enjoys all the empty dishes, then feigns drunkenness after drinking the imaginary wine, and knocks down the prince. Seeing the comedy of the situation and the wisdom of the Schacabac, the prince provides him with a real feast. Hence Barmecide refers to any attractive illusion.

Barnes, Jake. Hero of Ernest Hemingway's *The Sun Also Rises* (1926); a journalist made impotent by a war wound, in love with the beautiful and promiscuous Brett Ashley. A defensive cynicism, drinking, sport and friendship help him live with his inner torment. See also: **Ashley, Brett**.

Bassanio. **Portia**'s fiance in Shakespeare's *The Merchant of Venice*. He wins her by choosing a lead casket, showing his lack of avarice, and receives the money which his friend **Antonio** borrowed from the Jew **Shylock** in order to help him woo her.

Bathsheba. The wife of Uriah, and beloved of King **David**. After Bathsheba became his mistress, David ordered that Uriah be killed in the forefront of battle. The King subsequently married her, and she bore him **Solomon** (II Samuel 11).

Baucis.   See **Philemon and Baucis**.

Bazarov, Yevgeny Vassilyitch.   The arrogant, intellectual hero of Turgenev's *Fathers and Sons* (1862). Almost despite himself, he holds only with reason and progress, rejecting traditional human beliefs and affections. He represents the generation of "nihilists" in mid-19th-century Russia.

Beatitudes.   The opening words of the **Sermon on the Mount** (Matthew 5:3-11) are nine short verses, each beginning with the word "blessed" (Latin: *beatus*) and called on that account the "beautitudes." In context, they constitute an eschatological prophecy that the humble of this world will inherit the messianic kingdom. In modern quotations they are cited separately and applied as needed; for example, "blessed are the peacemakers."

Beatrice.   (1) The beloved of Dante, and symbol of divine love, who leads the poet through his allegorical journey of damnation and salvation in the *Divine Comedy*. In the *New Life* Dante sang of his love for her. (2) The sharp-tongued, quick-witted heroine of Shakespeare's *Much Ado About Nothing* (1598-99) who falls in love with **Benedick**, the man she professes to loathe and with whom she carries on continual, pointed banter.

Beauty and the beast.   A fairy tale in which a merchant, in order to bring presents to his daughters, makes certain commitments to an ugly monster. When called to account, he is forced to surrender to the monster his youngest and most beautiful daughter. This "Beauty" sacrifices herself and goes with the Beast, gradually grows full of pity and then affection for him and consents to marry him—whereupon he is transformed into a handsome Prince, freed by her love from a wicked enchantment.

Beelzebub.   Literally "the lord of the flies," the prince of devils, and generally one of **Satan**'s closest chiefs. He is mentioned in Matthew 10:25, 12:24-27, Mark 3:22, Luke 11:15-19 and figures prominently in Milton's *Paradise Lost*.

Be fruitful and multiply.   "Be fruitful, and multiply and replenish the earth" (Genesis 1:28; 9:1). God's commandment to **Adam** and to **Noah** is sometimes cited as an argument against either contraception or clerical celibacy, depending on whether one is Catholic or Protestant. By any interpretation, it implies that man's procreative powers are expressly sanctioned by God.

Begats.   *Begat* is an archaic form of *beget*. The word recurs like a refrain in the genealogical sections of Genesis (Genesis 5, 10, 11) which are called in consequence "the begats." These chapters are notorious as the dullest in the entire Bible.

Behemoth.   Literally "great beast." The behemoth is cited in **Job** 40:15-24 by the voice out of the whirlwind as representing the Lord's creative power. Today the word retains its original meaning.

Belch, Sir Toby.   A character in Shakespeare's *Twelfth Night*, Sir Toby Belch is given to riotous drinking bouts, which he finances by persuading the stupid Sir Andrew Aguecheek that he is promoting Sir Andrew's courtship of his niece, Olivia. See also: **Aguecheek, Sir Andrew**.

Bellerophon.   Legendary hero of Corinth. When the guest of King Proetus of Argos, he rejected the advances of Queen Antea. Enraged, she accused him of attempting to seduce her, and Proetus sent him to Iobates, King of Lycia, with a sealed letter requesting Iobates to put the bearer to death. Iobates sent Bellerophon to fight the monster **Chimaera**, but with the assistance of **Athena**, Bellerophon caught the winged horse, **Pegasus**, who helped him slay the Chimaera. Later, Bellerophon attempted to ascend to heaven upon Pegasus, but fell off its back to the earth, while Pegasus flew on to the stars among which he dwells.

Belshazzar.   Son of **Nebuchadnezzar**, and the last Chaldean king of **Babylon**. It was at Belshazzar's feast (Daniel 5:1-30) that "the handwriting on the wall" appeared. (See **Mene, mene, tekel, upharsin**.) When Belshazzar saw it, he was shaken by palsy. "Belshazzar's palsy" may be applied to a fevered ague from many causes. Belshazzar is an archetypally corrupt and decadent ruler tottering on the brink of overthrow or disaster.

Benedick.   The witty misogynist in Shakespeare's *Much Ado About Nothing*. He becomes devoted to **Beatrice**, thinking she loves him, and in the end marries her. His name is often used to describe a reluctant lover or bachelor. Beatrice and Benedick are the archetypes for all lovers who commence their affection by trading quips and joking insults.

Ben-Hur. Lew Wallace's novel, *Ben-Hur, a Tale of the Christ* (1880), is set in Rome at the time of Christ. Ben-Hur is a Jew high in Roman favor. After the treachery of his friend Messala, whom Ben-Hur defeats and cripples in a chariot race, Ben-Hur follows Christ and is converted.

Benjamin. Youngest of two children born to **Jacob** and his second wife, **Rachel**, and founder of one of the twelve tribes of Israel.

Bennet, Elizabeth. The sharply intelligent, quick-tongued and rather overly self-assured heroine of Jane Austen's (1775-1817) novel *Pride and Prejudice* (1913). Her parents, designated in the novel simply as Mr. and Mrs. Bennet, offer a study in contrasts: her father, a gentleman with a modest estate in Hertfordshire, is drily humorous, sarcastic and rather remote from the cares of marrying off five daughters with only modest portions, while the silly, frivolous, gossiping Mrs. Bennet cares for nothing else. Despite her confirmed prejudice against the haughty aristocrat Fitzwilliam Darcy, Elizabeth ends up falling in love with him and agreeing to be his wife. See also: **Darcy, Fitzwilliam**.

Beowulf. Perhaps the earliest poem of any substance in a modern language, an epic in alliterative Old English verse of approximately 3,200 lines. The poem's hero Beowulf is the strongest and bravest vassal at the court of Hygelac, King of the Geats. Beowulf battles the monster **Grendel** and finally, through an act of superhuman endurance and strength, defeats him. The subject matter, originating in Norse legend, blends myth with historical event, and finally fuses with Christianity. Beowulf was written down, probably by a single, unknown poet, about the year 700 A.D.

Berling, Gösta. In Swedish novelist S.O.L. Lagerlöf's (1858-1940) *Gösta Berling's Saga* (1891), an unfrocked clergyman turned vagabond; a warm-hearted, impulsive man, the leading spirit among the gentleman pensioners at Ekeby.

Bethel. In Hebrew, "the house of God." For the story of the founding of the shrine at Bethel, see **Jacob's ladder**. In English usage, a Bethel (as a common noun) is a nonconformist chapel.

Bethesda, Pool of. A pool in Jerusalem. It cured whoever stepped into it of whatever disease he had. A cripple complained to Jesus that he had waited 38 years by the pool but someone always "steppeth down before me;" whereupon Christ cured the man (John 5:1-9). Hence the term would be used in allusion for a situation of unfair preferment or a situation where one is passed over through some physical or mental incapacity.

Better to marry than to burn. "I say therefore to the unmarried and widows, It is good for them if they abide even as I. But if they cannot contain, let them marry: for it is better to marry than to burn" (I Corinthians 7:8-9). Paul's estimate of matrimony may strike married people as churlish and insensitive, but then, Paul was a bachelor. "To burn" is translated in the Revised Standard Version as "to be aflame with passion." There is no indication, as some have thought, that it means "to burn in Hell as a punishment for fornication." See also: **Paul, Saint**.

Between Scylla and Charybdis. See **Scylla and Charybdis.**

Big Brother. In George Orwell's *1984* (published in 1949), the despotic leader of a society, whose ubiquitous image stares out of countless posters above the slogan "Big Brother is watching you." He represents the pervasive presence of totalitarian rule.

Big-Endians and Little-Endians. During his sojourn among the Lilliputians in Swift's *Gulliver's Travels*, *Gulliver* describes a war caused by a controversy concerning whether an egg is properly broken at the big end (the heretic view) or the little end (orthodox view). The petty factionalism satirizes Catholic-Protestant theological disputes. See also: **Lilliput**.

Blessed are the meek. "Blessed are the meek: for they shall inherit the earth" (Matthew 5:5). See also: **Beatitudes; Sermon on the Mount, The.**

Blifil, Master. Squire Allworthy's nephew and Tom's half-brother in Henry Fielding's *Tom Jones* (1749). He pretends to be honest and virtuous, but is actually hypocritical, scheming and vindictive. See also: **Jones, Tom**.

Bligh, Lieutenant William.   Real-life British naval officer, commander of H.M.S. *Bounty*, fictionally characterized as a fanatical, raging, and at times nearly insane captain in Charles Nordhoff (1887-1947) and James Norman Hall's (1887-1951) *Mutiny on the Bounty* (1932).

Blind Bard, The.   An appellation of **Homer**.

Blind lead the blind.   "Let them alone: they be blind leaders of the blind. And if the blind lead the blind, both shall fall into the ditch" (Matthew 15:14; Luke 6:39). Jesus' condemnation of the **Pharisees** (q.v.) is often applied generally to any misguided leadership or instruction.

Bloom, Leopold.   Hero of James Joyce's *Ulysses* (1921). Joyce's celebrated novel follows the modern "Ulysses" as he voyages through a complete day in Dublin on June 16, 1904. (June 16 has since become known as Bloomsday.) His common rounds as he canvasses for ads, remembers his past, encounters the perils and pleasures of his city, correspond to the heroic episodes of **Homer**'s epic. Bloom, a Jew, is kind, generous, helpful and scientifically-minded. A persecuted but forgiving victim of a decaying world. See also: **Odysseus**.

Bluebeard.   The ogre-hero of Charles Perrault's tale (1697). Bluebeard entrusts his latest young wife with the key to a room never opened and goes on a trip; curiosity overcomes the young woman, who finds in the room the bodies of Bluebeard's erstwhile spouses. The key acquires an unremovable red stain, and Bluebeard on his return is about to kill her when she is saved by the arrival of her brothers. "Bluebeard" now means any murderous spouse or man who deliberately plans the death of a wife or mistress.

The blue bird of happiness.   The object of a search by the woodcutter's children, Tyltyl and Mytyl, in Maurice Maeterlinck's drama *The Blue Bird* (1909). Used symbolically today for "happiness."

Bone of my bones.   **Adam** said, "This is now bone of my bones and flesh of my flesh" (Genesis 2:23). The fact that Eve was made of Adam's body was formerly used as an argument for the natural subordination of women (see **Adam's rib**). Today the phrase "bone of my bones" is used to indicate any very close relationship, as between parent and child. Grammatically it illustrates the Hebrew "genitive superlative," cf. "Song of Songs," "holy of holies."

Bones, Billy.   In R.L. Stevenson's *Treasure Island* (1883), a mysterious guest at the Admiral Benbow Inn. An ex-pirate, he possesses the map of Treasure Island, which after his death falls into the hands of Jim Hawkins. See also: **Hawkins, Jim**.

Bonnard, Sylvestre.   The modest, shy scholar of Anatole France's *The Crime of Sylvestre Bonnard* (1881). He tries to do good by involving himself in the lives of other people.

Book of life.   The book in which the names of those who are to be saved on Judgment Day are written, "and whosoever was not found written in the book of life was cast into the lake of fire" (Revelations 3:5; 20:12-15; 21:27).

Books, Of making many.   "Of making many books there is no end, and much study is a weariness of the flesh" (Ecclesiastes 12:12).

Boreas.   Generally understood as the north wind, Boreas was in Greek mythology the son of Astraeus and **Eos**, and brother of the other winds, **Zephyrus** (the west wind), Notus (the south wind) and Eurus (the east wind).

Bottom, Nick.   In Shakespeare's comedy *A Midsummer Night's Dream*, the oafish Bottom, the weaver, becomes the tool of the mischievous sprite **Puck**, who affixes an ass's head to him, and so bewitches **Titania**, queen of the fairies, that she becomes enamored of Bottom when she awakens.

Bottomless pit.   See **Abaddon**.

Bountiful, Lady.   The name for a kind and benevolent lady, from a character so named in Farquhar's *The Beaux' Stratagem*. (1707).

Bovary, Emma.   Heroine of Gustave Flaubert's novel *Madame Bovary* (1857). Raised on romantic illusions, she becomes disenchanted and then mortally bored with her marriage to the mediocre Charles Bovary. She seeks adventure and passion in two adulterous affairs with men who are merely exploiting her, becomes more and more immersed in vice and debt until she escapes through suicide by poison. Her fate symbolizes the humiliating traps and moral emptiness of bourgeois experience.

Bowels of compassion.   "Whose hath this world's good, and seeth his brother have need, and shutteth up his bowels of compassion from him, how dwelleth the love of God in him?" (I John 3:17). The bowels were anciently believed to be the seat of the emotions; to shut up the bowels of compassion is to withhold compassion.

Brahma.   The Hindu Godhead or Absolute, conceived in his personal form. In the Hindu "**tri murti**," or three forms of the godhead, Brahma is the creator. See also: **Vishnu; Shiva**.

Brand of Cain   (Mark of Cain). See **Cain and Abel**.

Brave new world.   In Shakespeare's *Tempest*, **Prospero**'s daughter **Miranda**, who has been brought up in isolation on an island, proclaims the words "O brave new world/That has such people in't" (Act V, 1:182-3), on seeing the persons whom her father has assembled on the island and on whom he has practiced his magic during the play. Aldous Huxley used the phrase ironically as the title of his dystopian novel, *Brave New World* (1932). Current usage is generally ironic, referring to the sterile uniformity and bureaucratization of modern life.

Bread cast upon the waters.   "Cast thy bread upon the waters: for thou shalt find it after many days" (Ecclesiastes 11:15). That is, be generous without thought of reward, and the reward will come to you.

Bread of affliction.   "Feed him with bread of affliction and with water of affliction" (I Kings 22:27; II Chronicles 18:26). A metaphor for suffering. No distinction is intended between the bread and water affliction; this is an example of emphatic reduplication characteristic of Biblical language.

Breath of life. "And the Lord God formed man of the dust of the ground, and breathed into his nostrils the breath of life, and man became a living soul" (Genesis 2:7; also, 6:17; 7:15, 22). Many ancient peoples identified the soul with the physical breath, as is shown by the fact that in many languages the same word means both "spirit" and "wind" or "breath"; for instance, the Latin *spiritus* (cf. respiration); the Greek *pneuma* (cf. pneumatic); the Hebrew *Ruach*.

Bricks without straw. "And Pharaoh commanded the same day the taskmasters of the people . . . saying, Ye shall no more give the people straw to make brick, as heretofore: let them go and gather straw for themselves" (Exodus 5:6-7). Straw was used to bind the clay for making bricks. The Hebrews were thus obliged to provide their own raw materials for their work, on their own time, and without any reduction in their quota of production. Thus the phrase now means to require work under unreasonable or impossible conditions.

Brimstone and fire. Brimstone is sulphur, which burns with a suffocating smell. Fire and brimstone are repeatedly mentioned in the Bible as symbols of divine punishment for evildoers, both in this world and the next. Examples may be found in Genesis 19:24; Deuteronomy 29:23; Job 18:15; Psalms 11:6; Isaiah 30:33; 34:9; Revelations 21:8. See also: **Lake of fire and brimstone**.

Brobdingnagians. The race of giants **Gulliver** meets in Book Two of Swift's *Gulliver's Travels* (1726). Though the kingdom of giants is peaceful and orderly, the king of Brobdingnag nonetheless keeps a standing army. Swift uses the giants to satirize the grossness and selfishness of mankind. Today Brobdingnagian means huge or colossal.

Brother's keeper, Am I my? See **Cain and Abel**.

Brownlow, Mr. The benefactor of Oliver Twist in Dickens' *Oliver Twist* (1838). He saves Oliver from the vicious courts, cares for him, and adopts him. See also: **Twist, Oliver**.

Brynhild   (or Brunhild). A princess loved by the hero **Sigurd** in the *Volsunga Saga*. In the Teutonic version, she is known as Brunhild, and she is a Valkyrie, one of the maidens who ride through the air in full armor and oversee the battles of men. Her beloved in this version is known as Seigfried. She is one of the major characters in Richard Wagner's cycle of operas *The Ring of the Nibelungs*.

Budd, Billy.   The handsome, honest and innocent sailor in Melville's *Billy Budd* (written in 1891, published in 1924). He is falsely accused by the vicious and envious John Claggart of mutiny, and strikes him a fatal blow when Claggart lies to Captain Vere. Billy is then court-martialed and sentenced to death by hanging. Today signifies an innocent, naive and perhaps simple-minded youth.

Buddenbrooks.   A novel (1901) by the German writer Thomas Mann (1875-1955) about the declining fortunes of a family of wealthy German merchants, the Buddenbrooks. Johann Buddenbrook, the family patriarch, established the family's fortune through less than scrupulous business practices and elevated their status; but with each succeeding generation, the Buddenbrook heirs grow increasingly antibourgeois. As their will to pursue financial gain dwindles, so does their strength, their health and their fortune.

Buddha.   The Buddha is considered in some religions of the East to be one of the last incarnations of the Godhead, and the founder of Buddhism. His historical name is Siddhartha Gautama and he is said to have lived in the sixth century B.C. The son of a princely family, he renounced all worldly possessions and led the life of an ascetic, teaching that enlightenment and escape from life's endless cycles can only be achieved through freeing oneself from desire.

Bumppo, Natty.   The brave, loyal, "natural man" protagonist of James Fenimore Cooper's *Leatherstocking Tales* (1823-41), he remains an outcast from white society, preferring the life of the forest and trail. The archetypal frontiersman.

Bunyan, Paul.   American folk hero, a lumberman of fantastically huge proportions who figures in the tall tales of James Stevens.

Burning bush. "Now **Moses** kept the flock of Jethro his father in law, the priest of Midian: and he led the flock to the backside of the desert, and came to the mountain of God, even to Horeb. And the angel of the Lord appeared unto him in a flame of fire out of the midst of a bush: and he looked, and, behold, the bush was not consumed. And . . . God called to him out of the midst of the bush, and said, Moses, Moses, . . . I am the God of Isaac, and the God of Jacob. And Moses hid his face; for he was afraid to look upon God" (Exodus 3:1-6). The episode of the burning bush is one of several epiphanies (appearances of the deity) of **Yahweh** in the form of fire. The angel of the Lord is identical with the Lord himself; at this early period the angels are not a separate order of beings, but rather a temporary embodiment of the deity. The burning bush is a symbol of God's immanence in nature; the crucial element in the image is the power of the divine fire to burn without consuming.

Butler, Rhett. Swashbuckling blockade-runner, in love with Scarlett O'Hara, in Margaret Mitchell's Civil War novel *Gone With the Wind* (1936). Although she's in love with Ashley Wilkes, her refined though weak neighbor, Scarlett takes Rhett as her third husband, losing him just when she realizes she loves him more than Ashley. Butler represents the pragmatic, materialistic values of the emerging new South, while the ineffectual Ashley clings to the chivalric code of that South destroyed by the Civil War. See also: **O'Hara, Scarlett.**

Buzfuz, Serjeant. The barrister who pleads **Mrs. Bardell**'s case in court against Mr. **Pickwick** in Charles Dickens' *Pickwick Papers* (1836-37).

By bread alone. "It is written, Man shall not live by bread alone, but by every word that proceedeth out of the mouth of God" (Matthew 4:4; Luke 4:4; cf. Deuteronomy 8:3). The phrase "not by bread alone" is still used as a rebuke against materialistic values.

By their fruits ye shall know them. See **False prophets.**

Byzantine. From the ancient city of Byzantium, on whose site in 330 A.D. the Emperor Constantine established Constantinople (now Istanbul) as the capital of the Eastern sector of the Roman Empire. Labyrinthine; intricately involved; turgid.

C

Cabala. From the Hebrew word *gabbalah* (tradition); a tradition of mystical interpretations of scripture that arose between the 9th and 13th centuries. It was based on a doctrine of "emanations" which linked infinite to finite, and a conviction that hidden truths were revealed in the numbers which emerged from manipulating the letters of a given text.

Cadmus. Founder of the ancient Greek city of Thebes and its first ruler. He slew a dragon that guarded a sacred well and, on the instructions of **Athena**, sowed its teeth in the earth. The teeth sprang up into armed men who at once entered into battle; the five who survived became the founding fathers of Thebes. In their old age, Cadmus and his wife Harmonia were transformed into immortal serpents.

Caduceus. The wand carried by **Hermes** (usually represented with two serpents twined around it) and later by Greek and Roman heralds in token of messages they bore.

Caesar's wife. "Caesar's wife must be above suspicion." Pompeia, wife of Caesar, was discovered to be having an affair with Clodius, a profligate young noble. Clodius was tried and Caesar divorced Pompeia. At the trial, Caesar declared that he knew nothing of the details of the affair. Asked why he had then divorced his wife, Caesar replied, according to Roman historian Suetonius (75-150 A.D.), "My family should be free not only from guilt but even from suspicion," or, according to Greek writer Plutarch (46-120 A.D.), "Because I thought that my wife should not even come under suspicion." Hence the modern expression that, "like Caesar's wife," a person in high office must act in such a way that no suspicion can fall on him.

Caiaphas.   After Jesus had raised **Lazarus** from the dead, Caiaphas, the Jewish high priest, prophesied that Jesus would die for the nation, it being "expedient for us that one man should die for the people, and that the whole nation perish not" (Matthew 26:3, 57; John 18:14, 24, 28). He made sure that Jesus was found guilty at his trial. Caiaphas is a type of the cold-blooded, hypocritical politician.

Cain and Abel.   "And Cain talked with Abel his brother: and it came to pass, when they were in the field, that Cain rose up against Abel his brother, and slew him. And the Lord said unto Cain, Where is Abel thy brother? And he said, I know not: *Am I my brother's keeper?* And he said, What hast thou done? the voice of *thy brother's blood crieth unto me from the ground*. And Cain said unto the Lord, my punishment is greater than I can bear. . . . it shall come to pass that every one that findeth me shall slay me. And the Lord said unto him, Therefore whosoever slayeth Cain, vengeance shall be taken on him sevenfold. And the Lord set a *mark upon Cain*, lest any finding him should kill him. And Cain went out from the presence of the Lord and dwelt in the **Land of Nod**, on the **east of Eden**" (Genesis 4:8-16). The conflict between Cain and Abel is now remembered as the original and archetypal fratricide. The question "Am I my brother's keeper?" is always quoted ironically, since the only correct answer is "Yes." Asking this question is equivalent to asking whether one has a responsibility to one's fellow man. The **mark** (or brand) **of Cain** was meant both to identify the fratricide and to protect from punishment, but in later literature it is understood as the stigma of punishment itself, and usually conceived (as in Shelley's "**Adonais**") as a scarlet mark upon the forehead.
Nod means "wandering"; the Land of Nod in the sense of "Dreamland" is a misinterpretation possible only in English.

Calchas.   The wisest of the Greek seers at the time of the **Trojan War**, who accompanied the Greeks to Troy. At Aulis he told the

Greeks that they must sacrifice **Iphigenia** to appease **Artemis** so that the fleet could set sail. In the ***Iliad*** (Book I) he tells **Agamemnon** that he must give up Chryseis, his prize, to her father, Chryses, to stop the plague sent by **Apollo** against the Greeks. In the ***Aeneid***, II,122, Sinon claims that Calchas was the one who designated him for sacrifice. Calchas died brokenhearted because another soothsayer, Mopsus, proved to be better in predicting things to come.

Calf, Golden.   "And when the people saw that **Moses** delayed to come down out of the mount, the people gathered themselves together unto **Aaron** and said . . . make us gods which shall go before us . . . And Aaron said unto them, Break off the golden earrings which are in the ears of your wives . . . and bring them unto me. And he received them at their hand and fashioned it with a graving tool, after he had made it a molten calf: and he said, These be thy gods, O Israel, which brought thee up out of the land of Egypt" (Exodus 32:1-4). When Moses returned from Sinai and discovered the idolatry of the people, he broke the tablets of the Law in his anger. The episode is recalled (in Psalms 106:20) as a shocking apostasy, and today to worship a golden calf means to worship false ideals, especially wealth.

Caliban.   In Shakespeare's *Tempest*, the deformed, grotesque monster whom **Prospero** binds into his service after defeating his mother, Sycorax the witch, in a duel of magic. Sired by a devil, Caliban represents instinctive and bestial evil. His opposite is **Ariel**, sprite of the air.

Calliope.   The muse of epic poetry. (See **Muses**.) Also, a musical instrument.

Calvary.   The hill of Calvary, or **Golgotha**, where Christ was crucified (Luke 23:33). From the Latin *Calvaria*, "skull." Symbolic of a place of agony.

Calypso.   In Homer's ***Odyssey***, Book V, the nymph who detains **Odysseus** for seven years on the island of **Ogygia**. Pining for **Penelope**, his wife, by day and playing the lover of the nymph by night, Odysseus resists all Calypso's lures to induce him to remain permanently (including the offer of immortality). Finally, at a command of **Zeus** brought by **Hermes**, Calypso abandons her desire and assists the hero to complete his return to Ithaca. Also, a musical style today.

Camelot.   In Arthurian legend, the site of King **Arthur**'s court. By extension, any center of power where youth and beauty hold sway and the arts flourish. The news media dubbed Washington, D.C., Camelot during President Kennedy's era.

Camel through a needle's eye.   "Then said Jesus unto his disciples, Verily I say unto you, That a rich man shall hardly enter into the kingdom of heaven. And again I say unto you, It is easier for a *camel* to go through the eye of a needle, than for a rich man to enter into the kingdom of God" (Matthew 19:23-24; Mark 10:23-25; Luke 18:24-25). For a camel to go through a needle's eye is a fine, bold, proverbial expression of an impossibility; it should not be weakened by trying to read "camel" as a Greek word for "rope," or by suggesting that the "needle's eye" was the name of a narrow gate. The same phrase appears in the Koran, and the Talmud has a similar one about an elephant. Millionaires who are discouraged by this text may take consolation from the verses that follow: "And they were astonished out of measure, saying among themselves, Who then can be saved? And Jesus . . . saith, With men it is impossible, but not with God: for with God all things are possible" (Mark 10:25-26).

Camille.   The poor seamstress become courtesan in Alexandre Dumas' *Camille* (1852). She falls in love with Armand Duval, foregoing a rich lover for his sake, but gives him up because of the family scandal created by the affair. As she is dying of tuberculosis, she tells Armand why she left him. Camille is the archetype of the courtesan capable of a true if tragic love, and of romantic self-sacrifice.

Canaan.   Of the three sons of **Noah**, Ham, the father of Canaan, looked on his father naked in his tent, for which Noah declared that Canaan was cursed, "a servant of servants shall he be unto his brethren." The words have been interpreted as justifying slavery, since the descendants of Canaan are traditionally said to be Africans (Genesis 9:18-27).

Canaan, Land of. See **Promised land**.

Candide. Subtitled "Optimism," Voltaire's (1694-1778) best and most well-known satire (published in 1759) tells of the catastrophic adventures of a naive youth named Candide. Candide's misadventures are always counterpointed with the precept of his foolish tutor Dr. Pangloss (see **Pangloss, Dr.**) that everything "is for the best in this best of all possible worlds." Through Pangloss, Voltaire is attacking the rational causality of Leibnitz. The satire closes with the frequently quoted statement "We must cultivate our garden," i.e., we must attend to our own affairs with practical application rather than absurd theories. Candide has become synonymous with the innocence and sunny idealism of youth.

Captian Nemo. In the novel *Twenty Thousand Leagues Under the Sea* (1870) by Jules Verne (1828-1905), Captian Nemo is a genius, the captain of the fantastic submarine "Nautilus," who lives undersea because he is a misanthrope.

Capulet. Juliet's hot-tempered father in Shakespeare's *Romeo and Juliet* (1594). Unreasonable when crossed, he destroys his daughter's love and life.

Carey, Phillip. The hero of W. Somerset Maugham's novel *Of Human Bondage* (1915). Carey, a shy, sensitive orphan afflicted with a club foot, is raised by his aunt and uncle, who have little feeling for him. The novel is concerned with his efforts to achieve independence and maturity, his struggles in a difficult love-affair with a waitress named Mildred, and, most of all, his search for intellectual illumination and artistic realization. These high aspirations are never fulfilled, and Carey finishes his studies in medicine, marries, and takes on a career as a doctor.

Carmen. The heroine of Prosper Mérimée's novelette *Carmen* (1846), which inspired Bizet's opera. A volatile gypsy, she lures Don José away from his military duties, causing him to kill a lieutenant in a quarrel over her. Don José kills Carmen when she tells him she no longer loves him. A type of the passionate, untamed Romantic heroine.

Carton, Sydney. One of the protagonists of Dickens' *A Tale of Two Cities*. He is a romantic, dissolute, feckless lawyer who gives his life for love of Lucie Manette, taking her husband's place on the guillotine and declaring at the moment of his death, "It is a far, far better thing that I do, than I have ever done; it is a far, far better rest, that I go to, than I have ever known." See also: **Manette, Lucie.**

Casanova de Seingalt, Giacomo. The Italian adventurer (1725-1798), gambler and charlatan, most famous for his exploits in love. His scandalous, checkered and sometimes influential career took him to most of the great places and put him in touch with most of the great personages of his time. His unreliable but historically interesting *Mémoires* were published in 12 volumes between 1826 and 1838. A *Casanova* is a name popularly applied to a philanderer, a promiscuous lover. Also see: **Don Juan.**

Cassandra. The daughter of **Priam**, King of Troy, Cassandra was loved by the god **Apollo**. He gave her the gift of prophecy, but as Cassandra resisted his wooing, Apollo saw to it that no one would believe her forecasts. She foretold the fall of Troy, and was taken by **Agamemnon** as his prize of war. Her prophecy of his end was fulfilled when his wife murdered him. A "Cassandra" is thus anyone with the wisdom of prophecy who is ignored by those who most need to take heed.

Cast money changers out of the temple. "And Jesus went into the temple of God, and cast out all them that sold and bought in the temple, and overthrew the tables of the money changers, and the seats of them that sold doves, and said unto them, It is written, My house shall be called the house of prayer; but ye have made it a **den of thieves**" (Matthew 21:12-13; cf. Mark 11:15-17; Luke 19:45-46; John 2: 13-16; Jeremiah 7:11). The money changers performed a necessary function: Doves were sold for ritual sacrifices, and changers exchanged Roman money for Hebrew to pay the temple taxes. Inevitably they introduced an inappropriate commercial note to the premises. The episode is proverbial for any attack on commercialism in religion or any other spiritual endeavor.

Castor and Pollux. The "Heavenly Twins" or Dioscuri, "Sons of Zeus." Children of **Leda** and **Zeus** and by tradition the brothers of Helen (see **Helen of Troy**). They participated in many adventures, during one of which Castor was killed. Pollux wished to join Castor in **Hades**, but Zeus allowed them to spend alternate days on earth and finally placed them in the heavens as the constellation "Gemini" ("Twins"), a name much used in the space program of the U.S.A.

Castorp, Hans.   Hero of Thomas Mann's novel *The Magic Mountain* (1924). Hans is a North German engineer who goes to visit his tuberculous cousin, Lt. Joachim Ziemssen, in a sanatorium in Switzerland. There he discovers he too is infected, and remains seven years. Under the erotic stimulation of Claudia Chauchat and the intellectual stimulation of Settembrini, an Italian humanist-liberal-rationalist, and Naphta, a Jew turned Jesuit, and the influence of the powerful personality of Mynheer Pieperkorn, Hans' character expands and he explores all branches of knowledge. Despite his development, he cannot return to the active world of duty in the "Flatland" until World War I begins, when he becomes a soldier and presumably dies on the battlefield.

Cast the first stone.   "And the scribes and Pharisees brought unto him a woman taken in adultery . . . They say unto him, . . . Moses in the law commanded us, that such should be stoned: but what sayest thou? . . . But Jesus . . . said unto them, **He that is without sin** among you, let him first cast a stone at her . . ." (John 8:3-8). Jesus' defense of the woman taken in adultery is a warning against self-righteousness and a reminder that all men are sinners.

Cattle of the sun.   During one of the adventures of **Odysseus** on the way home from Troy, he and his men landed on the Island of the Sun with specific instructions not to harm the sacred cattle grazing there. The sailors were becalmed, and without food, and when Odysseus left them to pray alone, they slew and ate some of the sacred animals. The Sun God took almost immediate revenge, destroying their ship and killing all aboard except Odysseus himself.

Caulfield, Holden.   Hero of J.D. Salinger's *The Catcher in the Rye* (1951). He is a 17-year-old boy who believes that the world is dominated by phonies and is in frantic search of some refuge. He has become a symbol for all alienated, searching youth.

Celestial City. The goal of **Christian**'s pilgrimage in John Bunyan's (1628-1688) *The Pilgrim's Progress* (1678). Hence, Heaven.

Centaurs. Mythic creatures half horse and half man, the centaurs represented to the Greeks the bestial and grotesque aspect of mankind. The successful war of the Lapiths, a Thessalian tribe wholly human, against these monsters, is celebrated on a frieze of the **Parthenon**. The most famous of the centaurs was Chiron, wise and good, who was **Achilles**' tutor.

Cerberus, A sop to. When the **Cumaean Sibyl**, in Vergil's *Aeneid*, conducted **Aeneas** to the underworld, she made Cerberus, hell's vicious three-headed guard dog, sleep by giving him a cake of honey and poppy. Hence a "sop to Cerberus" is any bribe or pacification to a dangerous person.

Ceres. See **Demeter**.

Chanticleer. In the story of *Reynard the Fox* (12th century), Reynard fools Chanticleer the cock into believing he does not eat meat any longer. Chanticleer becomes less watchful, and Reynard eats his children. In Chaucer's *The Canterbury Tales*, Chanticleer, rather pompous and strutting, is blinded to danger by his own vanity—associations that the name retains today.

Chaos. According to early Greek cosmology, the condition of the world in its original state, without limits, without the pattern imposed by the mind of god. The Greeks personified Chaos and made it the parent of Night and **Erebus**. The antonym is "cosmos," a word which we use to embody the ideas of harmony and beauty. Today chaos signifies any unorganized, ungoverned, confused condition.

Chariot of fire. "Behold, there appeared a chariot of fire, and horses of fire, and **Elijah** went up by a whirlwind into heaven" (II Kings 2:11). The story of Elijah's translation to heaven is part of a large body of miraculous legend about the prophet. Marvelous chariots appear in the folklore of many nations as vehicles for heavenly beings, and fire is especially associated with the God of the Old Testament. Since Elijah went to heaven without dying first, popular piety looked for his eventual return as the forerunner of the **Messiah** (Luke 9:19). A chariot of fire is thus an image of transcendence or miraculous overcoming of natural obstacles. William Blake uses it in his prefatory hymn to the long poem "Milton," and this usage was alluded to in the title of the recent film *Chariots of Fire* (1981).

Charon.   Son of **Erebus**; ferryman who transported the souls of the dead across the River **Styx** to **Hades**. As a fee he received a small coin which had been placed in the mouth of the dead at burial. Charon was described as an old man in tattered clothes, sordid and squalid in appearance with unkempt and matted locks. He appears in Book VI of Vergil's ***Aeneid***, in *The Frogs* of **Aristophanes**, and in Lucian's *Dialogues of the Dead*.

Charybdis.   The sea monster, and great hazard to ships, daughter of **Poseidon** and **Gaea**. She gulped down huge mouthfuls of water and then spewed them forth. She was later associated with the whirlpool off the Sicilian coast. "Between **Scylla and Charybdis**" means colloquially to be "between the devil and the deep blue sea," to be hemmed in by perils with only the narrowest margin of escape. See also: **Odysseus**.

Cherub.   In the Bible, the cherubim were celestial beings who carried the throne of God; theologians assigned them the place of angels of the second order. In Western art they are usually represented as beautiful, chubby babies with wings. The adjective cherubic implies sweet, childish innocence.

Cheshire cat, The.   The gossipy cat with the famous grin that remains behind while he vanishes; in Lewis Carroll's *Alice in Wonderland* (1865). See also: **Alice**.

Children's teeth set on edge.   "In those days they shall say no more, The fathers have eaten a sour grape, and the children's teeth are set on edge. But everyone shall die for his own iniquity" (Jeremiah 31:29-30; Ezekiel 18:2-3). Both Jeremiah and Ezekiel are quoting a familiar proverb which asserted the joint moral responsibility of all members of a family. Both prophets, in rejecting the proverb, are proclaiming the more modern and individualistic doctrine of separate responsibility.

Chillingworth, Roger. Husband of Hester Prynne in Hawthorne's *The Scarlet Letter* (1850). He disappears and is supposed dead, but returns after Hester bears Dimmesdale's child. He is an incarnation of evil and vengeance. See also: **Dimmesdale, Arthur; Prynne, Hester**.

Chimaera. A mythological creature who was lion in her fore-third, goat in her middle-third and serpent in her hind-third. She was supposed to be invincible, but proved an easy contest for the hero **Bellerophon**, who, mounted on his horse **Pegasus**, vanquished her with arrows shot from above. Today a chimera signifies a grotesque, fearful creature of the imagination; an illusion. Chimerical means wildly fanciful or fantastic.

Chingachgook. The chief of the Mohicans and the loyal friend of Natty Bumppo (Hawkeye), in Cooper's *The Last of the Mohicans* (1826). See also: **Bumppo, Natty**.

Chosen people. The Jews, chosen by God in the Old Testament to fulfill His purpose on earth.

Christ. See **Jesus' entry into Jerusalem; Messiah; Seven last words**.

Christian. The central figure in *The Pilgrim's Progress* (1678) by John Bunyan (1628-1688), Christian is a simple-hearted, earnest man who leaves behind his worldly existence in the City of Destruction to seek salvation. His pilgrimage brings many encounters with danger, temptation, hardship and doubt—and these encounters make up the literal story of this allegorical narrative. In the end, Christian reaches the **Celestial City**.

Christian, Fletcher. Historical figure and leader of an 18th-century mutiny, fictionalized in *Mutiny on the Bounty* (1932) by Charles Nordhoff and James Norman Hall. Dark, handsome, moody and headstrong, Christian is a type of romantic hero.

Cid, El (The Cid). One of the renowned medieval figures in chivalry: the Spanish knight, Rodrigo (or Ruy) Diaz de Bivar (c. 1043-1099), who became famous for military conquests against the Moors. His heroic exploits are celebrated in *El Cid* (from the

Arabic *Sidi*, "Lord"), the Spanish epic poem written around 1140 by an unknown Castilian poet. His various adventures culminate in the taking of Valencia in 1094.

Cimmerian darkness.   See **Cimmerians**.

Cimmerians.   A tribe in ancient mythology placed by **Homer** in a gloomy, dark land just this side of **Hades**, a locale hardly distinguishable from the land of the dead; hence "Cimmerian darkness" denotes extreme darkness, the ends of the world.

Circe.   In **Homer**'s *Odyssey*, Circe was a beautiful sorceress who turned men into swine when they arrived at her palace. After **Odysseus'** advance guard suffered this fate, the hero himself on advice from **Hermes** confronted the enchantress, threatened her with his sword and thus broke her magic. After remaining a year with the repentant Circe, Odysseus received directions from her which enabled him to visit with the shades of the dead in **Hades**. Then, with his men restored to human form, he continued his voyage. By extension, "Circe" today refers to a temptress.

Circumlocution Office, The.   In *Little Dorrit* (1857) Charles Dickens invented this archetypal department of red tape, the government office in which evasiveness has become a high bureaucratic art; hence, any government department obstructive to public information.

Clare, Angel.   In Hardy's *Tess of the d'Urbervilles* (1891), he is Tess's husband, a rather selfish and self-righteous man, who opposes antiquated traditions and effete customs. Thinking she is a country girl (Tess Durbeyfield), he leaves her upon finding she descends from the d'Urberville family and has been seduced by Alec d'Urberville. He returns, but too late to prevent her from murdering Alec, who had continued to hound her.

Claudius.   In Shakespeare's *Hamlet*, brother and murderer of King Hamlet; uncle of Prince Hamlet, and husband of Queen Gertrude, Hamlet's mother. He is, as Hamlet puts it, lecherous and treacherous. Although Claudius has won a measure of sympathy from some critics, who point to his decisiveness, his desire to repent and his ability to maintain order in Denmark, at least for a while, he nevertheless plots Hamlet's assassination to the end of the action.

Clay in the potter's hand.   "As the clay is in the potter's hand, so are ye in mine hand" (Jeremiah 18:6). In current usage it has come to mean easily led or influenced.

Cleopatra.   Born in 69 B.C., of pure Greek descent, she ruled Egypt jointly with her younger brother, Ptolemy XIII (51 B.C.), whom she married but expelled. After his death, she married, by order of Caesar, Ptolemy XIV, whose murder she contrived. Noted for her ambition, governing ability, beauty and wit, Cleopatra is best remembered for her love affairs with Julius Caesar and Mark Antony (see **Antony, Mark**). Her son by Caesar, Caesarion, whom she made nominal co-ruler of Egypt, was put to death by order of Octavian in 30 B.C. She accompanied Caesar to Rome but left for Egypt after his assassination in 44 B.C. She so thoroughly captivated the triumvir Mark Antony in Tarsus that he followed her to Egypt, eventually divorced his wife, Octavia (sister of the other trimuvir, Octavian), and married Cleopatra. After the defeat of their navy at **Actium** (31 B.C.), in a war with Octavian, Antony died in her arms and she committed suicide, either by poison or the self-inflicted bite of an asp. Shakespeare's *Antony and Cleopatra* is the most famous dramatization of their love and death.

Clio.   The muse of history. See **Muses**.

Clotho.   See **Fates**.

Cloud like a man's hand.   "And it came to pass at the seventh time, that he said, Behold, there ariseth a little cloud out of the sea, like a man's hand . . . And it came to pass . . . that the heaven was black with clouds and wind, and there was a great rain" (I Kings 18:44-45). "A cloud like a man's hand" proverbially means "a modest forerunner of great events."

Cloven hoof.   **Moses** declared that only animals with cloven hoofs were fit for eating or sacrifice. Later medieval tradition depicted or described the devil with a cloven hoof, a trait borrowed from the pagan gods, who were often bovine. Hence the association of "cloven hoofed" with the demonic or grotesque (Leviticus 11:3, 7, 26; Deuteronomy 14:7). See also: **Satan**.

Clytemnestra.   **Agamemnon**'s wife, the daughter of **Leda** and King Tyndareus of Sparta. Incensed by the sacrifice of her daughter **Iphegenia**, Clytemnestra killed her husband on his return from the **Trojan War**.

Coat of many colors.   **Joseph**, favorite son of **Jacob**, and **Rachel**'s first-born, was given a "coat of many colors" as a symbol of affection and preference. The jealousy aroused in his older brothers led them to sell Joseph into slavery. They stained his coat with blood, brought it to Jacob and told him Joseph had been devoured by a wild animal (Genesis 30).

Colossus of Rhodes, The.   See **Seven wonders of the ancient world**.

Columbine.   One of the stock female characters of the *commedia del l'Arte*; sharp, witty and usually loved by the Harlequin. From the Italian *colombina*, "dovelike."

Come, let us reason together.   "Come now, And let us reason together, saith the Lord: Though your sins be as scarlet, they shall be as white as snow; though they be red like crimson, they shall be as wool" (Isaiah 1:18). Cited frequently as an offering of hope to the fallen and depraved.

Connecticut Yankee, The.   Hero of Mark Twain's *A Connecticut Yankee at King Arthur's Court* (1889), a shrewd New Englander who receives a blow on the head and awakens in **Arthur**'s England of 528. With the advantage of 19th-century knowledge, he gains control of the kingdom and institutes various reforms.

Constantin, Abbé.   Hero of Ludovic Halévy's (1834-1908) *The Abbé Constantin* (1882), a beneficent, kindly and generous curé, living in the French countryside in the late 19th century.

Cordelia.   The youngest daughter of King **Lear** in Shakespeare's *King Lear* (1606). Though she truly loves her father, she refuses to put a value on that love as her wicked sisters **Goneril** and **Regan** do. For this, the irascible king banishes her. Lear and Cordelia are reunited briefly at the tragedy's end. She is a paragon of goodness and faithfulness.

Cornucopia.   The horn of plenty, containing an endless supply of food and drink. The gift of **Zeus** to Amalthea. Colloquially, any unending, overflowing supply.

Corybantes.   The ecstatic priests of **Cybele**, the fertility goddess, who celebrated the rites of the goddess with frenzied beating of cymbals. The infant god **Zeus**, hunted by his father, was saved by the Corybantes, whose din drowned out his crying.

Counsel of perfection.   "Jesus said unto him, If thou wilt be perfect, go and sell that thou hast, and give to the poor . . . But when the young man heard that saying, he went away sorrowing, for he had great possessions" (Matthew 19:21-22; Mark 10:21-22; Luke 18:22-23). In this episode, a rich youth who has lived virtuously according to the law asks Jesus what he must do to receive eternal life; Jesus' advice is beyond his moral capacity. The phrase "counsel of perfection," referring to any impossible ideal, derives from this story, though the exact words do not appear in the Bible. See also: **Camel through a needle's eye**.

Crane, Ichabod.   The shrewd, yet naive, timid and awkward schoolmaster in Washington Irving's *Legend of Sleepy Hollow* (in *The Sketch Book*, 1820). His rival disguises himself as the **Headless Horseman** and scares Crane away from the community. An archetypal yokel.

Cratchit, Bob.   The poor, mistreated employee of the miserly Scrooge in Dickens' *A Christmas Carol* (1843); he maintains a sunny outlook on life despite his troubles. His youngest son, **Tiny Tim**, is frail and sickly but possessed of a will to survive—which he does, thanks to the charity that Ebenezer Scrooge bestows after he sees the light. See also: **Ghosts of Christmas Past, Present and Yet to Come; Scrooge, Ebenezer**.

Crawley, Rawdon.   The husband of the scheming Becky Sharp in William Makepeace Thackeray's *Vanity Fair* (1847-48), he exiles himself to Coventry Island after he learns of his wife's perfidy. See also: **Sharp, Becky**.

Creakle, Mr.   In Dickens' *David Copperfield* (1850), the headmaster of the miserable school attended by David. He substitutes harsh discipline for any real teaching.

Creon.   (1) Brother of **Jocasta** (wife of **Oedipus**) and uncle of **Antigone**, Eteocles and Polyneices. He was twice king of Thebes. He appears in **Sophocles'** *Oedipus the King*, *Oedipus at Colonus* and *Antigone*. (2) King of Corinth, father of Glauce. When **Jason** cast off **Medea** to marry Glauce, Medea brought about the deaths of both Creon and Glauce.

Cressida.   See **Troilus and Cressida.**

Cretan bull.   The bull for which **Pasiphaë**, wife of Minos, king of Crete, conceived an unnatural passion. She coupled with the bull by concealing herself in a wooden cow fashioned for her by **Daedalus**; the issue of the union was the half-man half-bull **Minotaur**, whom Minos imprisoned in his labyrinth.

Crichton, William.   The butler of the Earl of Loam in James M. Barrie's *The Admirable Crichton* (1902). Crichton believes in the justice of the social order and the natural selection of leaders. His own abilities make him leader of a group of upper-class people stranded on an island.

Croesus.   The king of Lydia (fl. 550 B.C.) who was fabled for his great wealth. Misinterpreting an oracle, Croesus attacked Persia, and suffered defeat. Sentenced to death by Cyrus, the Persian king, Croesus called out the name of Solon, who had prophesied Croesus' fall, and on learning the whole ironic tale, Cyrus made Croesus his adviser. The story, told by Herodotus, is historically impossible and was intended as an illustration of the Greek proverb "Count no man happy until he ıs dead." Croesus' name is now primarily associated with great wealth, as in the common expression "rich as Croesus."

Cronos,   or Cronus. A Titan, son of **Uranus** and **Gaea**. His Roman counterpart was Saturn. With the help of his mother, Cronus dethrᴏ ᴠed his father. During his rule there was a **Golden Age** on earth. ᴊecausᴇ of a prophecy that one of his children would dethrone him, Cronus swallowed them as they were born, but his wife, **Rhea**, helped **Zeus** escape and tricked Cronus into disgorging the other children. Finally, aided by the **Cyclopes**, some of the

Giants, Themis and **Prometheus**, Zeus and his brothers fought against Cronus and the **Titans**, defeated them and confined them to **Tartarus**. The other children of Cronus and Rhea were **Hades** and **Poseidon**, **Demeter**, **Hera** and **Hestia**.

Crooked shall be made straight. "The crooked shall be made straight, and the rough places plain" (Isaiah 40:4; cf. Isaiah 45:2; Luke 3:5). One of the prophecies about the coming of the **Messiah**.

Crossing of the Red Sea. When the Hebrews, led out of Egypt by **Moses** and pursued by the Egyptians, came to the barrier of the Red Sea, the waters were parted by a strong east wind sent by God. After the Hebrews had all passed through the corridor in the waters, Moses lifted his hand and the waters engulfed the Egyptians (Exodus 10:19; 14:1-31). In allusion, the phrase signifies either a miraculous escape or an act of divine intervention and destruction.

Crossing the Rubicon. In 49 B.C. Julius Caesar, under ban of Rome, returned from his province of Cisalpine Gaul and precipitated a civil war. The fateful, irrevocable decision to march against Pompey was made at the Rubicon, a small river separating the province from Italy, Caesar crossed uttering the words, "Jacta alea est"—"The die is cast." Today it means a fateful decision, or a decision from which there is no turning back.

Cross over Jordan. The Isrealites under the leadership of **Joshua** invaded **Canaan** from the east, and so had to cross the Jordan. According to Joshua 3, the waters stopped flowing and piled up in a heap until the whole nation had passed over. In certain Negro spirituals, to cross over Jordan and to enter the **Promised Land** are metaphors for going to heaven.

Crown of thorns. In the **New Testament**, Jesus is taken by Pilate's soldiers "and when they had plaited a crown of thorns, they put it upon his head . . . and they bowed the knee before him and mocked him, saying, Hail, King of the Jews" (Matthew 27:29, Mark 15:17; John 19:2-5). A symbol of suffering and humiliation. See also: **Pilate, Pontius**.

Cruncher, Jerry.   In Dickens' *A Tale of Two Cities* (1859), a bank employee who helps Charles Darnay escape from France. By day a messenger for Tellson's, Jerry is at night a "resurrectionist," a supplier of cadavers for medical dissection. See also: **Darnay, Charles.**

Crusoe, Robinson.   The central character in Daniel Defoe's *Robinson Crusoe* (1719). On one of his adventures, Crusoe is wrecked on a small, uninhabited island. Utilizing all his practical skills and knowledge, he makes a comfortable home for himself. He is later joined by **Friday**, a savage whom he rescues from cannibals. Friday becomes his servant and companion. Crusoe spends 24 years on the island—self-sufficient and quite content, until his rescue.

Cuchulain.   In Irish legend, the "Irish **Achilles**," an heroic pagan warrior whose fabulous adventures are celebrated primarily in the Ulster Cycle of Gaelic literature. His deeds are the subject of poems and plays by the Irish poet W.B. Yeats (1865-1939).

Cultivate our garden, We must.   See *Candide*.

Cumaean, sibyl.   The sibyl or prophetess of the Temple of **Apollo** at Cumae in Italy who guided **Aeneas** through the underworld.

Cunegonde.   See *Candide*.

Cupid.   The Roman name for **Eros**, son of **Aphrodite** and god of love.

Cupid and Psyche.   A romance with fairy tale elements included by Apuleius, a Latin author (second century A.D.) of North Africa, in his collection called *The Golden Ass*. Psyche, a mortal loved by the god of love, has promised her lover not to try to discover his true identity. He has kept this a secret, only visiting her by night. After many trials and hardships (for Psyche under the urging of her sisters, has broken her promise to Cupid and has found out who he is) all turns out well.

Cup runneth over. "Thou preparest a table before me in the presence of mine enemies: thy anointest my head with oil; my cup runneth over" (**Psalms** 23:5). Probably no chapter in the Bible is more universally known and loved than the 23rd Psalm, from which these three sentences come. All are images of God's super-abundant generosity. Oil, a valuable product throughout the Mediterranean world, was a symbol of gladness and prosperity; it was used for the consecration of priests, but also by private persons for their own pleasure.

Cybele. The earth mother goddess of Asia Minor, identified with the Greek goddess **Rhea** and the Roman Magna Mater. Worshippers celebrated her cult with orgiastic and often bloody rituals.

Cyclopes. Greek, "round eyes"; *Cyclops* is the singular. According to Hesiod, there were only three Cyclopes, one-eyed **Giants** who were the sons of the primordial gods, **Uranus** and **Gaea**. They provided **Zeus** with lightning and thunderbolts and were later killed by **Apollo**. **Homer**, however, believed there were many Cyclopes, monstrous, gigantic creatures with one eye in the center of the forehead. They lived in Sicily and along the west Italian coast, tended sheep, and were cannibalistic. The most interesting story about them is the encounter of their leader, **Polyphemus**, with **Odysseus**. To the Cyclopes was attributed the building of huge, prehistoric structures; the word *cyclopean* is applied to a type of building, still visible in many places, such as Mycenae, Greece, and Tarragona, Spain, in which massive stones were piled atop each other.

Cymbeline. A king of Britain during the Roman occupation (first century B.C.) and the title character of the play (1609) by Shakespeare. During the rule of the historical Cymbeline, the Britons lived at peace with their Roman conquerors, to whom they paid a regular tribute. Shakespeare's play, categorized as a romance, is something of a fairy tale in which the hot-tempered but good-hearted king forgives his estranged daughter and is reunited with his long-lost sons.

Cyrano de Bergerac. The historical Cyrano de Bergerac (1619-1655), French author, playwright, soldier, adventurer and freethinker, is perhaps less well known popularly than the fictive hero of Edmond Rostand's 1897 play which bears his name. The historical Cyrano is famed for comic fantasies, the dramatic comedy *Le Pedant joue* (1654), the tragedy *La Mort d'Agrippine* (1654) (both estimable works poetically), his ability at dueling, and, of course, his very long nose. The fictive Cyrano hides his shyness and self-consciousness about his nose behind swagger; he possesses a heart of gold and is moved by an extreme sense of honor.

D

Daedalus. The first artisan-inventor and engineer. Employed by Minos, king of Crete, he fashioned the wooden cow wherein Minos's Queen **Pasiphaë** was able to satisfy her unnatural desire for a bull; the issue of this union, the half-bull half-man **Minotaur**, was so monstrous he required an extraordinary prison. This Daedalus furnished in the form of the **Labyrinth**, in which Minos sacrificed to the Minotaur twelve Athenian youths and maidens each year—until **Theseus** succeeded in killing the monster. In order to keep Daedalus in his service, Minos imprisoned him in his own escape-proof labyrinth along with his son, **Icarus**. Daedalus effected their escape by fashioning two pairs of wings. They flew out; unfortunately, Icarus did not heed his father's warning not to fly too near the sun. The wax holding the feathers melted and Icarus fell to his death. The modern reference to Daedalus is to his symbolism as an inventor.

Daily bread. "Give us this day our daily bread" (Matthew 6:11). One of the petitions of the Lord's Prayer, it implies that man may legitimately ask that his physical needs be met, but it also inculcates a spirit of trust that is not overly concerned for the future (cf. Matthew 6:25-34). Roman Catholics are authorized to understand the words as applying to the bread of the Eucharist, but this interpretation is not mandatory.

Damocles, Sword of. Damocles, sycophantic retainer of Dionysius, tyrant of Syracuse, was invited to share the luxury he

envied. At a great feast, Damocles observed a sword hung by a
thread over his head, and could not move. Hence "the sword of
Damocles" defines a situation of extreme precariousness or im-
pending danger.

Damon and Pythias   (Phintias). In the story told by Cicero
(*De Officiis*, II, x, 45) the name is Phintias but *Pythias* has become
established in English usage. Damon and Pythias, followers of
Pythagoras, were named by Cicero as examples of perfect friendship and their names have become proverbial for this relationship,
like those of **David** and **Jonathan**. The tyrant Dionysius of Syracuse, Sicily, had ordered Pythias to be put to death. The latter
begged to be allowed a few days' reprieve that he might look after
his family. Damon agreed to become surety for him, agreeing that
he himself would be executed if Pythias should not return. On the
appointed day, Phythias returned and Dionysius was so overcome
by the loyalty of these two friends that he pardoned them both and
asked to become a third member of their society of friendship.

Danae.   The mother of the hero **Perseus** and daughter of King
Acrisius of Argos. The king shut his daughter up in a tower of
bronze because an oracle said the girl would bear a son who would
slay him. **Zeus** came down to Danae in a shower of gold and thus
impregnated her with Perseus.

Daniel in the lion's den.   "Then the king comanded, and they
brought Daniel, and cast him into the den of lions . . ." (Daniel 6:16).
Daniel was a Jew who retained his faith during the **Babylonian
Captivity** under Kings **Nebuchadnezzar**, **Belshazzar** and Darius.
He interpreted dreams and foretold the future (see **Mene, mene,
tekel, upharsin**). When the princes of Babylon plotted against
Daniel and caused him to be sealed inside a den of lions, God
miraculously shut the lions' mouths. The story signifies faith and
courage in the face of extreme danger.

Dantes, Edmond.   In Alexandre Dumas père's *The Count of
Monte Cristo* (1845), he is unjustly imprisoned for 14 years. He
escapes, and spends his life as the Count of Monte Cristo, avenging
himself on those who conspired to imprison him. See also: **Monte
Cristo, Count of.**

Dan to Beersheba. These two cities were situated at the extreme northern and southern ends of the Holy Land. Today, from Dan to Beersheba means from one end of a country to another, or from one end of the world to another.

Daphne. The daughter of the river Peneus, who was pursued by the enamored god **Apollo**. In flight, Daphne begged the help of the gods and was changed into a laurel tree, which henceforth became Apollo's favorite. Laurel wreaths were the traditional crowns for the finest classical poets and singers.

Daphnis and Chloë. The best-known and most admired work of ancient fiction, a Greek pastoral romance written by Longus, of whom nothing more is known (date is set at anywhere from second to fifth century A.D.). Two children are found in adjoining fields near Lesbos in Mytilene. They eventually meet, fall in love, go through various adventures and separations, finally are found by their parents, are married, and "live happily forever after." The atmosphere is truly that of **Arcadia**, and the romance served as the prototype of later works of the genre, such as *Paul et Virginie* (1788) by Bernardin St. Pierre. The story is the basis of the ballet *Daphnis et Chloe*, set to music by Maurice Ravel in 1912.

Darcy, Fitzwilliam. The proud aristocrat in Jane Austen's *Pride and Prejudice* (1813). His offer of marriage to Elizabeth Bennet, the heroine, is refused; but after he becomes less snobbish, and she less prejudiced, they marry. See also: **Bennet, Elizabeth**.

Darnay, Charles. In Dickens' *A Tale of Two Cities* (1859), a French aristocrat who renounces his title and goes to England to live happily with his wife. He returns to France to help his family agent, who has been captured by the revolutionists. Arrested and condemned to die, Darnay is rescued by his wife and Sydney Carton. See also: **Carton, Sydney**.

d'Artagnan, Charles de Baatz. The dashing soldier-hero whose exploits are the subject of Alexandre Dumas père's *The Three Musketeers* (1844). See also: **Athos, Porthos and Aramis**.

David. The famous king of the Hebrews, whose name means "beloved" or "chieftain." He is noted for his songs, for the miraculous slaying of **Goliath** with his sling when still a boy, for his friendship with **Jonathan**, for his many wives, the most famous among whom was **Bathsheba** (whose husband Uriah was sent by David into the heat of the battle to die) and for his anguish at the treachery of his son Absalom. He is represented as wise, brave, prudent and handsome. Luke traces the ancestry of Christ back to David (I and II Samuel, *passim*). See also: **Absalom, O my son**.

David Copperfield.   The hero and the title of a novel written in 1850 by Charles Dickens (1812-1870). Though his early life is happy, David experiences great hardship at the hands of cruel head-masters, brutal employers and a tyrannical stepfather before he finds happiness in love and success as an author.

Day of judgment.   The day following the ultimate destruction of the world, when the Lord will judge each soul as good or evil and pronounce its salvation or its doom (Revelation 20:11-15). Also referred to as Judgment Day, Doomsday or the Last Judgment.

Days of our years.   "The days of our years are threescore years and ten," sings the psalmist in meditating on the swiftness of pass-ing time (Psalms 90:10).

Dead bury their dead.   "And another of his disciples said unto him, Lord, suffer me the first to go and bury my father. But Jesus said unto him, Follow me; and let the dead bury their dead" (Matthew 8:21-22; Luke 9:60). The burial of the dead is an act of piety so im-perative that Jesus' hearers must have been shocked by his insis-tence on the still greater urgency of the kingdom of God. His reply should not be understood as flippant or callous. Today it is used with a weakened application, meaning simply, "Let us think about the concerns of the present time, not the past."

Deadeye, Dick.   A deformed sailor who transforms everything to ugliness in W.S. Gilbert's operetta *H.M.S. Pinafore* (1878, music by Arthur Sullivan). His pleasure is in foiling and betraying Ralph and Josephine, the lovers, but the happy ending frustrates his machinations.

Dead Sea fruit.   Proverbially, the fruit grown at Sodom, near the Dead Sea, was beautiful to look at but bitter to the taste. Because of the reputation of the Sodomites for sensuality, this fruit lent itself to an obvious moral or allegorical application. The expression "apples of Sodom" or Dead Sea fruit" now means any bitter disappointment. See also: **Sodom and Gomorrah**.

Death, where is thy sting?   "So when this corruptible shall have put on incorruption, and this mortal shall have put on immortality, then shall be brought to pass the saying that is written, Death is swallowed up in victory. O death, where is thy sting? O grave, where is thy victory?" (I Corinthians 15:54-55). This passage is especially familiar because of its use at funerals; see, for example, the Book of Common Prayer.

Deborah.   A prophetess and judge of the Israelites. She directed Barak to lead his army against Sisera, the captain of the Canaanite forces, and sang a great ode, called "the song of Deborah," to celebrate the victory (Judges 4, 5).

Decalogue.   See **Ten Commandments, The**.

Dedalus, Stephen.   Hero of James Joyce's *Portrait of the Artist as a Young Man* (1914); he struggles against the fetters of family, nation and church to realize himself as an artist. He appears also in *Ulysses* as a highly intellectualized young man, unable to make peace with himself or his environment. Stephen himself believes his last name links him spiritually with the Greek mythological inventor and artificer, **Daedalus**.

Deep calleth unto deep.   "Deep calleth unto deep" (Psalms 43:7). In the original context, this phrase refers to the tumult of a storm at sea; now used symbolically in reference to a profound spritual communion or response.

Defarge, Madame Therese.   In Dickens' *A Tale of Two Cities* (1859), a relentless woman who hates all aristocrats. She keeps count of each decapitation by the guillotine with stitches in her knitting. See also: **Carton, Sydney**; **Darney, Charles**; **Manette, Lucie**.

Delectable Mountains.   In John Bunyan's *Pilgrim's Progress* (1678), a range of hills from whose summit the **Celestial City** is visible.

Delilah. The seductress responsible for discovering the secret that Samson's great strength lay in his long hair. While he slept, she cut his hair, and betrayed him to the **Philistines**, who blinded and imprisoned him (Judges 16:1-21). By extension, any treacherous woman. See also: **Samson and Delilah**.

Delphi. See **Delphic oracle**.

Delphic oracle. The oracle at Delphi on the southern slope of Mount **Parnassus**. It was very old, having been successively the possession of the goddesses Ge, Themis and **Phoebe**. During the later tradition the oracle was under the protection of **Apollo**. The priestess Pythia sat upon a tripod over a crevice in the rock and, in a deep trance, uttered the incomprehensible **oracles** which were then interpreted by a priest. This oracle was the highest authority in religious matters, and is the source of many prophecies in Greek literature. Inscribed on the temple of Apollo at Delphi there were at least three maxims, known as the Delphic maxims: "Know theyself"; "Nothing is excess"; and "Give security [a pledge] and trouble will follow."

Deluge. See **Noah**.

Demeter. Identified with Ceres by the Romans; an earth goddess of wheat and grain, who spread knowledge of agricultural arts; daughter of **Cronos** and **Rhea**, and mother of **Persephone**. When the latter was abducted by **Hades**, Demeter roamed over the earth in search of her. Disguised as an old woman she came to Eleusis, where she was received kindly by King Celeus and his wife, Metaneira. Eventually Demeter disclosed her identity and instructed that certain rites in her honor should be inaugurated at Eleusis. She taught Triptolemus, a son of Celeus and Metaneira, the agricultural arts and supplied him with a chariot drawn by dragons, in which he traversed the world, passing on her lore to mankind.

Demiurge. "A worker for the people"—**Plato**'s term for a lesser god that creates the world. In Gnosticism, a supernatural being that creates the material world and is sometimes considered the originator of evil.

Demogorgon.   Name given to a vaguely mysterious, powerful, terrifying god of the nether region; "The Highest of the Triple Universe, whom it is forbidden to know," according to a commentator of the fifth century B.C., who first used this name. Demogorgon is taken to be a mistaken name for **Demiurge**. In medieval literature, Demogorgon was considered to be the primitive god of ancient mythology, and his name was invoked in magic ritual. Shelley used Demogorgon as a character in *Prometheus Unbound* to represent eternal power at war against false gods.

Den of thieves.   When Jesus threw the money changers out of the temple, he accused them of making the house of prayer into a den of thieves (Matthew 21:12-23; Mark 11:15-17; Luke 19:45-46). See also: **Cast money changers out of the temple**.

De Rerum Natura.   "On the Nature of Things," a scientific-philosophical poem by the Roman poet Lucretius (98-55 B.C.), in which the poet presents an explanation of the nature and operation of things based on the ideas of Democritus and Epicurus. The work is largely materialistic, and quite modern in its basic approach, attempting to demonstrate the inherent laws by which things exist, and denying animation by supernatural or "spritual" causes.

Desdemona.   In Shakespeare's *Othello* (1604), the gentle-born daughter of a Venetian senator who falls in love with and marries **Othello**, a Moorish general who is serving in Venice. The treacherous **Iago** convinces Othello that Desdemona is carrying on an adulterous affair. Though as innocent as she is pure of heart, Desdemona falls into a trap set by Iago. At the play's end, Othello, maddened by mistaken jealousy, murders her.

Desert shall blossom.   "The desert shall rejoice, and blossom as the rose. It shall blossom abundantly, and rejoice even with joy and singing" (Isaiah 35:1,2). A messianic prophecy of the restoration of the exiles to Zion; frequently quoted today with reference to land reclamation projects in Israel and elsewhere. See also: **Messiah**.

Des Esseintes, Duc Jean Floressas.   Main figure in J.K. Huysman's novel *A rebours* ("Against the Grain," 1884). Effeminate and voluptuous, he eventually retires into a wholly artifical world of pleasure. He represents the ideas of aestheticism in extreme degree and is the archetypal decadent.

Deucalion.   A kind of **Noah** of Greek legend, Deucalion built a ship to save himself and his wife, **Pyrrha**, when **Zeus** sent a deluge over the earth. After the flood receded, the ship came to rest on Mount **Parnassus**. Instructed by the **Delphic oracle** of Themis how to reconstitute the human race, Deucalion cast stones, the bones of Mother Earth, behind him, which became men; those cast by Pyrrha became women.

Deuteronomy.   The last book of the **Pentateuch**. It restates the laws of **Moses**, records the final events of Moses' life, and ends with his death.

Deus ex machina.   Literally, "the god from the machine"; this mechanical device in Greek drama lowered onto the stage the god who intervened to provide a solution to the dramatic conflict. Now the term has come to mean any rescuing agency introduced by the author to bring about a desired conclusion, usually without regard to the logic of character or situation.

Diana.   See **Artemis**.

Dido.   The queen of Carthage who received **Aeneas** after he was shipwrecked on the journey from Troy to Latium. She fell in love with Aeneas and committed suicide after he left her at the command of Jupiter (**Zeus**). See **Aeneas**.

Dies irae.   Latin, "Day of Wrath"; referring to the **Day of judgment**, the opening words of a medieval Latin hymn used in a Requiem Mass, or Mass for the Repose of the Dead.

Dimmesdale, Arthur.   The religious and intellectual minister in Nathaniel Hawthorne's 1850 novel *The Scarlet Letter*. He is the heroine Hester Prynne's partner in adultery and father of their child, Pearl. He suffers both physically and spiritually for his sin and his inability to confess it. See also: **Prynne, Hester**.

Dionysos   (or Dionysus). Also known as Bacchos to the Greeks, and **Bacchus** to the Romans; son of **Zeus** and Semele. At first a god of vegetation, he came to be especially worshipped as the god of wine. He is supposed to have wandered over a great part of the earth, even as far as India, spreading his cult, celebrated in frenzied festivals (see **Bacchae**; **Maenads**; **Bacchanalia**). He became associated with poetry and music; early choral odes known as dithyrambs were connected with his worship and from such choral pieces tragedy developed. In fact, tragedy and satyr plays were presented in Athens at the Greater Dionysia, a festival in honor of Dionysos. Although not included among the Olympian gods in the Homeric pantheon, Dionysos later displaced **Hestia** when his worship became more widespread. Mystic elements pertaining to regeneration and resurrection became part of the ritual associated with the worship of Dionysos, who was identified with the Egyptian **Osiris**. (See **Adonis**; **Eleusinian mysteries**; **Orphic mysteries**.) Dionysian, originally descriptive of the orgiastic rituals connected with the god, now signifies frenzied, ecstatic, wildly uninhibited rites or activities. Its opposite is Apollonian.

Dioscuri.   See **Castor and Pollux**.

Dis.   The Roman name for **Pluto** or **Hades**, god of the underworld; thus the lower world, Hell. Dante calls one part of his Inferno "the city of Dis."

Dives.   See **Lazarus and Dives**.

Divide the sheep from the goats.   "The Son of man shall come in all his glory, . . . and before him shall be gathered all the nations: and he shall separate them one from another, as a shepherd divideth his sheep from the goats: And he shall set the sheep on his right hand, but the goats on the left" (Matthew 25:31-33). In this prophecy of the Last Judgment the sheep and the goats symbolize the righteous and the wicked, respectively. See also: **Day of judgment**.

Dobson, Zuleika.   Max Beerbohm's beautiful enchantress in *Zuleika Dobson* (1911). All the Oxford undergraduates fall in love with her, but she can love only someone who does not love her. When all at Oxford have committed suicide for her, she goes to Cambridge for a try there.

Dogberry.   The pompous and confused constable in Shakespeare's *Much Ado About Nothing* (1598).

Don Juan.   Don Juan Tenorio, son of a prominent 14th-century family in Seville, had a reputation for seducing women. He killed the commander of Ulloa after seducing his daughter, and was eventually lured into a Franciscan monastery, where the monks killed him. His life provided the model for the Don Juan legend, utilized by Mozart in his opera *Don Giovanni*, by Byron in his poem *Don Juan*, and by George Bernard Shaw in his "Don Juan in Hell," part of *Man and Superman*. Today used, like **Casanova** and **Lothario**, for a man who pursues amorous adventures with many women.

Don Quixote.   The hero of Cervantes' novel *Don Quixote* (1605, 1615), who as an old man sets out to accomplish the ideals of knight-errantry. In a suit of armor and accompanied by his pragmatic squire, Sancho Panza, he experiences a series of sometimes humorous, sometimes comic and sometimes tragic adventures, through all of which he upholds his fervent idealism in the face of the corruptions and brutality of the world about him. Quixotic, derived from his name, means visionary, extravagantly romantic and impractical. See also: **Dulcinea del Toboso**; **Panza, Sancho**.

Doolittle, Eliza.   Ragged and uneducated flower girl in George Bernard Shaw's *Pygmalion* (1913). Henry Higgins, a linguist, bets he can pass her off as a duchess in six months by teaching her to speak and behave properly. He succeeds, but he refuses to acknowledge her as a woman with feelings who is grateful and fond of him. She finally marries Freddy Hill, slavishly devoted to her, and they open a flower shop. See also: **Higgins, Henry**; **Pygmalion**.

Doomsday.   The Last Judgment. The word "doom" originally meant simply a legal decision, but because of the association with the awesome images in the Book of Revelation and elsewhere in the Bible, it has come to mean any terrible fate. Doomsday in current usage refers usually to the threat of world destruction through a human agency, as in a nuclear war. See also: **Day of judgment**.

Doubting Thomas. "But he said unto them, Except I shall see in his hands the print of the nails, and thrust my hand into his side, I will not believe" (John 20:25). The disciple Thomas would not believe the resurrection except upon tangible proof, and Jesus, though permitting him to satisfy his doubts, nevertheless rebuked them. In popular speech, a doubting Thomas is the equivalent of the proverbial man from Missouri (the "show me state"), who must see in order to believe.

Douglas, Widow. Kind, well-meaning lady who attempts to "civilize" Huck in Mark Twain's *The Adventures of Huckleberry Finn* (1885). See also: **Huck Finn**.

Dove of Noah. After the 40 days of rain had ceased and the **flood** waters had begun to recede, **Noah** released a dove which returned to him with an olive leaf held in her beak, signifying that the land had emerged (Genesis 8:8-12). The dove and the olive branch are symbols of peace.

Draco. The seventh-century B.C. lawgiver of Athens noted for the severity of the laws he laid down. "Draconian" thus refers to any unusually harsh law or code.

Dracula, Count. Vampire hero of Bram Stoker's *Dracula* (1897). Dracula, a corpse by day and a bloodsucker by night, is hundreds of years old. His death is made irrevocable by a stake driven through his heart. The subject of numerous films and plays.

Drouet, Charles. In Dreiser's *Sister Carrie* (1900), the traveling salesman who is Carrie's first lover and introduces her to the "good life." He is flashy, boyish and utterly superficial.

Dryads. The tree nymphs (also called "hamadryads") of Greek mythology, specifically **nymphs** of the oak tree (*drys* meaning "oak" or "tree") but later generalized; they died with the trees they lived in. Most famous of the dryads was *Eurydice*, the wife of **Orpheus**.

Dulcinea del Toboso. In Miguel de Cervantes' *Don Quixote* (1605), Dulcinea is, in the Don's mind, the womanly incarnation of the chivalric ideal. In actuality she is an ordinary country wench, whose condition the Don takes to be an evil enchantment. He dedicates himself to breaking this enchantment and restoring Dulcinea to heavenly beauty.

Duncan.   The old king of Scotland, murdered in his sleep by **Macbeth** in Shakespeare's *Macbeth* (1605.).

Dust and ashes.   "Behold now, I have taken upon me to speak unto the Lord, which am but dust and ashes" (Genesis 18:27; also Job 30:19; 42:6). Here, dust and ashes means something worthless, and the phrase expresses humility and repentance. The formula "Ashes to ashes, dust to dust" is familiar from its use in the Book of Common Prayer for the burial of the dead; in that context it simply refers to the mortality of the physical or "earthly" body. See also: **Sackcloth and ashes**.

E

Earnshaw, Catherine. In Emily Brontë's *Wuthering Heights* (1847), she has a strange and passionate affinity for the brooding, wild **Heathcliff**, but rejects him for social reasons, forcing him to leave. He returns for revenge when she has been married and tamed by the mild Edgar Linton. Their fierce love destroys them, and Catherine dies giving birth to Linton's daughter, Cathy.

Earthly paradise. According to the Bible, after **Adam** and Eve's explusion from **Eden**, there is no **Paradise** open to man except that which awaits the righteous after death. Mankind, however, is still haunted by the dream of achieving an ideally happy life on this earth. It is not surprising, therefore, to find the earthly paradise, often conceived as an island, a garden, or an isolated valley, appearing as an archetypal image in hundreds of forms and in many cultures. It appears in the classical tradition of **Arcadia** and the **Golden Age**, in the Celtic tradition of **Avalon**, in the Peng-lai of Chinese myth, in Spenser's Garden of Adonis, in the **Shangri-la** of the novel *Lost Horizon*, in Camoens' *Lusiads* and in Melville's South Sea paradise in *Typee*. *The Earthly Paradise* is the title of a long narrative poem by William Morris (1870).

Earth shaker. One of the epithets for the sea god **Poseidon**, who could by his storms and huge waves shake the earth. By extension, used today as an epithet for a man who is a "world" shaker in his power over events; or, in the form "earthshaking," for an event or occurrence of enormous, worldwide significance, or one that challenges fundamental attitudes or beliefs.

East of Eden.   The place to which Cain was exiled after he killed his brother Abel (Genesis 4:16). John Steinbeck used the phrase as the title for a novel about conflict between brothers. See also: **Cain and Abel**.

Eat, drink and be merry.   This phrase is from Jesus' parable of the rich man who looked forward to enjoying the wealth he had accumulated, without knowing that his soul would be required of him that very night (Luke 12:16-20; cf. Ecclesiastes 8:19; Isaiah 22:13). The expression is proverbial for any short-sighted enjoyment.

Ecclesiastes, Book of.   The **Old Testament** book characterized by its pessimistic and cynical indictment of all worldly things; the book is perhaps most famous for its emphatic statement of worldly fatuity and futility: "Vanity of vanities; **all is vanity**, saith the preacher . . . " (Ecclesiastes 1:2; 2:11, 17, 26; 4:4, 16; 6:9, etc.).

Echo.   The nymph of Greek myth, who was hopelessly in love with **Narcissus** and pined away until nothing was left of her but her voice.

Eddas.   The *Elder Edda* is a collection of Old Norse mythological poems originating in the twelfth century and collected in the thirteenth; the *Younger Edda* is a guide to poets and poetry, in prose and verse, by Snorri Sturluson (d. 1242). Synonymous with Norse sagas.

Eden, Garden of.   The garden described as an **earthly paradise** in the Book of **Genesis**, the locale of the brief life of innocence and grace of **Adam** and Eve before **Satan** tempted them to taste the forbidden fruit of the Tree of the Knowledge of Good and Evil, causing their fall into sin. After they ate of this fruit, they were banished from the garden of paradise to a land "to the **east of Eden**." Today the term signifies any blissful and perfectly innocent place or state of being. See also: **Tree of Life, Tree of Knowledge**.

Egyptian darkness.   See **Plagues of Egypt**.

Elaine. "The Lily Maid of Astolat" of Arthurian legend. In Tennyson's *Idylls of the King*, she loves **Lancelot** in vain and is in turn vainly loved by **Gawain**. She dies of grief, and is buried at **Camelot**.

Electra. Daughter of **Agamemnon** and **Clytemnestra**, and sister of **Orestes**, whom she had sent away for his safety when Clytemnestra and Aegisthus killed Agamemnon on his return from Troy. Years later, when Orestes and his friend Pylades returned, Electra, filled with hatred for her mother, persuaded him to kill their mother and her lover. Electra later married Pylades. The story of Electra has been told by all three of the great Greek writers of tragedy: by **Aeschylus** in the *Libation Bearers* (second play of the trilogy, the **Oresteia**); by **Sophocles** in his *Electra*; and by Euripides in his play of the same name. Hofmannsthal's libretto of Richard Strauss' powerful, violent opera *Electra* (1909) is based on the play by Sophocles. The term "Electra complex" used in Freudian psychoanalysis refers to erotic attachment of a daughter to her father; it is the female counterpart of the "**Oedipus complex**."

Eleusinian Mysteries. Celebrated at Eleusis, a town near Athens, these were the most famous of the Greek mysteries or secret worships, whose rituals were a secret known only to the initiates. The exact rites are unknown but they were dedicated to **Demeter** and **Persephone** and were associated with fertility and the sowing of the grain, since the mysteries seem to have developed from an agrarian festival. Some idea of the preliminary activities of the mysteries can be found in the Homeric *Hymn to Demeter*. In later times, **Dionysos**, under the name of Iacchos, came to be associated with the mysteries as a god of fertility and regeneration of the earth; consequently, part of the festival consisted of a preoccupation with the descent to the Lower World and the life hereafter.

Eli, Eli Lamma Sabacthani. Aramaic for "My God, my God, why has thou forsaken me?" (Matthew 27:46). One of Jesus' last words or sentences, on the cross. See also: **Seven Last Words**.

Elijah. After King **Ahab** and **Jezebel** became followers of the god **Baal**, Elijah challenged the prophets of Baal to test the true God. Baal did not answer his prophets, and Elijah mocked them, building his own altar surrounded by a trench filled with water.

God's fire then came down, and "licked up the water that was in the trench." Elijah went up to heaven in a "**chariot of fire**," an apotheosis witnessed by Elisha, who happened to be plowing a field. The mantle of Elijah then fell to Elisha, who had asked that "a double portion of [Elijah's] spirit be upon me" (I Kings 18:17-40; 19:19; II Kings 2:8-14).

Eliza   (Harris). A sweet, brave, loving slave in Harriet Beecher Stowe's (1811-1896) *Uncle Tom's Cabin* (1852). When she learns that her child is about to be sold into slavery, she runs away with the child, crossing the Ohio River by jumping from one ice floe to another. See also: **Uncle Tom**.

Elmo, Saint.   In Christian hagiography, the patron saint of sailors. St. Elmo's fire refers to luminous effects surrounding ships during storms or great darkness.

Elohim.   See **Jehovah**.

Elysian Fields.   Called "The Elysian Plain" in Homer's *Odyssey* (IV, 563), a blessed and happy land at the world's end, ruled by Rhadamanthus, a judge of the dead. Here a select few favored by the gods come to a kind of paradise where "life is easiest for men," and where there is no snow, storms or rain. In Book VI of the *Aeneid*, **Vergil** places the Elysian Fields in the Lower World and to them are admitted the purified souls of all who have led an upright life. These souls spend their time joyously in a region of eternal spring and sunlight. One of the most beautiful boulevards in Paris is named *Les Champs Elysees*, "The Elysian Fields." In contemporary usage, another name for paradise. See also: **Earthly paradise**; **Islands of the Blessed**.

Elysium.   Latin, from the Greek, "*Elysion*." See **Elysian Fields**.

Endor, Witch of.   Facing the Philistine army, King **Saul** consulted a certain sorceress of Endor and had her raise the shade of the dead prophet **Samuel**, who correctly foretold his defeat and death at the hands of the enemy (I Samuel 28:3-25).

Endymion.   The best-known version of the story of Endymion is that he was a young and extremely handsome shepherd with whom

Selene, the Moon, fell passionately in love, and that at her request **Zeus** granted him a wish. Wanting to remain perpetually young, Endymion asked for eternal sleep. Each night Selene came down to kiss him without his being aware of her presence. The story forms the theme of Keats' long poem *Endymion* (1818), which opens with the famous line, "A thing of beauty is a joy forever."

Enoch.   The father of **Methuselah** and the archetype of the upright man (Genesis 5:21-24).

Eos.   The goddess of dawn, called **Aurora** by the Romans. Rosy-fingered, Homer's epithet for the goddess, has been frequently repeated in English poetry.

Eppie.   In George Eliot's ***Silas Marner*** (1861), the unacknowledged, illegitimate daughter of Godfrey Cass and adopted daughter of Silas, whom she loves and cares for in his old age. She is blond, blue-eyed and captivating.

Erato.   The muse of love poetry. See **Muses**.

Erebus.   Darkness; from Erebus and Nyx (Night) were born Hemera, "Day," and Aether, "Sky," according to **Hesiod**. Later poets identified Erebus with **Hades** or Hell, a meaning it retains.

Erinyes.   Also known as the Furies from the Latin, *Furiae*. Primitive avenging spirits called upon to punish crimes, especially those committed against one's kin. They were merciless. In artistic representations, they look stern and fierce, but not ugly, are winged, and may carry or be encircled by snakes. The most famous reference to them is their pursuit of **Orestes** for his murder of **Clytemnestra**, his mother. The conflict is resolved in the *Eumenides* of **Aeschylus**, the last play of his trilogy the *Oresteia*, in which the Furies and Orestes plead their cases before a court in Athens at which **Athena** casts the deciding vote of acquittal. The Furies are appeased when Athena promises them honor and a permanent home in Attica. Moreover, their name is changed to the Eumenides, "The Kind Ones." The interpretation is that the rule of tribal custom and revenge has given way to a code of law where all factors, including intent, are weighed in judging the penalty for a crime.

Erl-King.   The malevolent "king of the elves" was believed in folk tradition to lure persons, notably children, to their death; the theme was popularized in Goethe's well known ballad *Der Erlkönig*, set to music by Schubert.

Eros.   Identified with Amor (love) or Cupido (Cupid, desire) by the Romans. In early Greek cults, Eros, the spirit of loveliness in youth, was a powerful, primal force arising from **Chaos** (according to **Hesiod**). Later, he became the god of romantic love, was held to be the son of **Aphrodite**, and was represented as a mischievous, winged boy carrying torches and shooting arrows at gods and men that caused the victims to fall in love. Eros today refers to sexual love or the sexual instinct (libido). See also: **Cupid and Psyche**.

Esau.   The elder son of **Isaac** and **Rebekah**, described as a red, hairy man and a skillful hunter. **Jacob**, his crafty younger twin brother, fought with him while they were still in the womb, and later tricked Esau out of his birthright and Isaac's paternal blessing. Esau became the progenitor of the Edomites, whose traditional rivalry with the Israelites was thus explained. Later Jacob took pains to be reconciled with his brother (Genesis 25, 27, 33).

Esther.   In the **Old Testament** Book of Esther, King Ahasuerus of Persia, at a seven-day feast, ordered Queen Vashti to appear before the guests. She refused and was deposed, and Esther was then chosen from among the virgins in the kingdom to replace her. Subsequently her cousin Mordecai aroused the anger of **Haman**, the king's counselor, because he refused to bow to him. Haman determined to kill all the captive Jews and execute Mordecai. Esther, however, dissuaded the king, and when Haman himself was killed, the Jews triumphed over their enemies. The feast of Purim commemorates these events. Esther remains one of the best-loved heroines of the Jews.

Eternal City.   In Latin, *Urbs Aeterna*: Rome. The epithet given to the city, very early, by Ovid, Tibullus and other Roman writers.

Eumenides.   See **Erinyes**.

Euphrosyne.   Daughter of **Zeus**, one of the three **Graces**, epitome of joy and beauty. The other two Graces were Aglaia and **Thalia**.

Europa.   Daughter of Agenor, king of Tyre. Falling in love with her, **Zeus** assumed the form of a gentle white bull. When she climbed on his back in the spirit of play, he leaped into the sea and swam with her to Crete, where she bore him three sons: Minos, Rhadamanthus and Sarpedon.

Eurydice.   A **dryad**, wife of **Orpheus**. In trying to escape the attentions of a certain Aristaeus, she stepped upon a snake, which gave her a fatal bite. For the rest of the story, see **Orpheus**.

Euterpe.   The muse of lyric poetry and of the flute. See **Muses**.

Eva, Little.   In Harriet Beecher's Stowe's *Uncle Tom's Cabin*, a lovely, golden-haired girl whose goodness and love are almost saintly. See also: **Uncle Tom**.

Evangelist.   From the Greek *euangelion*, meaning good news. **Matthew**, **Mark**, **Luke** and **John**, the writers of the four Gospels, are known as the four evangelists, or bringers of good news. In latter usage, an evangelist came to mean any preacher of the gospel, especially an itinerant preacher or Protestant revivalist. By extension, any fervent supporter of a moral or religious cause.

Eve.   See **Adam**.

Excalibur.   In Arthurian legend, the sword which was embedded in a stone in a churchyard. Excalibur could be withdrawn only by the rightful king of England. Young **Arthur** was recognized as heir of Uther **Pendragon** and king when he pulled the sword from the stone.

Exodus.   The second book of the **Old Testament**, from the Greek *exodos*, "marching out." It chronicles the birth of **Moses**, the Israelites' bondage in Egypt and their final escape into the desert. With Moses as their leader, they cross the Red Sea. Thereafter, they wander in the Sinai wilderness for 40 years until they reach the promised land of **Canaan**. By extension, any departure of a large group of people, a mass migration.

Eye for an eye.   "Ye have heard that it hath been said, An eye for an eye, and a tooth for a tooth: But I say unto you, That ye resist not evil: but whosoever shall smite thee on thy right cheek, turn to him the other also" (Matthew 5:38-39). The allusion here is to the *lex talionis*, "principle of retaliation," in the Mosaic law (see Exodus 21:23-24; Leviticus 24:19-20; Deuteronomy 19:21). In its original context, the *lex talionis* was not an expression of vindictiveness so much as an attempt to set limits to vengeance. Jesus' injunction to eschew vengeance entirely therefore does not deny the law but extends it. Today the expression is used primarily to refer to any harsh and primitive system of justice that requires retribution to be exactly equal to the crime. See also: **Sermon on the Mount**; **Turn the other cheek**.

Eyre, Jane.   The heroine of a novel by the same name written by Charlotte Brontë (1816-1855) in 1847. Orphaned early in life, Jane grows up to be a sensitive, intelligent and self-reliant woman who earns her living as a governess and schoolmistress. The story of her love for the brooding, mysterious **Rochester** is at the heart of the novel.

F

Fagin. The evil old Jewish leader of a band of boys whom he trains to be thieves and pickpockets in Dickens' *Oliver Twist* (1838). He is finally arrested and condemned to die. See also: **Twist, Oliver**.

Faith that moves mountains. "Verily I say unto you, if ye have faith, and doubt not . . . if ye shall say unto this mountian, Be thou removed and be thou cast into the sea, it shall be done" (Matthew 21:21). Today the phrase is used to evoke the power of belief.

Fall, The. The "fall" of **Adam** and Eve from God's grace, and their subsequent exile from the **Garden of Eden** for disobeying His command not to eat of the Tree of the Knowledge of Good and Evil (Genesis 3). The title of Albert Camus' novel (in French, *La Chute*, 1956). Now used as a metaphor for any lapse from a happy or blessed state. See also: **Tree of Life, Tree of Knowledge**.

Fallen angel. One of the angels who sided with **Lucifer** (**Satan**) in his rebellion against God and was thrown with him from Heaven into Hell. The story of this revolt may derive from some Canaanite myth (Isaiah 14:12; cf. Revelations 12:7). It was elaborated on in later Jewish and Christian tradition, and, for the English-speaking world, achieved its definitive form in Milton's *Paradise Lost*. In current usage the phrase might be applied to anyone who has descended from a state of grace or happiness.

Fall of Jericho.   See **Jericho**.

Fall of a sparrow.   Jesus said to the apostles, "Are not two sparrows sold for a farthing? and one of them shall not fall on the ground without your Father. . . . Fear ye not therefore, ye are of more value than many sparrows" (Matthew 10:29). The phrase signifies God's presence in and guidance of every minute particular in His creation.

False prophets.   "Beware of false prophets, which come to you in sheep's clothing, but inwardly they are ravening wolves. Ye shall know them by their fruits. Do men gather grapes of thorns or figs of thistles? Even so every good tree bringeth forth good fruit; but a corrupt tree bringeth forth evil fruit" (Matthew 7:15-17). "Wolf in sheep's clothing" is a proverb now used with no awareness of its Biblical origin; it can apply to "false prophets" or to anyone who is dangerous but deceptively fairspoken.

Falstaff, Sir John.   One of Shakespeare's most successful and celebrated comic characters, Falstaff appears in *Henry IV*, Parts I and II, *The Merry Wives of Windsor* and *Henry V*. He is the fat, gloriously bibulous, lying, wenching, knavish knight, friend of young Prince Hal, unscrupulous, cowardly and despicable except for his wit, charm and his lack of hypocrisy.

Fata Morgana.   Italian, for "fairy mirage," also known as **Morgan le Fay**, a female fairy in medieval chivalric tales and Arthurian legend; usually controlled by the **Demogorgon** and involved in various nefarious and treacherous activities. The Fata Morgana is also a mirage seen in the sea or in the air above the sea, especially around the Straits of Messina where Morgan le Fay was reported to live.

Fates.   Known also as the Parcae or the Greek Moirae; three sister goddesses who preside over the birth, life and death of men. Clotho fabricated the thread of a man's life at his birth. Lachesis measured its length and determined its character and Atropos cut it off with her shears. These fates were unappeasable and inexorable.

Father forgive them; for they know not what they do.   See **Seven Last Words**.

Father William. In Lewis Carroll's *Alice in Wonderland* (1865), the ex-athlete who figures in the poem **Alice** recites that begins "You are old, Father William." Despite his age, Father William can still turn "a back-somersault in at the door" and balance an eel on the end of his nose.

Fat of the land. "I will give you the gold of the land of Egypt, and ye shall eat the fat of the land" (Genesis 45:18). Now a proverbial expression meaning to live in luxury.

Fatted calf, Kill the. See **Prodigal son**.

Faunus. A Roman god of nature and fertility, identified with the Greek **Pan**. His wife was the Roman earth-mother Fauna, also known as the Bona Dea (good goddess). Remarkable for her chastity, she never set eyes on a man after her marriage to Faunus. Fauns were minor rural deities represented as men with ears, horns, tails and hind legs of goats. They are identified with the Greek **satyrs**.

Feet of clay. "Thou, O king, sawest, and behold a great image . . . This image's head was of fine gold, his breast and his arms of silver, his belly and his thighs of brass, His legs of iron, his feet part of iron and part of clay" (Daniel 2:31-33). In Daniel's prophecy, the two feet of the image are the kingdoms of the Seleucids and Ptolemies (Macedonian and Greek dynasties that ruled in Asia Minor and Egypt from the fourth century B.C.); in current usage an "idol with feet of clay" means anything that is much admired, but proves to have a fatal weakness.

Ferdinand. (1) In Shakespeare's *The Tempest* (1611), the son of Alonso, the King of Naples, he is among the party shipwrecked on **Prospero's** island. At the end of the play, Ferdinand is betrothed to Prospero's daughter **Miranda**. (2) A gentle, noncombative bull who has delighted small children (in *The Story of Ferdinand*) by preferring to smell the flowers rather than take part in the bullfight in the ring.

Fergus. One of the great warrior kings of Celtic mythology. His name means "virility." The 20th-century Irish poet W.B. Yeats (1856-1939) celebrated the exploits of Fergus in a number of his poems.

Fiery furnace.   See **Shadrach, Meshach and Abednego**.

Fig leaves.   "Then the eyes of them both were opened, and they knew that they were naked; and they sewed fig leaves together, and made themselves aprons" (Genesis 3:7). The act of **Adam** and Eve was an expression of sexual shame springing from their loss of innocence. In the 19th century, museum curators regularly provided their Greek statues with fig leaves, and a good many works in the Papal collections of the Vatican still wear them. Consequently the fig leaf has become a symbol of Victorian prudery.

Fire and brimstone.   See **Lake of fire and brimstone**.

First born of Egypt, The slaying of.   In the **Old Testament**, the tenth plague that the Lord inflicted upon Pharaoh and the Egyptians: "And it came to pass that at midnight the Lord smote all the first born in the land of Egypt, from the firstborn of Pharaoh that sat on his throne unto the firstborn of the captive that was in the dungeon, and all the firstborn of the cattle" (Exodus 11:4-6; 12:29-30). The Angel of Death did not strike the firstborn of the Hebrews because **Moses** had instructed the people "to strike the lintel and the two side posts" of their doors with "a bunch of hyssop" dipped in the blood of a lamb (Exodus 12:21-28). See also: **Plagues of Egypt**.

Fishers of men.   "Jesus, walking by the sea of Galilee, saw two brethren, Simon called Peter, and Andrew his brother, casting a net into the sea, for they were fishers. And he saith unto them, Follow me, and I will make you *fishers of men*. And they straightway left their nets, and followed him" (Matthew 4:18-20; repeated in Mark 1:16-18; Luke 5:10; John 1:35-41). "Fishers of men" is a metaphor for "winners of souls." Since the Roman Pontiff is heir to Saint Peter, the ring used for the investiture of the Pope is called the "fisherman's ring."

Flaming sword.   After their disobedience, God drove **Adam** and Eve out of the Garden of Eden, keeping them from the Tree of Life with a flaming sword "which turned every way" (Genesis 3:24). See also: **Eden, Garden of**.

Flesh pots of Egypt. The children of Israel murmured against **Moses** and **Aaron** in the wilderness: "Would to God we had died by the hand of the Lord in the land of Egypt, when we sat by the flesh pots, and when we did eat bread to the full: for ye have brought us forth into the wilderness, to kill this assembly with hunger." Usually "flesh pots . . ." means sinful luxuries (Exodus 16:3).

Flood. See **Deucalion**; **Noah**.

Flora. The ancient Roman goddess of flowers and of spring, depicted in Botticelli's *Primavera*.

Fly in the ointment. "Dead flies cause the ointment of the apothecary to send forth a stinking savor: so doth a little folly him that is in reputation for wisdom and honour" (Ecclesiastes 10:1). The proverb now means simply the one drawback in an otherwise satisfactory situation.

Forbidden fruit. Specifically the fruit of the Tree of Knowledge of Good and Evil, which God commanded **Adam** and Eve never to eat. He expelled them from the Garden of Eden when, heeding the temptation of the snake, they did so anyway (Genesis 3:1-16). By extension, any desired but prohibited object. See also: **Eden, Garden of; Tree of Life, Tree of Knowledge**.

Forsyte. The upper-middle-class English family whose passions and fortunes John Galsworthy (1867-1933) chronicles in the series of novels known as *The Forsyte Saga*, which include *The Man of Property* (1906), *In Chancery* (1920) and *To Let* (1921). Among the more important members of the Forsyte family are James, the stiff-necked, strait-laced founder of the firm of solicitors "Forsyte, Bustard, and Forsyte"; Jolyon, James's older brother and a very wealthy tea merchant as well as the only Forsyte with a true appreciation for beauty; Soames, a solicitor who considers himself a connoisseur of art; and Irene, Soames's unhappy wife and most beautiful possession.

Fortunate Isles. Also called the Isles of the Blessed or the Happy Isles; a place of eternal felicity. Later they were associated with the Canary or Madeira Islands. See also: **Happy Islands; Islands of the Blessed**.

Four Horsemen of the Apocalypse. Four riders symboliz-ing Pestilence, War, Death and Famine (Revelation 6:1-8).

Frankenstein. The name of Mary Wollstonecraft Shelley's 1818 romance, subtitled *A Modern Prometheus*. Frankenstein, a medical student, succeeds by means of galvanism in bringing to life a monster formed of graveyard corpses and dissecting-room remains. The monster, who in the course of time has usurped the name of his creator, initially yearns for human sympathy. Rejected, he turns on his maker and, destroying everyone he loves, hounds him to his death. Symbolically, the creation that turns on its creator.

Frankenstein's monster. See **Frankenstein**.

Frankincense, gold and myrrh. See **Magi**.

Friar Laurence. In Shakespeare's ***Romeo and Juliet*** (1594), the Franciscan monk who marries Romeo and Juliet hoping, in vain, that their marriage will end the feuding between their two families, the **Montagues** and the **Capulets**.

Friar Tuck. The fat, merry friar, and friend of the legendary **Robin Hood**.

Friday. In Daniel Defoe's *Robinson Crusoe* (1717), the savage whom Robinson Crusoe rescues from cannibals. Friday quickly adjusts to Crusoe's way of life. He learns to speak English and becomes servant, friend and companion to Robinson Crusoe. Today a "Girl Friday" or "Man Friday" is a constant, loyal, almost indispensable helper. See also: **Crusoe, Robinson**.

Frome, Ethan. Hero of Edith Wharton's novel *Ethan Frome* (1911). A farmer and frustrated engineer, Ethan bears with a sick and nagging wife until Mattie Silver, his wife's cousin, comes to live with them. They fall in love, but when forced to separate, they de-cide on suicide. They are both injured, and Ethan's wife nurses them for the rest of their lives. See also: **Silver, Mattie**.

Furies. See **Erinyes**.

G

Gabriel.   One of the archangels, and messenger of God. He was the interpreter of **Daniel**'s vision, and announced the births of **John the Baptist** and Jesus Christ (Daniel 8:16; 9:21; Luke 1:19, 26). In Christian eschatology, Gabriel's trumpet will announce the **Day of judgment**; in Islamic tradition, Gabriel dictated the Koran to Mohammed.

Gadarene swine.   See **My name is legion**.

Gaea   or Gaia. Greek personification of the earth as goddess. Gaea is the mother or source of **Uranus** (the Heavens) and joined with him to produce the **Titans**, among others.

Galahad, Sir.   One of the Arthurian Knights of the **Round Table**, son of Sir **Lancelot** and **Elaine**, and the most pure and chaste of the knights. He is the rightful occupant of the **Siege Perilous** and reaches the Holy **Grail**. See also: **Arthur**.

Galatea.   The sculptor **Pygmalion** scorned living women for their imperfections, and resolved to create a perfect woman. In revenge, **Aphrodite** caused him to fall in love with a cold stone statue, but finally relented and brought it to life as the mortal Galatea. The inspiration for G.B. Shaw's play *Pygmalion* and the musical *My Fair Lady*.

Gamp, Sarah   ("Sairy Gamp"). The disreputable, low-class, drunken midwife in Dickens' *Martin Chuzzlewit* (1843). She carries an umbrella, and validates her opinions through the sanction of an imaginary "Mrs. Harris."

Gant, Eugene. Hero of Thomas Wolfe's *Look Homeward, Angel* (1929). The youngest in a large family, he is a brooding dreamer, hungry for life, love, beauty. His father Oliver is a huge, exuberant, eloquent man harried by his sharp-tongued and avaricious wife Eliza. The book's title is itself an allusion to a line in Milton's elegiac poem "Lycidas" (1638).

Ganymede.   A young man of Phrygia so beautiful that **Zeus** had him brought to heaven by an eagle to become his cupbearer. Might be applied today to any youth of extraordinary beauty.

Garden of Eden.   See **Eden, Garden of.**

Garden of the Hesperides.   The garden where **Hera**'s apples were guarded by the nymphs called **Hesperides** and by a dread dragon. One of **Heracles'** labors was to bring back the golden apples.

Gargantua.   The hero of Rabelais' satirical narrative *Gargantua and Pantagruel* (1533). A likable and gigantic prince, he undergoes a series of adventures, fighting wars, mediating disputes, and assisting friends to achieve their desires. "Gargantuan" in common usage means enormous, gigantic.

Gargery, Joe.   The kind and gentle blacksmith who raises Pip, the hero of Dickens' *Great Expectations* (1860).

Gates of Janus.   See **Janus.**

Gatsby, Jay.   Born James Gatz, he is the tragic hero of F. Scott Fitzgerald's *The Great Gatsby* (1925). He has made money by bootlegging and peddling phony stocks. Gatsby creates an image for himself of larger-than-life fortune and glamor and tries to live up to it. Reckless and romantic, he suggests the emptiness of the American success myth.

Gautama.   The full name of the historical **Buddha** (meaning "enlightened one") who founded Buddhism was Gautama Siddhartha.

Gawain.   In Arthurian legend, one of the knights of the **Round Table**, a nephew of King **Arthur**. He is one of the original heroes of the **Grail** quest, and is described by medieval writers as "sage" and "courteous." He is the hero of the great medieval poem "Sir Gawain and the Green Knight."

Gehenna.   From the Hebrew *ge-hinnom*, literally, "valley of the son of Hinnom," a valley where bloody sacrifices of children were made by their parents in the worship of the god **Moloch**; also called **Tophet**, hence the expression "as hot as Tophet" (II Kings 23:10; Isaiah 30:33; Jeremiah 7:31-32; 19:1-5; 32:35). Today it signifies hell.

Generation of vipers.   "O generation of vipers, who hath warned you to flee from the wrath to come?" (Matthew 3:7; 12:34; 23:33; Luke 3:7). An attack on the **Pharisees** (q.v.).

Genesis.   From the root of the Greek word meaning "to be born." The first book of the **Old Testament**, it deals with the creation of the world, followed by accounts of Israel's patriarchs: Abraham, **Isaac**, **Jacob**, **Joseph**. See also: **Abraham's Bosom**.

Genius.   Protective spirits supposedly assigned to men at birth or resident in places (*genius loci*). The Romans believed each man had his own individual genuis who watched over him. By extension, genius means the unique character of a language, an historical period, a country, and *genius loci* means the peculiar character of a place or distinctive impression it makes on the mind. "Evil genius" is a person who exercises a harmful influence upon the actions and character of another. The sense of genius as extraordinary intellectual power or instinctive and supreme creative ability (or the person born with such powers) came into English usage much later, though this is what the word most commonly signifies today.

Geryon.   In Greek myth, the monstrous son of Chrysaor and Callirhoe, with three merged bodies and three heads. He owned a cannibalistic herd of cattle and a two-headed dog, Orthus, who guarded them. **Heracles** killed Geryon and Orthus and presented the herd to Eurystheus. In Canto 17 of Dante's *Inferno*, Geryon is the winged monster of fraud who bears Dante and Vergil into the pit of lower Hell.

Gethsemane. "Then cometh Jesus with them unto a place called Gethsemane, and saith unto the disciples, Sit ye here, while I go and pray yonder . . . My soul is exceeding sorrowful, even unto death" (Matthew 26:36-38; Mark 14:32-34; Luke 22:39 ff.). Gethsemane was a garden at the foot of Mount Olivet, about a mile from Jerusalem, where Jesus went to pray on the night of his betrayal. Although he asked his disciples to watch with him, they fell asleep, leaving him alone. Thus Gethsemane now typifies any lonely ordeal or describes any scene of suffering. This incident is also known as "the agony in the garden." See also: **Mount of Olives**.

Get thee behind me, Satan. "Get thee behind me, Satan: thou art an offence unto me: for thou savourest not the things that be of God, but those that be of men" (Matthew 16:23; Mark 8:33). The words of Jesus to **Peter**, when the latter suggested that Jesus ought not to be crucified. Now a proverbial formula for renouncing a temptation.

Ghosts of Christmas Past, Present and Yet to Come. The three apparitions that appear before the mean, penny-pinching Ebenezer Scrooge in *A Christmas Carol* (1843) by Charles Dickens (1812-70). Together the three ghosts show Scrooge the evil of his ways in an attempt to reform his soul. Light emanates from the head of Christmas Past; Christmas Present reveals to Scrooge the joys he is missing at Christmastide; while the fearful Ghost of Christmas Yet to Come points to the dreadful consequences, including a neglected grave, of Scrooge's inhumanity. See also: **Scrooge, Ebenezer**.

Giants. A race of monstrous beings, children of **Gaea**, the earth, and **Uranus**, the sky. In the Greek cosmology, they came into existence just after the earth's creation, before it took essential form. In the usual version of the myth, they rebelled against the Olympian gods, were defeated, and were hurled by **Zeus** to **Tartarus**. See also: **Olympians, The Twelve**.

Giants in the earth. "There were giants in the earth in those days" (Genesis 6:4). **Genesis** contains a fragment of an old myth about a race of giants (Nephilim) sprung from marriage between earthly women and heavenly beings ("the sons of God"). The Biblical tradition is that the wickedness of the Nephilim was so great that they provoked God to send the Flood (see **Noah**); modern allusions to this passage, however, usually ignore the wickedness of the giants and apply the text in the context of the lines that follow: "The same became mighty men which were of old, men of renown." Thus used in reference to greatness and glory of mankind in bygone days.

Gideon.   A man of great religious zeal and military ability, who led the Israelites in their combat against the Midianites and Amalekites (Judges 6-8). The Gideon Society, which places Bibles in hotel rooms, is named after him.

Gifts of the Magi.   See **Magi**.

Gilgamesh.   Hero of the ancient Mesopotamian epic *Gilgamesh*; a demi-god and king of Uruk, one of the cities of ancient Sumeria. In titanic combat he defeats his rival Enkidu, and then becomes his friend. After Enkidu's death, the stricken Gilgamesh looks for him in the land of the dead.

Gird up the loins.   "And the hand of the Lord was on **Elijah**; and he girded up his loins and ran before Ahab" (I Kings 46; cf. II Kings 4:29; 9:1). A common expression meaning to tighten one's belt in preparation for action.

Girondists.   Members of a moderate political group known as the Gironde, important in the French Revolution. Their name derives from the French department of the Gironde, a region near Bordeaux that supplied many of their leaders. Mostly middle-class businessmen, they supported political but not social democracy and lost their power when the pendulum of Revolution swung toward a more radical faction which brought on the Reign of Terror.

God and Mammon.   See **Mammon**.

Godiva, Lady.   The patroness of Coventry, England, who sought to have removed certain exactions that Leofric, Earl of Mercia, imposed on his tenants in 1040. According to legend, Leofric agreed to do so if Lady Godiva rode naked through the town at noon. She did so, and he kept his word. All the townspeople stayed indoors but a tailor peeped at her through a window and, in consequence, was blinded. See also: **Peeping Tom**.

Go down to the sea in ships.   "They that go down to the sea in ships, that do business in great waters; These see the works of the Lord, and his wonders in the deep" (Psalms 107:23). Novelists and poets have used this allusion as a way of creating an aura of solemnity around the journeys of seafarers.

Godunov, Boris.   The cruel, ruthless protagonist of Pushkin's *Boris Godunov* (1831). The story is set in the late 16th century. Boris has Crown Prince Dimitri assassinated, and becomes czar himself. Before Boris dies of illness during the campaign against him, he names his son as the new czar. The real Godunov was czar from 1598 to 1605.

Gog and Magog.   Two nations who will wage war with **Satan** against the people of God (Revelation 20:8). They signify the coming of the great war of the **Apocalypse**.

Golden Age.   The initial stage of man's history on earth, characterized by great happiness, prosperity and harmony, man living at one with nature and his fellow man. Today, any particularly prosperous and creative era. See also: **Eden, Garden of**.

Golden bowl be broken.   See **Silver cord be loosed**.

Golden calf.   The idol of the golden calf was made from jewelry by **Aaron**, and worshipped by the Israelites when **Moses** had gone to **Mount Sinai** (Exodus 32:1-14). Colloquially, today: money or materialism.

Golden fleece.   The fleece of a pure gold, winged ram. Phrixus and Helle escaped Boeotia by flying on the ram's back, but only Phrixus reached Colchis. In some versions, Phrixus gave the ram as a gift to Aeetes, king of Colchis, who offered it as a sacrifice to **Zeus**. The golden fleece hung from a tree in a sacred grove in Colchis, until **Jason** and the **Argonauts** stole it with the help of **Medea** and carried it off.

Golden rule.   "Do unto others as you would have others do unto you," as tradition has paraphrased the original lines in Matthew 7:12, a part of Christ's **Sermon on the Mount**.

Golgotha.   See **Calvary**.

Goliath.   The huge, supposedly invincible warrior who daily came out to challenge any Israelite. **David**, while still a young shepherd, accepted the challenge and slew Goliath with a stone from his sling (I Samuel 17:23-54).

Gomorrah.   See **Sodom and Gomorrah**.

Goneril.   The savagely cruel elder daughter of **Lear** in Shakespeare's *King Lear*. She joins her evil sister **Regan** in humiliating Lear, contests with her over Edmund, and kills herself after poisoning Regan.

Good Samaritan.   "A certain lawyer . . . willing to justify himself, said unto Jesus, And who is my neighbour? And Jesus answering said, A certain man went down from Jerusalem to Jericho, and fell among thieves, which stripped him of his raiment, and wounded him, and departed, leaving him half dead. . . . But a certain Samaritan, as he journeyed, came where he was: . . . And went to him, and bound up his wounds, pouring in oil and wine, and set him on his own beast, and brought him to an inn, and took care of him . . . Which now of these three, thinkest thou, was neighbour unto him that fell among thieves? And he said, He that showed mercy on him. Then said Jesus unto him, Go, and do thou likewise" (Luke 10:30-37). The Samaritans were a schismatic Jewish sect who accepted only the **Pentateuch** as canonical. The rivalry between Samaria and Judea is mentioned in Ezra 4 and Nehemiah 4. In Jesus' time Jews still regarded Samaritans with contempt (John 4:9, 8, 48, etc.). In choosing a Samaritan as hero of his parable, Jesus intended a rebuke to national pride and religious intolerance. The word now applies to any charitable person, especially one who, like the man in the parable, rescues or helps out a needy stranger.

Good shepherd.   The Bible abounds with images of sheep and shepherds, the latter used as metaphors for the Lord (Psalms 23) or for the pastor of a Christian congregation (John 23). Thus the good shepherd, in the biblical sense, is someone charged with the religious care and guidance of others.

Good tidings of great joy.   The news brought to the shepherds in the field by the angel of the Lord, informing them of Christ's birth (Luke 2:10).

Gordian knot.   Gordias, a peasant, became king of Phrygia when the Phrygians, in obedience to an oracle, crowned the first person to drive up to the temple of **Zeus** in a wagon. Gordias tied the wagon's yoke to the pole inside the temple with an extremely complex knot. The oracle decreed that whoever was able to untie it would become emperor of Asia. Alexander the Great cut the knot with a single stroke of his sword. Hence a "Gordian knot" is any complex problem, and "cutting the Gordian knot" is a particularly decisive way of solving it.

Gorgons.   The Gorgons were three extraordinarily ugly sisters, Stheno, Euryale and Medusa. The sight of Medusa could turn an onlooker to stone. Their hair was laced with serpents, their hands were of brass, their bodies covered with scales, their teeth like tusks. Medusa, the most famous, was beheaded by **Perseus**; her sisters were immortal.

Goriot, Father.   Hero of Balzac's *Père Goriot* (1835). He is totally devoted to his two selfish, ungrateful daughters who exploit his paternal love and drain him of all his money. He dies still praising them, but they do not attend his funeral.

Go and sin no more.   When the scribes and **Pharisees** brought to Christ the woman taken in adultery and asked what to do, Christ replied, "He that is without sin among you, let him first cast a stone at her . . . And they which heard it, being convicted by their own conscience, went out one by one . . . and Jesus was left alone, and the woman standing in the midst. When Jesus . . . saw none but the woman, he said unto her, Woman, where are those thine accusers? hath no man condemned thee? She said, No man, Lord. And Jesus said unto her, Neither do I condemn thee: go and sin no more" (John 8:9-11). A rebuke to hypocrisy.

Gospel. Literally, "good tidings" or "good news," from the Anglo-Saxon "godspell," a translation of the Latin *evangelium*, which derives from the Greek *euangelion* (see **Evangelist**). Refers to the written accounts of the life of Jesus collected in the **New Testament** and ascribed to **Matthew**, **Mark**, **Luke** and John (known as the four evangelists) (see **John, Saint**). Also a general term for the teachings of Christ, the Christian revelation. By extension, the word has come to mean an assertion or statement of unimpeachable source or character, as in "the gospel truth," or a teaching or cause propounded with great fervor.

Goths. A teutonic tribe which invaded and destroyed much of Southern Europe between the third and fifth centuries. "Goths" now stands for any cruel, untutored barbarians. The term Gothic, derived from the name of this tribe, refers primarily to the style of architecture very common in Europe from the 12th to the 16th centuries. A Gothic novel, however, is a form of popular fiction that originated in England during the late 18th century. These novels employ lonely settings, often drawn from history, and mysterious, "brooding" characters to play out stories of gloom, terror, violence and the supernatural.

Götterdämmerung. The twilight of the gods. In Germanic mythology, the destruction of the gods and the world in a cosmic battle with the powers of evil. The last opera in Wagner's *Ring* tetralogy. See also: **Nibelungenlied**.

Graces. The graces were three daughters of **Zeus**: Euphrosyne (Mirth), Aglaia (Splendor) and **Thalia** (Good Cheer); the embodiment of charm and beauty, they give life its grace and loveliness.

Gradgrind, Thomas. In Dickens' *Hard Times* (1854) the founder of a school where only scientific fact is taught and where the warmth and imagination of human character are stifled. He victimizes himself, his wife and his children by his harsh views and even harsher discipline.

Grail (Holy Grail, Graal, Sangraal). The Holy Grail figures prominently in Arthurian legend (see **Arthur**) as a sacred object. According to the most familiar version, it was a dish or cup used by Jesus at the **Last Supper**, in which Joseph of Arimathea later caught some of Jesus' blood at the Crucifixion. It was carried to Britain, but the world becoming too sinful for so holy a relic, it disappeared. From time to time, however, it manifested itself to a chosen few. The quest for the Grail occupied many of the knights of King Arthur's **Round Table**. The legend is known to English readers mainly in the accounts of Thomas Malory in the 15th century and Alfred Tennyson in the 19th. There are medieval French versions by Chretien de Troyes and others. The best known German treatments are by Wolfram von Eschenbach and Richard Wagner. In popular speech and allusion, the Grail still carries some suggestion of ancient religious awe. It often symbolizes any high ideal or object of a spritual quest.

Gray, Dorian.   In Oscar Wilde's *The Picture of Dorian Gray* (1891), a rich, extraordinarily handsome young man of the London of the 1890s. His life of sodden debauchery leaves its mark not on his own face but on the face of his portrait, which becomes the visible barometer of his inner corruption.

Greater love hath no man.   "Greater love hath no man than this, that a man lay down his life for his friends" (John 15:13). This line is from Jesus' last address to his disciples, recorded only by John; Jesus continues by explaining, "I have called you friends, for all things that I have heard of my Father I have made known to you."

Greeks bearing gifts.   See **Timeo Danaos et dona ferentes**.

Green pastures.   "The Lord is my shepherd; I shall not want. He maketh me to lie down in green pastures: he leadeth me beside the still waters; he restoreth my soul" (Psalms 23:1-3). Probably as familiar as any other passage in the Bible, these lines are spoken especially at funerals. "Green pastures" refers to any pleasant place.

Grendel.   In , the monster who kidnaps and devours King Hrothgar's warriors. He is killed in a struggle with Beowulf.

Griselda.   The quintessential patient, obedient wife. Geoffrey Chaucer (1340?-1400) includes an unforgettable version of her story in his *Canterbury Tales* ("The Clerk of Oxenford").

Grove(s) of Academe.   This expression, often used to mean a college, university, or academic circles, comes from Milton's *Paradise Regained* (IX-244): "The olive grove of Academe, / Plato's retirement...." *Academe* was the public grove in Athens where the philosopher **Plato** taught. The term derived originally from Academus, an **Arcadian** citizen who owned the estate that became a meeting place for the philosophers of Athens.

Grundy, Mrs.   From the phrase in Tom Morton's *Speed the Plough* (1798): "What will Mrs. Grundy say?" that is, what will the proper-thinking neighbors say. "Mrs. Grundy" now epitomizes the rigid and Puritanical-minded person who condemns the slightest departure from conventional behavior.

Grushenka.   In Dostoevsky's *The Brothers Karamazov* (1880), the earthy, unstable, vital, primitive, beautiful woman loved by Dmitri Karamazov and pursued by his father. See also: **Karamazov, Fyodor Pavlovitch**.

Guermantes, Prince de.   A representative of the older aristocracy in Marcel Proust's *Remembrance of Things Past* (1918-22). See also: **Swann, M.**

Guinevere.   Wife of King **Arthur**. She is abducted and seduced by Sir **Lancelot**. While Arthur is away, **Mordred**, Arthur's son, usurps the Kingdom. His desire to marry Guinevere brings on the final tragedy that ends in his and Arthur's death, and leads to the dissolution of the **Round Table**. Guinevere renounces Sir Lancelot and takes the veil at Almesbury where she dies.

Gulliver.   Hero of Swift's *Gulliver's Travels* (1726). A satire on some of the customs, institutions and innovations of the time, the book is divided into four parts. In part one, Lemuel Gulliver is ship-wrecked on the island of the Lilliputians, a people only six inches in height and of petty moral stature as well. In the second part, Gulliver finds himself among the **Brobdingnagians**, a race of giants. In the third part, he travels to various islands where reason and science are prostituted by the grotesque "projectors," and in the fourth he finds himself among a race of horses called the **Houyhnhnms**, who embody reason, serenity and justice, and who dominate a race of filthy barbaric, ape-like creatures with human forms and vices, called the **Yahoos**. See also: **Lilliput**.

Gummidge, Mrs. The forlorn widow of Daniel Peggotty's partner in Dickens' *David Copperfield* (1850); she constantly wails that she is a "love-lorn creature."

Gunn, Ben. A half-crazed pirate marooned for three years on Tresure Island in R.L. Stevenson's *Treasure Island* (1883). See also: **Hawkins, Jim**.

Gynt, Peer. The fantastical, imaginative, Faustian hero of Ibsen's *Peer Gynt* (1867), who cannot accept the pure and ideal love of Solveig, and makes his life a detour through the evil kingdom of the Trolls and the world at large. At the play's end, Peer returns to Solveig, his sole hope of salvation.

H

Hades.   The brother of **Zeus**, lord over the world of the dead. The name is also used to signify the lower world itself, more commonly referred to today as hell.

Halcyon.   Halcyone, daughter of **Aeolus** and wife of Ceyx, dreamed of her husband's shipwreck and death. She found the body on the shore the next morning and after three days of extreme grief, cast herself into the sea. She and her husband were then changed into kingfishers, birds whose nesting time always occurs when the surface of the sea is very peaceful. Today the term means particularly calm and happy, as in the phrase "halcyon days."

Hamadryads.   Tree nymphs. See also: **Dryads**; **Nymphs**.

Haman.   Angered by the Jew Mordecai's refusal to bow down before the Persian King **Ahasuerus**, Haman, an enemy of the Jews, plotted to kill the captive Jews and hang Mordecai. **Esther**, the Jewish wife of Ahasuerus, frustrated his plan and it was Haman who was hanged. This episode from the Book of Esther is celebrated at the Jewish festival of Purim. The *hamantaschen* or triangular filled pastries eaten at the season are "Haman's purses."

Hamlet.   The tormented and obsessively introspective prince of Denmark and protagonist of Shakespeare's tragedy *Hamlet* (c. 1600), Hamlet is regarded by many as the first truly modern character in English literature. Hamlet's brooding about the death

93

of his father, the remarriage of his mother to **Claudius**, his father's brother and murderer, his feigned (or possibly real) madness, and his contemplation of suicide have given rise to numerous interpretations. Unable to act or to live at peace without acting, fascinated by the playing of roles, aware of the corruption around him but powerless to move against it, Hamlet embodies the paralyzing consciousness and self-consciousness of Western man in our era. The play contains some of Shakespeare's most famous and memorable lines, including Hamlet's soliloquy on suicide that begins, "To be, or not to be, that is the question."

Handwriting on the wall.   See **Belshazzar**; **Mene, mene, tekel, upharsin**.

Hanging gardens of Babylon.   See **Seven wonders of the ancient world**.

Hannah.   Mother of the prophet **Samuel**. She was barren until God answered her prayers and gave her a son (I Samuel 1:2).

Happy Islands   (or Isles). Another name for the **Islands of the Blessed**, as in Tennyson's "Ulysses":

> It may be we shall touch the Happy Isles
> And see the Great **Achilles**, whom we knew.

See also: **Odysseus**.

Harpies.   Literally, "snatchers, robbers." They were considered personifications of the winds that could carry persons away, or as souls of the dead that could snatch away the souls of the living. They are depicted as winged maidens or as repulsive-looking birds with heads of maidens and long claws. In modern usage, a "harpy" means any grasping person, generally female but sometimes male, or a mean-tempered, shrewish woman.

Hawkins, Jim.   In R.L. Stevenson's *Treasure Island* (1883), the brave young narrator and hero of the story, who becomes cabin boy aboard the *Hispaniola*.

Headless Horseman, The.   A figure of mock horror in Washington Irving's (1783-1859) "Legend of Sleepy Hollow," from his

The Sketch Book of Geoffrey Crayon Gent (1820). The local schoolmaster, Ichabod Crane, is enamored of the lovable Katrina Van Tass. But his courtship of Katrina is broken up by his rival, Brom Bones, who, dressed as a headless horseman, scares Ichabod out of his wits and out of town. See also: **Crane, Ichabod**.

Heap coals of fire. "If thine enemy be hungry, give him bread to eat; and if he be thirsty, give him water to drink: For thou shalt heap coals of fire upon his head, and the Lord shall reward thee" (Proverbs 25:21-22). In other words, evil is best overcome by repaying it with goodness. The coals of fire may be understood as the embarassment and remorse felt by the enemy.

Heathcliff. The violent and passionate hero of Emily Brontë's *Wuthering Heights* (1847). Brought as an untamed child into the Earnshaw household, he is badly treated by Hindley, the family's weak and snobbish son. He loves and is loved by Catherine, but leaves, vowing revenge against Hindley. When he returns years later to achieve it, he has become a man something more and less than human, with a fund of demonic energy fed by his unfulfilled passion for Catherine. Heathcliff is a type of romantic hero. See also: **Earnshaw, Catherine**.

Heaven's gate. After **Jacob** awoke from his vision of **Jacob's ladder**, he exclaimed, "How dreadful is this place! This is none other but the House of God, and this is the gate of heaven" (Genesis 28:16-17).

Hebe. The daughter of Zeus and Hera, and goddess of youth; Hebe was cupbearer to the gods before she was replaced by **Ganymede**.

Hecate. At first considered a mighty goddess who helped men to achieve success in war, to acquire wealth or to gain good crops, she was later indentified with her cousin **Artemis**. According to some versions, Hecate was one aspect of the triple-formed Artemis, who was Selene, the moon-goddess, in the sky, Artemis on earth, and Hecate in the underworld. Finally, she became a goddess of the lower world, of witchcraft, ghosts, magic and necromancy. She was especially worshiped at crossroads, since these were associated with magic. She appears briefly with the **Weird Sisters** in

Shakespeare's *Macbeth* and today represents the spirit of ancient witchcraft.

Hector.   In the *Iliad*, the oldest son of **Priam** and **Hecuba**, husband of **Andromache**, and father of Astyanax. Hector typifies the greatest virtues of the code of the ancient warrior, preferring death to dishonor, but he also possesses the most outstanding human virtues: compassion, affection, loyalty, piety, devotion to family and parents. While **Achilles** is sulking in his tent, Hector fights with the greatest of the other Greek warriors and carries the fighting to the Greek ships. Finally he kills **Patroclus**, the dear friend of Achilles, and strips him of Achilles' armor. Achilles then comes out to fight and drives the Trojans back behind their walls, but Hector remains to fight Achilles alone. With the help of **Athena**, Achilles mortally wounds Hector, drags his body around the walls of Troy and denies it burial. Finally, the gods intervene to cause Achilles to allow the body to be buried. As the *Iliad* began with the wrath of Achilles, the Greek hero, it ends with the funeral of Hector, the Trojan hero. See also: **Trojan War**.

Hecuba.   Wife of **Priam**, king of Troy, and mother of many children, among them **Hector**, **Paris**, **Cassandra**, Polyxena, Polydorus. In the *Iliad* she witnesses one sad scene after another as so many of her sons are slain, culminating with the killing of Hector by **Achilles** and the desecration of his body. When Troy is taken, Hecuba falls by lot to **Odysseus**. The grief and despair she feels over her own fate are exacerbated by the news of the sacrifice of her daughter Polyxena on the tomb of Achilles. To pile sorrow on sorrow, she has to prepare for burial the broken body of her little grandson Astyanax, son of Hector and **Andromache**, whom the Greeks have just killed. All this is poignantly told in *The Trojan Women* (415 B.C.) by Euripides. Hecuba has become a symbol of intense grief and devastating misfortune. See also: **Trojan War**.

Heep, Uriah.   One of the best-known characters in literature; the conniving, shrewd, falsely "umble" clerk of Mr. Wickfield in Dickens' *David Copperfield* (1850). His name is colloquially synonymous with untrustworthy humbleness.

Hegira.   From the Arabic word meaning "departure"; the journey of **Mohammed** from **Mecca** to Medina after his expulsion on July

16, 622. This marked the beginning of the Muslim era. By extension, a hegira is any departure for a more favorable or promising place.

Helen of Troy.   Daughter of **Zeus** by **Leda** (wife of Tyndareus), and sister of **Clytemnestra, Castor** and **Pollux.** Helen grew into the most beautiful woman in the world, and her many suitors agreed among themselves that whoever eventually married her would be defended by the others. She married **Menelaus**, and when Paris carried her off to Troy, the Greek leaders organized the expedition against Troy. After the end of the **Trojan War**, Helen returned with Menelaus to Sparta. Her name signifies the power of a woman's beauty to change the course of history. See also: **Apple of discord.**

Helicon.   A mountain in Boeotia, an ancient Greek district northwest of Athens, the dwelling place of the **Muses**; here flowed the Hippocrene, a spring that inspired poetry. Today, a reference to poetic inspiration.

Helios.   The Greek sun god (corresponds with the Roman Sol), the son of **Hyperion.**

Hellas.   The Greek name for Greece after the time of the Homeric poems. The Greeks themselves were called Hellenes, though **Homer** refers to them as *Achaeans. Greece* comes from the Latin word *Graec:a*, which the Romans formed from the name of the first tribe in Hellas with which they came into contact.

Hellenic.   Adjective referring to the culture of Hellas, or Greece, from about the date of the First Olympiad, 776 B.C., to the death of Alexander the Great, 323 B.C. See also: **Hellas.**

Hellespont.   "Sea of Helle"; named after Helle, a girl who fell into the body of water now called the Dardanelles, the strait that separates Europe and Asia in Turkey leading from the Aegean Sea to the Sea of Marmora. This story is part of the legend of the **Golden Fleece.** See also: **Hero and Leander.**

Henry V.   Son of Henry IV and historic king of England (from 1413 to 1422). As portrayed in Shakespeare's historical dramas

Henry IV Part I and *Part II*, Prince Hal (as the future Henry V is known) is a wild and boisterous youth, the drinking companion of the sot **Falstaff** and his gang of rowdy hangers-on. Showing his father's fears about his worthiness for the role of king to be unfounded, Prince Hal rises nobly to his new position, dismissing the loose companions of his youth and effectively establishing his power. In the play *Henry V*, Shakespeare portrays King Henry as a fearless and able military leader, the deliverer of rousing battlefield rhetoric and the heroic victor of the Battle of Agincourt against the French.

Henry IV.   Historic king of England (from 1399-1413) whose rise to power and troubled reign Shakespeare depicts in his historical plays, *Richard II*, *Henry IV Part I* and *Henry IV Part II*. Shakespeare portrays Henry IV as a rather ruthless political animal who seized power by deposing the effete Richard II and allowing him to be murdered. As an old man, Henry is haunted by the political violence of his early career and worries that his wild and irresponsible son, Prince Hal (see **Henry V**), can never rise to the responsibility of monarchy.

Henry, Frederic.   In Hemingway's *A Farewell to Arms* (1929), an American lieutenant serving in the Italian ambulance corps during World War I. Uprooted, haunted by life's emptiness, disheartened by his own cynical escapism, he searches—at first indifferently, then desperately—for a truth to sustain his spirit. The focus of the novel is his love for the beautiful English nurse Catherine Barkley, played out against the violence of the war. See also: **Barkley, Catherine**.

Hephaestus.   Known to the Romans as Vulcan, the god of the forge and the guardian of fire. Ugly, and also lame, he had a gentle and kind disposition, which was often taxed by the affairs of his wife, **Aphrodite**, goddess of love. He crafted the glorious armor of the gods, made **Achilles'** famous shield, and produced **Zeus'** thunderbolts and **Artemis'** arrows.

Hera.   Called Juno by the Romans, Daughter of Cronus and **Rhea**, sister and wife of **Zeus**, goddess of marriage, protectress of married women. She was the mother of **Ares**, **Hebe**, **Hephaestus**, and Eileithyia, a goddess of childbirth. Hera was one of the three goddesses who contended for the Golden Apple (see **Apple of dis-**

cord) awarded to **Aphrodite** by the **Judgment of Paris**. A great part of her time and energy was spent in thwarting the amorous designs of Zeus or in wreaking vengeance upon the women he loved or their offspring (see **Heracles**). Most myths and ancient poems depict her as petty, jealous, wrathful and implacable.

Heracles.   Known to the Romans as Hercules. Noted not only for his prodigious strength but also for his good nature and compassion, he has the longest list of exploits of any of the Greek heroes; in fact, many deeds that may have been accomplished by lesser heroes were later attributed to him. Heracles' feats began in the cradle, where he strangled two serpents that **Hera**, jealous of this child produced by the love of **Zeus** and the mortal Alcmene, sent to kill him. Hera's enmity followed him throughout his life. It brought on the madness which led him to kill his wife Megara and their children. On the advice of the **Delphic oracle**, he then performed the celebrated **Twelve Labors** (see **Labors of Heracles**) to expiate his crime. After their completion, Heracles married Dejanira. How he met his death is told in the story of the **Shirt of Nessus**. From the funeral pyre, his soul rose to take its place among the gods; a reconciliation was effected with Hera. He then married her daughter **Hebe**. For other incidents related to Heracles, see **Argonauts**; **Alcestis**. Heracles is the archetype of the powerful and fearless hero. The most frequent references are to his twelve formidable labors ("herculean" tasks).

Hermes.   Known as Mercury to the Romans; son of **Zeus** and Maia. As an infant, he fashioned a lyre out of tortoiseshell and stole the cattle of **Apollo**. Noted for his inventiveness, he also became the god of traders and thieves, the messenger of the gods, and conductor of souls to the lower world. In art he is generally represented as a young god wearing a wide hat called a petasos, winged sandals (*talaria*), and carrying a wand with serpents twined about it (**caduceus**).

Hermes Trismegistus.   In late classical times, the Neoplatonists identified the Greek god **Hermes** with the Egyptian god **Thoth**—scribe of the gods, inventor of numbers and god of human knowledge, especially magic—and called him Hermes Trismegistus, literally Hermes "thrice-greatest." The so-called *Hermetic Writings* of magical and mystical lore were attributed to

Hermes Trismegistus, who continued to be an important figure in magic and alchemy throughout the Middle Ages. Our word hermetic, meaning either sealed airtight or pertaining to the occult sciences, particularly alchemy, derives from Hermes Trismegistus.

Herod Antipas. Pontius Pilate sent Christ before Herod Antipas, who "set him at nought, and mocked him" (Luke 23:7-15). The son of **Herod the Great**, he served as tetrarch (ruler of one quarter of a Roman province) from 4 B.C. to 39 A.D. His marriage to his niece, Herodias, was denounced by **John the Baptist**, whose beheading was sought by **Salome**. Herod Antipas was eventually exiled to Gaul in 39 A.D. He is remembered chiefly for the beheading of John the Baptist. See also: **Pilate, Pontius**.

Herod the Great.   Not to be confused with **Herod Antipas**, he was king of Judea at the time of Christ's birth; he ordered the **Massacre of the Innocents**, hoping by killing all male children under two years of age to destroy the "Prince" who was prophesied to take his throne from him. Unjustly suspecting his wife Mariamne of adultery, he ordered her executed. Allusions to Herod (73 B.C.-4 B.C.) usually refer to the ferocious cruelty of his slaughtering innocent children. Quick to lash out at what he feared and could not control, he stands as an archetypal tyrant.

Hero and Leander.   Hero, a young priestess of **Aphrodite**, lived in Sestos, a city on the European side of the **Hellespont**. Directly opposite, in Abydos, there lived her lover, a young man named Leander, who swam across every night to see her, guided by a lamp (or torch) held by Hero. One night, the lamp was extinguished by a storm and Leander was drowned. When the body was washed ashore the next morning at the base of the tower on top of which Hero used to stand with her light, she threw herself into the sea. Hero and Leander are cited as proverbial examples of true and devoted lovers. The story, not properly a myth but rather a romantic folktale, has come down to us from a poem by the Greek poet Musaeus (sixth or fifth century A.D.).

Hesiod.   One of the earliest Greek poets (ca. 800 B.C.), Hesiod is the author of the *Theogony* (describing the myths of the gods) and *Works and Days* (describing peasant life).

Hesperides, The.   "The Daughters of Evening"—daughters of night, or of **Atlas** and Hesperis. Their number is usually given as three but varies from four to seven. They dwelled in the **Garden of the Hesperides**, located far to the west, either near the **Islands of the Blessed** or near Mt. Atlas. They guarded the tree bearing the golden apples given by **Gaea** to **Hera** when she married **Zeus.** They were aided by the dragon Ladon. One of the labors of **Heracles** was to carry off the golden apples.

Hestia.   Goddess of the hearth and one of the twelve Olympian deities. See also: **Olympians, The Twelve**.

He that is without sin.   See **Cast the first stone**.

He that runs may read.   God said to the Old Testament prophet Habakkuk, "Write the vision, and make it plain upon tables, that he may run that readeth it" (Habakkuk 2:2). Commonly quoted as "he that runs may read." The meaning is that the letters are so plain that they can be read "on the run."

Hewers of wood and drawers of water.   **Joshua** cursed the Gibeonites during his conquest of **Canaan**, saying "Now therefore ye are cursed, and there shall none of you be freed from being bondmen, and hewers of wood and drawers of water for the house of my God. . . . And Joshua made them that day hewers of wood and drawers of water for the congregation" (Joshua 9:23-27). "Hewers of wood and drawers of water" is now used generally for any persons who do hard, menial work.

Hezekiah.   A king of **Judah** who tries to abolish idolatry among the Israelites, and to restore the worship of **Jehovah** (II Kings 18).

Hide your light under a bushel.   See **Light of the world**.

Higgins, Henry.   The lingust in Shaw's *Pygmalion* (1913), who takes Eliza Doolittle, a ragged Cockney flower girl, and transforms her in six months into a woman accepted in society as a duchess. Professor Higgins is a bad-tempered bully, yet underneath he is kind and good-hearted and utterly without malice. Eliza becomes very fond of him, but he remains a bachelor. See also: **Doolittle, Eliza**.

Hippocrates   "The father of medicine," a Greek doctor (ca. 460-377 B.C.) born in the island of Cos, author of 87 treatises on aspects of medicine. Physicians today take the **Hippocratic oath**.

Hippocratic oath.   An oath attributed to **Hippocrates**, "the father of medicine," and enjoined upon his followers, setting up a canon of behavior, integrity and loyalty for doctors. One version begins with the words, "I swear by Apollo, the physician, by Aesculapius, by **Hygeia**, by Panacea, and by all the gods and goddesses . . . ." The so-called Hippocratic oath taken by the medical profession today is much shorter and somewhat different although the intent is in many respects the same.

Hippolyta   (or Hippolyte). Queen of the **Amazons** and, according to some myths, the mother of **Hippolytus** by **Theseus**. One of the twelve **Labors of Heracles** was to bring back the girdle of Hippolyta. In some versions, he killed her in order to get it, while in others she gave it to him willingly. In some myths, she is called Antiope, while in others the two are sisters.

Hippolytus.   The son of **Theseus** and the Amazon queen **Hippolyta** (in some versions her name is Antiope), Hippolytus was a handsome and chaste youth dedicated to **Artemis**, virgin goddess of the hunt, and utterly indifferent to love. **Phaedra**, whom Theseus married after Hippolyta died, fell madly in love with the young man, but he spurned her advances. In despair, Phaedra hanged herself, claiming that Hippolytus had seduced her and so shamed her into committing suicide. Theseus cursed his son and called upon the sea god **Poseidon** to fulfill his curse. A sea monster rose up and frightened the horses of Hippolytus; the chariot overturned and the innocent young man died of his wounds.

Holmes, Sherlock.   The hero of a series of detective stories by Sir Arthur Conan Doyle (1859-1930). His brilliantly deductive genius (and his eccentricities) have made him the most famous of professional detectives, and, with his foil, the amiable **Dr. Watson**, the protagonist of innumerable contemporary productions of the canon on theater screens and television.

Holofernes.   See **Judith**.

Holy City. A city which becomes holy through its association with a given religion, such as Jerusalem to Christians and Jews, Benares to Hindus, **Mecca** and Medina to the Muslims.

Homer. Commonly accepted as the author of the *Iliad* and the *Odyssey*, although for a long time various scholars argued that these were the works of different writers. No details of his life are known for certain. He is supposed to have been blind, and is often referred to as "The Blind Bard." It is not known where he was born, although tradition has it that he came from a city in Asia Minor, such as Smyrna, or from an Aegean island, such as Chios. His date has been fixed as anywhere from the ninth century B.C. down to the seventh. The epics of Homer, held in reverence in the classical age as in our own, formed the basis of the literary education of the ancient Greeks and contain a treasure house of Greek mythology. Today, "Homeric" carries the suggestion of herioc, larger-than-life.

Homeric laughter. In Homer's *Iliad* (I, 599) "unquenchable laughter" arose among the gods at their feast. Hence, "Homeric laughter" is unrestrained, and, by extension, very loud and cheerful, epic and heroic.

Hope deferred. "Hope deferred maketh the heart sick: but when the desire cometh, it is a tree of life" (Proverbs 13:12).

Horace. Great Roman lyric poet and satirist (65-8 B.C.) during the reign of the Emperor Augustus. Best known for *Odes* and *Epistles*. "Horatian" usually connotes a refined, balanced view of life that may be sharply satiric at times but is generally conservative and respectful of authority.

Horsemen of the Apocalypse. "And I saw, and behold a white horse: and he that sat on him had a bow; and a crown was given unto him: and he went forth conquering, and to conquer. . . . and there went out another horse that was red: and power was given to him that sat thereon to take peace from the earth. . . . And I beheld, and lo a black horse; and he that sat on him had a pair of balances in his hand. And I looked, and behold a pale horse: and his name that sat on him was Death, and Hell followed with him. And power was given unto them over the fourth part of the earth, to kill with sword, and with hunger, and with death, and with the beasts of the earth" (Revelation 6:2-8). In the apocalyptic vision of Saint John, when the Lamb opens the Book of the Seven Seals, John sees four horsemen symbolic of the last judgment. The rider on the red horse is war and bloodshed; the rider on the black horse represents famine; the rider on the pale horse represents death; the rider on the white horse is probably Christ (cf. Revelation 19:11). See also: **Apocalypse; Day of judgment; John of Patmos**.

Horus   (or Hor). God in the form of a falcon, whose eyes were the sun and the moon; son of Egyptian deity, **Osiris**. In battle with Osiris's enemy, **Set**, Horus's left eye was damaged and then healed by the god, **Thoth**. This was the mythological explanation of the phases of the moon. Egyptian kings or pharaohs also came to be viewed as incarnations of Horus and used his name as part of their own.

House divided.   "Every city or house divided against itself shall not stand" (Matthew 12:25; also Mark 3:25). The words of Jesus, referring to Satan and his kingdom. "House" means a household or family. Abraham Lincoln applied this allusion to the divided condition of the United States, "half slave and half free," in a speech delivered in 1858; today Lincoln's allusion is perhaps even better known than the original use of the phrase in the **New Testament**.

Household gods.   See **Lares and Penates**.

House of many mansions.   In his farewell sermon, Jesus said to his disciples, "Let not your heart be troubled: ye believe in God, believe also in me. In my Father's house are many mansions: if it were not so, I would have told you. I go to prepare a place for you" (John 14:2). In this passage, "mansion" means literally a separate place in a larger building, but the theological allusion is to a place of salvation for those who follow Jesus.

Houyhnhnms.   The race of rational, socially and morally perfect horses **Gulliver** meets in Book IV in Swift's *Gulliver's Travels* (1726). They dominate the nasty, brutish **Yahoos**, an inferior race alarmingly similar to man. Gulliver lives among them in their happy, harmonious and orderly society until they banish him, fearing corruption from Gulliver's human nature.

How are the mighty fallen.   "The beauty of Israel is slain upon thy high places: how are the mighty fallen!" (2 Samuel 1:19). From David's elegy for Saul and Jonathan, now generally applied in any appropriate context. See also: **Tell it not in Gath**.

Hubris.   Overweening pride, arrogance or insolence which causes a man to violate the moral code of the gods and ultilmately to challenge them directly. An example is Capaneus who saved himself from death in a raging storm by grasping a rock jutting out high on a cliff. Still hanging over the waters, he taunted **Zeus** with his skill and fortune; promptly the rock broke and Capaneus was dashed to death.

Huck Finn   (Huckleberry Finn). The hero of Mark Twain's novel *The Adventures of Huckleberry Finn* (1884). Huck flees from his alcoholic, reprobate father, and in company with **Jim**, a runaway slave, journeys down the Mississippi River on a raft. In the course of the trip, Huck undergoes a complete introduction to the evils, corruptions and hypocrisies in our society. From Jim he learns the values of human integrity and dignity. The trip ends with Jim's capture. Huck, reunited with Tom Sawyer, decides to go west rather than accept the values of civilized society. See also: **Sawyer, Tom**.

Hurstwood, George.   In Theodore Dreiser's *Sister Carrie* (1900), he is Carrie's second lover, a man of position but not great wealth. As a result of his love affair with Carrie, he loses his reputation and self-esteem, and ends his life as a sordid suicide in a flop house.

Hyacinth.   A beautiful youth loved by **Apollo**. Zephyr, the West Wind, who was jealous, caused Apollo to misdirect a discus throw, killing Hyacinth. The hyacinth flower grew from the spilled blood, and Apollo placed the youth's body amidst the constellations.

Hydra.   A mythical beast with nine heads, one of which was immortal and the others possessed of the power to grow back as two when chopped off. Killing the Hydra was one of the **Labors of Heracles**. Today a very complex and troublesome situation, which presents fresh difficulties as soon as one element is resolved, might be described as hydra-headed.

Hygeia   (or Hygiea). Goddess of health, daughter of **Asclepius**.

Hymen.   Also called Hymenaeus, son of **Dionysos** and **Aphrodite**, he is the god of marriage; represented as a handsome youth carrying a torch, and as leader of the wedding chorus and marriage feasts.

Hyperboreans.   A mythical people, the Hyperboreans (from Greek, *hyper*, "above, beyond," *Boreas*, "North Wind") lived far to the north, beyond both Europe and Asia, in a land of perpetual happiness not unlike the **Islands of the Blessed**. They were favored by **Apollo** who often visited them, and whom they especially worshipped. Some Roman poets used their own word for hyperborean to mean simply far to the north; today it carries the secondary meaning of arctic or frigid.

Hyperion. A **Titan**, son of **Uranus** and **Gaea**, *husband of Thea, father of* **Helios**, or the Sun, **Selene**, or the Moon, and **Eos**, or the Dawn. Homer also refers to Helios as Hyperion. Hyperion is often identified with the sun.

Hypnos. Also **Somnos** (in Roman mythology), god of sleep. Father of **Morpheus**, god of dreams.

I

Iago. The villain and personification of evil in Shakespeare's tragedy *Othello* (1604). He incites Othello to such rages of unfounded jealousy against his wife, **Desdemona**, that eventually Othello kills her. Few characters in world literature rival Iago for pure malevolence.

Icarus. The son of **Daedalus**, who was provided with wings of wax and feathers by his father during their escape from the **Labyrinth** of Minos. He failed to heed his father's warning not to fly too near the sun, and fell to his death when the wax melted.

Ichor. A clear fluid, the blood of the gods.

Ida, Mount. (1) A mountain in Asia Minor noted as the scene for both the carrying off of **Ganymede** and the **Judgment of Paris**; also the place from which the gods watched the battles around Troy. (2) A mountain in Crete where **Zeus** was said to have been born. See also: **Trojan War.**

If thy right eye offend thee. "And if thy right eye offend thee, pluck it out, and cast it from thee: for it is profitable for thee that one of thy members should perish, and not that thy whole body should be cast into hell" (Matthew 5:29). From the **Sermon on the Mount**. This text, with its rather ferocious insistence on righteousness, has sometimes been used as an argument for the explusion of unwanted church members.

I.H.S.   Monogram of the name of Jesus, in Greek *Iesous*. "H" is not the Roman "aitch," but the capital form of the Greek *eta*. The mistaken notion that these initials correspond to Roman letters gave rise to the erroneous interpretation that I.H.S. is a acronym for *Iesus Hominum Salvator*, "Jesus saviour of men," or worse still, "I have suffered." This monogram often appears on vestments, chalices, altar cloths, and other Christian ceremonial objects.

Iliad.   The great Greek epic poem by **Homer**, the first surviving piece of European literature, generally dated before 700 B.C.; from "Ilion," one of the names of Troy. Divided into 24 parts, called books, its basic themes are the **Trojan War** and the wrath of **Achilles**. The action covers 47 days of the tenth year of the war. Deeply offended because **Agamemnon**, leader of the Greeks, had taken the maiden Briseis from him, Achilles withdrew from combat and "sulked" in his tent. Achilles reentered the fight to avenge the death of his bosom friend **Patroclus**, slain and stripped of his armor by **Hector**, the Trojan hero. Achilles slew Hector and dragged his body around the walls of Troy. Hector's father, the Trojan King **Priam**, aided by **Hermes** in disguise, gained permission from Achilles to have Hector's body buried. The *Iliad* ends on a quiet note with the funeral of Hector. An epic of battle and death, the *Iliad* is filled with the peculiar sadness and moments of compassion that only war can arouse. The action takes place on two levels, divine and human, with the gods taking part in the affairs of men and at times suffering with them.

Imogen.   In Shakespeare's *Cymbeline* (1609), Cymbeline's daughter. An incarnation of supreme virtue, she is faithful, forgiving, loyal, courageous and independent.

In the beginning was the Word.   "In the beginning was the word, and the Word was with God, and the Word was God. . . . In him was life; and the life was the light of men" (John 1:1-5). From the Greek *logos*, "word." This term has a long history in Greek philosophy. In Heraclitus, it designates the principle of rational order amid the flux of things. The Stoics saw it as the principle of divine reason, from which all things derive. Philo Judaeus (Jewish theologian and philosopher who lived in Alexandria around the time of Christ) conceived of it as a kind of **demiurge,** distinct from God, but the instrument of His creation. John, in this passage from the fourth gospel, corrects Philo by asserting that *logos* is to be identified with God, and further declares (1:14) that the Word has become incarnate in Christ. John is using Greek concepts to reinterpret for his own time the Hebraic belief in a creative God and in the **Messiah.** This usage is not to be confused with "the word of God," in the sense of divine revelation, or scripture. See also: **John, Saint.**

Inherit the wind.   "He that troubleth his own house shall inherit the wind" (Proverbs 11:29; cf. Hosea 8:7). "House" means family, household. To inherit the wind is to cause trouble, to raise a storm.

Injun Joe.   In Mark Twain's *Tom Sawyer* (1876), an evil halfbreed who murders Dr. Robinson, is exposed by Tom, and nearly kills the boy later. Joe escapes, but is trapped in a cave and starves to death. See also: **Sawyer, Tom.**

In the sweat of thy face.   "In the sweat of thy face shalt thou eat bread" (Genesis 3:19). Part of **Adam**'s punishment for his disobedience to God; ever since **the fall** of Adam and Eve, men must toil and sweat for their livelihood, and for this reason work is sometimes called "Adam's curse."

Iphigenia.   Daughter of **Agamemnon** and **Clytemnestra**, sister of **Electra** and **Orestes**. When the Greek fleet was becalmed at Aulis, because Agamemnon had offended **Artemis**, the seer **Calchas** revealed that Agamemnon's daughter had to be sacrificed to appease the goddess. Clytemnestra and Iphigenia were summoned on the pretext that the latter was to be married to **Achilles**, who, of course, knew nothing about the match. Iphigenia was about to be sacrificed but, according to one version of the story, Artemis was moved to pity and substituted a deer in her place. The goddess carried her off to the land of the Tauri in the Crimea to become her priestess there. Eventually, Orestes and Pylades came there to remove the statue of the Taurian Artemis as expiation for Orestes' murder of Clytemnestra. When Iphigenia recognized her brother, she helped him escape with the image to Greece. Iphigenia appears in two plays by Euripides, *Iphigenia in Aulis* and *Iphigenia in Tauris.*

Iris.   Iris ("Rainbow") was goddess of the rainbow and messenger of the gods in the *Iliad*, and also in **Vergil**.

Isaac.   The son of Abraham and **Sarah**, born to them when they were 100 and 91 years respectively. To test Abraham's faith, God ordered him to sacrifice the boy, and when his readiness to do so was clear, God substituted the traditional ram for the human sacrifice (Genesis 21:1-8; 22:1-14). Isaac was the father of **Esau** and **Jacob** by his wife **Rebekah**.

Isaiah.   Hebrew prophet (eighth century B.C.) after whom the biblical *Book of Isaiah* is named. Isaiah foresaw the destruction of Israel by its enemies, the Assyrians, and warned his people that deliverance depended on their return to proper devotion to **Yahweh** (God) (see **Jehovah**). The later chapters prophesy the destruciton of Babylon and the return of the Jews to their homeland. Although the earlier chapters convey a grim message of doom, the *Book of Isaiah* is often quoted for its prophecy of peace, "and they shall beat their swords into plowshares, and their spears into pruninghooks: nation shall not lift up sword against nation, neither shall they learn war any more" (Isaiah 2:4). The Christian **Gospels** draw more heavily from the *Book of Isaiah* than from any other prophetic text.

Ishmael.   The disaffected, meditative narrator of Herman Melville's (1819-1891) *Moby Dick* (1851), which opens with the famous line, "Call me Ishmael." Ishmael, who goes to sea whenever life on land makes him restless and disenchanted, signs aboard the *Pequod* under **Ahab** and gets swept up in his mad pursuit of the white whale. The name is an allusion to the Biblical Ishmael, the son of Abraham and Hagar, the maid of Abraham's wife **Sarah**. When Sarah bears Abraham a child of her own (**Isaac**), she asks Abraham to drive Hagar and Ishmael away, and the two wander in the wilderness (Genesis: 11-12; 21:9-21). Ishmael, which means "God is hearing," is a prototype of the outlaw or dweller in the wilderness.

Isis.   The principal goddess of ancient Egypt, an equal of her husband-brother **Osiris** and her son **Horus**. She is a fertility/nature goddess, and there are many mystery cults associated with her; in addition, she is the patron of mariners and the goddess of the moon. The cow is her sacred animal.

Islands of the Blessed (Blest). According to **Hesiod, Zeus** settled some of the chosen men of the Heroic Age in a dwelling place at the ends of the earth where they lived a carefree existence. This place Hesiod called the Islands of the Blessed; it corresponds to Homer's Elysium or **Elysian Fields**. Some other poetical names for it are the **Fortunate Isles**, or Islands, the **Happy Islands**, or Isles. Now used as another term for heaven or paradise.

Ixion. A king of Thessaly, he murdered his father-in-law, Eioneus, and planned to seduce **Hera. Zeus** sought to prevent the seduction by creating a cloud in the shape of Hera. Ixion, drunk, made love to the cloud. Zeus thereupon ordered **Hermes** to tie Ixion to a wheel which revolves eternally across the sky. His name in allusion signifies treachery and the dire punishment meted out to it.

J

Jabberwock. A monster, resembling a dragon, described in Lewis Carroll's nonsense verse ballad "The Jabberwocky," in his *Through the Looking Glass* (1872).

Jacob. The patriarch of the book of **Genesis** whose twelve sons became the founders of the twelve tribes of Israel. As a young man he purchased the birthright of his brother **Esau** "for a mess of pottage," and then with the help of his mother Rebekah he impersonated Esau and obtained the blessing from his aged blind father, **Isaac.** When traveling to Padan-Aram to escape Esau's anger, he dreamed of the ladder "set up on earth, and the top of it reached to heaven: and behold the angels of God ascending and descending on it." (See **Jacob's ladder.**) Another well-known story of Jacob tells of how, when he was returning home one evening he wrestled with a man until the break of day, not releasing him until he blessed Jacob. The man was an angel of God, who then changed Jacob's name to Israel. His later life centers on his two sons by his wife Rachel, **Joseph** and **Benjamin** (Genesis 24-51).

Jacob's ladder. "And Jacob went out from Beersheba, and went toward Haran. And he lighted upon a certain place, and tarried there all night . . . And he dreamed, and behold a ladder set up on the earth, and the top of it reached to heaven: and behold the angels of God ascending and descending upon it. And behold the Lord stood above it . . . And Jacob awaked out of his sleep and said, Surely the Lord is in this place and I knew it not. . . . and he called the name of that place **Bethel**" (Genesis 28:10-19). Taken at face value, this story explains the origin of the shrine at Bethel (Hebrew for the house of God), which remained an important cult center until its destruction by King Josiah. Modern scholarship suggests that the place was already an established shrine where visitors who slept in the sacred precincts could consult the oracle in dreams. Jacob's exclamation, "This is the house of God," would then indicate the fusion of the local cult with the worship of Jacob's god, **Yahweh**. In modern allusion, the ladder from heaven to earth symbolizes the communion of man with the Divine.

Jacques.   In Shakespeare's *As You Like It* (1599), a melancholy, contemplative, cynical character attached to the banished Duke's court in the forest of **Arden**. His speech on "The Seven Ages of Man" contains some of Shakespeare's most often quoted lines:

> "All the world's a stage
> And all the men and women merely players.
> They have their exits and their entrances.
> And one man in his time plays many parts,
> His acts being seven ages."

Janus.   One of the oldest Roman deities, depicted with two faces, one facing forward, the other facing to the rear. He was thus a god of vigilance and wisdom, knowing the past and looking to the future. He was also the god of doors (Latin, *ianuae*) and came to be the god of exits and entrances, or beginnings and endings. Originally he was a god of light who opened the heavens at dawn and closed them at sunset. In time of peace, the doors to his temple were closed, but they were open in time of war. He is described by **Vergil** in the ***Aeneid*** (VII, 607 ff). Today, the reference is usually "two-faced" in the sense of deceitful or double-dealing.

Jason.   The Greek hero, son of Aeson, king of Iolcus. His throne was usurped by his uncle Pelias, and Jason was sent into exile, where he was raised by the centaur Chiron (see **Centaurs**). When Jason returned to claim his throne, he was told by Pelias that he could have it in exchange for the **Golden Fleece**. Jason set out in the ship *Argo* with a number of other famous heroes (the **Argonauts**), and arrived at Colchis where the Fleece was kept by King Aeëtes. With the help of the king's sorceress daughter, **Medea**, who had fallen in love with him, Jason obtained the prize and returned to Greece. Jason thereafter became king of Corinth and had two children by Medea. Later, however, Jason cast off Medea to marry Glauce. Medea avenged herself by killing her successor, and her own two children. She then fled to Athens. Jason is said to have become an outcast later in his life, and to have been killed by the falling prow of his old ship.

Javert, M.   The sternly conscientious, incorruptible police inspector of Victor Hugo's *Les Misérables* (1862). His duty is to return Jean Valjean to prison. However, when Valjean saves the inspector's life, when he could have escaped and let him die, Javert cannot resolve the conflict and commits suicide. See also: **Valjean, Jean.**

Jehosaphat.   One of the kings of Judah in the **Old Testament**, ruled 873-849 B.C. (I Kings 22). Today often used as a mild oath, sometimes in combination with "jumping."

Jehovah. The word used by Christians for the God of the **Old Testament**, whose incommunicable name is represented in Hebrew by the letters Y,H,W,H. Called the tetragrammaton, the word is never spoken when the Jews read scripture, but instead pronounced as Adonai or Elohim. The actual pronunciation has been lost, but may have been **Yahweh** or Yave. In any case, it was not Jehovah.

Jehu.   The son of Nimshi, who killed King Jehoram and overthrew the dynasty of **Ahab**, the evil Queen **Jezebel**, and all the pagan prophets. He is reputed to have driven his chariot fast and furiously on his way to kill the king (II Kings 9:20). By extension, a dangerous driver.

Jekyll and Hyde personality.   In Robert Louis Stevenson's 1886 novel, *The Strange Case of Dr. Jekyll and Mr. Hyde*, the good Dr. Jekyll invents a drug which transforms him into the evil Mr. Hyde, along with an antidote which will return him to his better self. Ultimately, Mr. Hyde is driven to murder, and when he is unable to make the antidote, he commits suicide. "Jekyll and Hyde" has come to refer to the "split" personality or someone who exhibits wildly contradictory character traits.

Jephtha's daughter. When Jephtha, judge of Israel, led the people against the invading Ammonites, he vowed to sacrifice to God, as the price of victory, the first creature who came to meet him on his return. This proved to be his daughter, his only child, but Jephtha kept his vow, after allowing her two months to go into the mountains to bewail the fact that she was dying a virgin (Judges 11:29-40). The theme of the rash promise is a common one in folklore, often with the detail added that the person making the vow expects to be greeted by his dog. Today, the story is remembered for its tragic quality, recalling the Greek legend of **Iphigenia**.

Jeremiad. A tragic lament after some catastrophe, from the lamentations of (the **Old Testament** prophet) **Jeremiah** after the fall of Jerusalem (*Book of Jeremiah*).

Jeremiah. One of the great prophets of the **Old Testament**, who lived during the time of the conquest of Jerusalem by the Babylonians and the period of despair that followed. After the temple was destroyed, Jeremiah stressed the individual rather than the nation and saw the source of religion in the human heart. His prophecies are in the *Book of Jeremiah*, and he is credited as author of the *Book of Lamentations*.

Jericho. "Now Jericho was straitly shut up because of the Children of Israel. See, I have given unto thine hand Jericho, and the king thereof, and the mighty men of valor. And ye shall compass the city. . . . And seven priests shall bear before the ark seven trumpets of rams' horns: and the seventh day ye shall compass the city seven times, and priests shall blow with the trumpets. . . . So the people shouted when the priests blew the trumpets. . . . that the wall fell down flat, so that the people went up into the city. . . . and they took the city" (Joshua 6:1-20). Jericho lies in the Dead Sea depression below Jerusalem. Archaeological evidence in part confirms and in part modifies the story in **Joshua**; the city was apparently destroyed not once but twice. The miraculous collapse of the walls of Jericho at the blast of a trumpet is sometimes used to describe a victory won without striking a blow.

Jeroboam. The son of Nebat, Jeroboam was known for his wickedness and idol-worship. He incited the ten tribes to rebel against Rehoboam, son of **Solomon**, and himself became king of the state that resulted. He is referred to as "a mighty man of valor," and hence the use of his name to denote a very large bottle or flagon (three liters, to be precise) (I Kings 11, 14).

Jessica. **Shylock**'s daughter in Shakespeare's comedy *The Merchant of Venice* (1596). She elopes with **Lorenzo**, taking much of Shylock's wealth with her.

Jesus' entry into Jerusalem. After Jesus had preached three years in various places in Palestine, he made a triumphal entry into Jerusalem the Sunday before his crucifixion, riding upon an ass. A crowd of worshipers "took branches of palm trees, and went forth to meet him, and cried, Hosanna." The entry is commemorated as Palm Sunday, the Sunday before Easter. Cf. Matthew 21:1–11; Mark 11:1-10; Luke 19:28-44; John 12:12-19.

Jesus' words on the cross. See **Seven Last Words**.

Jezebel. "And it came to pass, when Joram (Jehoram, son of **Ahab**) saw **Jehu**, that he said, Is it peace, Jehu? And he answered, What peace, so long as the whoredoms of thy mother Jezebel and her witchcrafts are so many" (II Kings 9:22). Jezebel, the queen of Ahab, king of Israel, was an abomination to **Elijah** and other worshippers of **Yahweh** because she imported the worship of **Baal** into the kingdom of the Israelites. The Jezebel of Revelations (2:20) was a false prophetess in the church of Thyatira who incited the faithful to immorality and to eat food offered to idols. Today, a Jezebel means any loose woman, often in the combination "painted Jezebel," since cosmetics were at one time regarded as virtually the sign of a prostitute.

Jim. In Mark Twain's *The Adventures of Huckleberry Finn* (1885), a Negro slave, illiterate and superstitious but brave, generous and good. Jim runs away from his owners and travels down the Mississippi with Huck, a runaway of a different sort. See also: **Huck Finn**.

Jingle, Mr. Alfred. A lovable, clever scoundrel in Dickens' *Pickwick Papers* (1836-37). He speaks in sentence fragments. **Mr. Pickwick** foils his plans to marry for money, and rescues him from prison.

Joad, Ma and Pa. The heads of the Joad clan in *The Grapes of Wrath* (1939), John Steinbeck's novel of the sufferings of refugees from the Oklahoma Dust Bowl during the years of the Great Depression. Ma, the matriarch, is a large woman, as ample in spirit as in body. She shoulders the responsibility of welding the family together in its time of despair. Pa, while hardworking, is dogged by troubles, spiritually tired and ineffectual.

Job. The upright, God-fearing, and good man of Uz, who was made to suffer greatly when God tested his faith and loyalty by allowing **Satan** to have his way with him. Despite his undeserving misfortunes, Job remained steadfast. In the end God restored his substance to him, and granted him happiness and prosperity (*Book of Job*). Job's patience in the face of suffering is proverbial.

Job's comforters. Eliphaz, Bildad and Zophar, all friends of Job, came to him in his greatest afflictions and tried to explain his misery as the result of his sins. Job rejected their interpretations. Hence, any comforters who add salt to one's wounds.

Jocasta. Wife of **Laius** and mother of **Oedipus**. She became the wife of her own son and killed herself when she realized what she had done.

John, Saint (Also called John the **Evangelist**, Saint John the Divine, John of Patmos). One of the twelve apostles of Christ and by tradition the author of the **Gospel** according to Saint John, the Epistles of John, and the *Book of Revelation* (see **Apocalypse**). His symbol is the eagle.

John the Baptist. The son of the aged Zacharias and Elizabeth, John the Baptist preached repentance and prophesied the coming of Christ, and later baptized Him in the river Jordan. Subsequently John denounced **Herod Antipas**, and was beheaded at the wish of his wife Herodias and her daughter, **Salome**.

John of Patmos. See **John, Saint.**

Jonah. Jonah, a minor Jewish prophet, refused to preach to the Ninevites, embarking instead on a ship for Tarshish. A storm arose, and the sailors threw Jonah overboard, knowing him to be the cause of the tempest. He was swallowed by a large fish (traditionally the whale) and spent three days in its belly. It then vomited Jonah out, and he went to preach to the Ninevites, although dismayed that God had granted them mercy (*Book of Jonah*). Jonah is often represented as a bearer of bad luck.

Jonathan.   The son of King **Saul**, famous for his friendship with **David** (I Samuel 20).

Jones, Tom.   The youthful, simple-hearted though often wild and foolishly impulsive hero of the comic novel *Tom Jones* (1749) by Henry Fielding (1707-1754). Through the treachery of the scheming Master Blifil, Tom, a foundling, is cast off by his foster father Squire Allworthy and sets out on a series of adventures and amorous entanglements. See also: **Blifil, Master.**

Joseph.   The son of **Jacob** by his wife **Rachel**. Joseph was favored by Jacob, thus incurring the jealousy of his older brothers. When he was given the "**coat of many colors**," they determined to kill him, but, relenting, instead they imprisoned him in a deep well and abandoned him, showing their father the coat stained with blood to deceive him into believing Joseph had been killed by wild animals. They then sold him into slavery in Egypt, where because of his general abilities and especially because of his interpretation of Pharaoh's dream as the coming of famine, he rose to a very high position. When the famine fell upon the land, Joseph's brothers came to Egypt begging grain from him. He was at last reconciled with them and returned to his father (Genesis 37-48). He is a model of the powerful person who loyally rescues his own, less privileged people.

Joseph, Saint.   Jesus Christ's earthly father. His life is described in the Gospel of the **New Testament**. He was a carpenter who married Mary, Jesus' mother (see **Mary, Mother of Jesus**). Upon finding her already pregnant, he was about to divorce her quietly when an angel told him that the child was the son of God. After Jesus' birth in Bethlehem, Joseph took Mary and the child to Egypt to escape King Herod (see **Herod the Great**), returning later to settle in Nazareth, in the province of Galilee. He is most commonly projected as a man of gentle protectiveness.

Joseph and his brothers. See **Joseph**.

Joseph and Potiphar's wife.   During his stay in Egypt, Joseph became overseer in the house of Potiphar, whose wife attempted to seduce him. The virtuous Joseph resisted, and the angry woman falsely accused Joseph to her husband, causing Joseph's imprisonment for a time (Genesis 39). Joseph's name in allusion thus signifies a man of scrupulous virtue in sexual matters.

Joshua.   After the death of **Moses**, the leader of the Israelites during the conquest of the **Promised Land**. Of his many exploits, popular imagination has fastened chiefly on the conquest of **Jericho**, where the city walls fell at the blast of a trumpet, and the victory over the Amorites, when **Joshua commands the sun and the moon to stand still** (Joshua 6:1-20; 10:12-14). The *Book of Joshua* is an idealized account of the conquest, contradicted in many details by the *Book of Judges*.

Joshua commands the sun and the moon to stand still.   "Then spake Joshua to the Lord in the day when the Lord delivered up the Amorites before the children of Israel, and he said in the sight of Israel, Sun stand thou still upon Gibeon; and thou, Moon, in the valley of Ajalon. And the sun stood still, and the moon stayed, until the people had avenged themselves upon their enemies (Joshua 10:2-3). The lines of Joshua's prayer are quoted from the now vanished *Book of Jasher*. What was presumably a bit of poetic hyperbole in the original context becomes in the *Book of Joshua* a prosaic and literal statement of fact which has tested the credulity of the faithful ever since.

Jove.   From Latin *Jovis*, an older name of **Jupiter** (*Jovis pater*, "Father Jove"). See **Zeus**. Invoked in the old-fashioned, mild expletive "By Jove!"

Jubal.   The son of Lamech and Adah, and brother of **Tubalcain**. He was the father of "all such as handle the harp and organ" (Genesis 4:21). He is remembered as the originator of song and music.

Jubilee.   The jubilee year was one year after the "space of the seven sabbaths of years," hence the fiftieth year, celebrated in commemoration of the Jews' liberation from Egypt (Leviticus 25;

Luke 4). The jubilee lasted an entire year and during this period Jewish slaves were freed, lands returned to their original owners or his heirs, and all agricultural work was halted. In the Catholic church, it is a year of plenary indulgence, usually occurring every 25 years. In common speech, the celebration of any major anniversary or any time of rejoicing.

Judah. (1) One of the sons of **Jacob.** (2) One of the twelve tribes, descended from Jacob. (3) After the division of Solomon's kingdom, the southern portion, with its capital at Jerusalem. Under Roman occupation, the same territory was called *Judea*. Judah was a common Jewish name, borne by **Judas Maccabaeus**, the patriot of the second century B.C., by **Judas Iscariot**, and by Saint Jude, one of the twelve apostles.

Judas Iscariot. One of the original twelve disciples of Jesus, who for thirty pieces of silver betrayed Him, with a kiss of identification, to the priests and elders of Jerusalem. Judas subsequently hanged himself from an elder tree. In common speech, a Judas is anyone who betrays a friend; a hypocrite and traitor. See also: **Apostle.**

Judas Maccabaeus. The leader of the Maccabee family; in 165 B.C. with his four brothers led guerrilla attacks on Jerusalem against the ruling Syrians and finally entered the city to restore the temple and achieve religious freedom and independence for the Jews. This autonomy lasted until 63 B.C. The celebration of Hanukkah, the Jewish festival of lights, stems from this reconsecration of the temple (Apocrypha: I and II Maccabees).

Judge not. "Judge not, that ye be not judged. For with what judgment ye judge, ye shall be judged; and with what measure ye mete, it shall be measured to you again. And why beholdest thou the mote that is in thy brother's eye, but considerest not the beam that is in thine own eye? Or how wilt thou say to thy brother, Let me pull out the mote out of thine eye; and, behold, a beam is in thine own eye. Thou hypocrite, first cast out the beam out of thine own eye; and then shalt thou see clearly to cast out the mote of thy brother's eye (Matthew 7:1-5). From the **Sermon on the Mount**; "To see the mote in your brother's eye" is to criticize the faults of others rather than one's own. "Judge not, that ye be not judged" is often cited as a reminder of the fallibility of all human decisions.

Judgment day.   See **Day of the Lord**.

Judgment of Paris.   Paris, the son of **Priam**, king of Troy, was traveling in Greece and was invited to a festival from which only Eris, the goddess of discord, was excluded. She cast into the feast an apple marked "For the fairest," over which three goddesses—**Hera**, **Athena** and **Aphrodite**—contended. Paris was chosen to decide the issue, and after weighing the bribes of the three goddesses, awarded the apple to Aphrodite, who had promised him the most beautiful woman in the world. She was Helen (see **Helen of Troy**), wife of **Menelaus**, and her abduction triggered the **Trojan War**. See also: **Apple of discord**.

Judgment of Solomon.   Two women both claimed to be mothers of a certain child and asked **Solomon** to decide which one was the real mother. He ordered the child to be cut into two halves, each mother keeping one. One woman agreed to this plan, but the other did not, renouncing her right over the child so that he might live. Solomon promptly identified her as the real mother, and awarded her the child (I Kings 3:16-28). An example of Solomon's proverbial wisdom, as well as a radical method of meting out justice. See also: **Solomon's judgment**.

Judith.   In the Old Testament, a rich and beautiful widow in Bethulia, which was put to siege by Holofernes, a Babylonian general. She volunteered to save her people and, going to Holofernes, she pretended to help him against the Jews and was royally entertained. When Holofernes fell into a drunken sleep, Judith cut off his head, and returned triumphantly to her town (*Book of Judith*).

Juggernaut   (Jagganath). A Hindu god, thought to be the remover of sin. During one of his festivals, when his image is placed on a great car and drawn to the temple, many of his fanatical worshipers would supposedly cast themselves beneath its huge wheels in the hope of achieving heaven immediately. Hence "juggernaut" has come to mean some machine of war, or ritual practice, which crushes the people ruthlessly or, more loosely, any powerful, destructive force.

Juliet.   See **Romeo and Juliet**.

Juno.   See **Hera**.

Jupiter.   See **Zeus**.

Jurgen.   Hero of James Branch Cabell's novel *Jurgen* (1919). He is a medieval pawnbroker yearning for his youth, which he magically regains. After fantastic experiences, he eventually expresses a desire to return to his wife and to his plain and peaceful life.

K

Kalevala. The great epic poem of Finland, now thought to date, in part, from the Middle Ages.

Karamazov, Fyodor Pavlovitch. The rich, debauched, self-pitying, buffoonish old man in Dostoyevski's novel *The Brothers Karamazov* (1880). He goads his son Dimitri into hating him and threatening to kill him for love of **Grushenka**, whose favors both seek. He is murdered by his servant and natural son, Smerdyakov.

Karenina, Anna. Heroine of Tolstoy's *Anna Karenina* (1875). Her conventionally stable marriage to Alexei Karenin, a cold and impersonal official, offers no inner satisfaction to the beautiful, passionate Anna, although she was hardly aware of this before she fell in love with Count Alexey Vronsky. Giving up everything, including her son, she elopes with him, bears his child, and, unable to get a divorce from Karenin, becomes ostracized by society. Unsure of Vronsky's love, she commits suicide. See also: **Vronsky, Count Alexey Kirilich**.

Karma. In Hindu and Buddhist thought, the sum total of one's actions and experiences in all previous earthly incarnations; it determines the nature of the next incarnation.

Kay, Sir. One of the gruffer, more boisterous knights of the **Round Table**.

Kennicott, Carol.   Heroine of Sinclair Lewis' novel *Main Street* (1920). An idealistic crusader, she wishes to transform the ugly, stereotyped and mediocre town of Gopher Prairie, Minnesota, into something more meaningful. Her brief rebellion and short-lived attempts to escape to other regions fail, and she realizes all of America is Gopher Prairie. She returns hoping that her children will attain her own goals.

Kill the fatted calf.   See **Prodigal son**.

King Log.   A king who rules peacefully and quietly, and whose subjects never feel his power. The name originated in a Greek fable in which the frogs ask **Zeus** for a king, but are dissatisfied with the log that he throws down to them. He then gives them a stork, which devours them.

King of Hearts, The.   The kind and timid playing-card king in Lewis Carroll's *Alice in Wonderland* (1865), who is intimidated by his shrewish wife, the Queen of Hearts. See also: **Alice**.

King of Kings.   As used in scripture, this expression refers to God; but it is often used secularly for any very powerful king.

Kiss of Judas.   See **Judas Iscariot**.

Knave of Hearts, The.   The timid playing-card knave in Lewis Carroll's *Alice in Wonderland* (1865), who writes poetry and is accused of stealing the Queen's tarts. See also: **Alice; King of Hearts, The**.

Know them by their fruits.   "Ye shall know them by their fruits. Do men gather grapes of thorns, or figs of thistles? Even so every good tree bringeth forth good fruit; but a corrupt tree bringeth forth evil fruit. A good tree cannot bring forth evil fruit, neither can a corrupt tree bring forth good fruit. Every tree that bringeth not forth good fruit is hewn down, and cast into the fire. Wherefore by their fruits ye shall know them" (Matthew 7:16-20). A warning against false prophets; from the **Sermon on the Mount**.

Ko-Ko.   The Lord High Executioner of W.S. Gilbert and Arthur Sullivan's operetta, *The Mikado* (1885). His tender heart makes it hard for him to execute anyone. He is married off to Katisha, an ugly old lady.

Koran. The Islamic Bible, the sacred book of Muslims. In it, the truth, considered the word of God, is revealed to **Mohammed** by the Angel **Gabriel**.

Krapp. The sole character in *Krapp's Last Tape* (1959), by Samuel Beckett. He is an aged derelict who listens to tape recordings of his glorious youth.

Kriemhild. The heroine of the *Nibelungenlied*. She marries the hero Siegfried (see **Sigurd**) but is robbed of part of the Nibelung's treasure after his death. She is Gudrun in the *Volsunga Saga* and Gutrune in Wagner's *The Ring of the Nibelungs* cycle of operas.

Krishna. One of the greatest of the Hindu gods, the deity of light, fire, storms, the heavens and the sun. One of the most popular Hindu gods, his cult experienced a resurgence in the 1960s and attracted many young American followers. See also: **Shiva**.

Krogstad, Nils. A bookkeeper in Torvald's bank in Ibsen's *A Doll's House* (1879); he is aware that **Nora** has forged the name of her dead father on a loan to enable Torvald to go to Italy for his health. He tries to blackmail Nora into getting Torvald to promote him. He also tries to regain his lost love, Christine Linde. When Christine accepts his proposal, Krogstad changes his mind and returns the forged bond.

Krull, Felix. Hero of Thomas Mann's early novelette, later expanded into a novel, *The Confessions of Felix Krull, Confidence Man* (1954). An audacious, charming, picaresque figure, Krull rises from a job as a bellhop to carry off a successful impersonation of a marquis.

Kyrie, Eleison. In Greek, "Lord, have mercy"; prayer that is part of the services of the Roman Catholic, Greek Orthodox, and Anglican churches (as a response in the last named); also, the musical setting of these words, as in a mass. Often called simply the *Kyrie*.

L

Laban. In the **Old Testament**, he is the uncle of **Jacob** and father of Leah and **Rachel**. Jacob served Laban for 14 years before he was allowed to marry Rachel.

Labors of Heracles. (Hercules). Imposed on Heracles by his cousin, King Eurystheus of Tiryns, the Twelve Labors were: (1) the killing of the supposedly invulnerable Nemean lion (he choked it and tore off its skin with its own claws); (2) the slaying of the many-headed Lernean **Hydra**, the water-serpent, with the help of his nephew, Ioleus; (3) the capturing alive of the Erymanthean boar, accomplished by casting a net over it in a field of snow; (4) the capturing of the Sacred Hind of **Arcadia**, after a year's pursuit, only to release it when **Artemis** claimed it; (5) the destruction of the Stymphalian birds; (6) the cleaning of the **Augean stables**; (7) the capture of the man-eating mares of Diomedes, the Thracian king; (8) the procuring of the girdle of **Hippolyta**, queen of the Amazons; (9) the capture of the **Cretan bull**; (10) the capture of the Oxen of **Geryon**, who lived far to the west; (11) the fetching of the Golden Apples of the **Hesperides**; (12) the most difficult labor, the removal of **Cerberus** from **Hades**. Hercules succeeded and then returned the dog to the Lower World. By extension, any near-impossible task or series of tasks. See also: **Heracles**.

Labyrinth. The building containing a maze which **Daedalus** constructed for King Minos of Crete as a place in which to confine the **Minotaur**. Each year, fourteen Athenian youths, sent as tribute for the murder in Athens of Androgeos, son of Minos, were offered up to the Minotaur in the Labyrinth. Today, "labyrinthine" signifies extremely intricate, tortuous.

Lachesis. See the **Fates**.

Lady Bountiful. The name for any kind and benevolent lady. She appears originally as a character in Farquhar's *The Beaux' Stratagem* (1707).

Lady Godiva. See **Godiva, Lady**.

Lady of the Lake. In Arthurian Legend she is Vivian or Viviane, the wily mistress of **Merlin**, living in an imaginary lake. She stole Lancelot in his infancy, raising him in her lake, and presented him in his manhood to King **Arthur**. The sword **Excalibur** was her gift to Arthur.

Laestrygonians. In Homeric legend, a tribe of cannibals encountered by **Odysseus** and his men on their long journey back to Ithaca. See also: *Odyssey*.

Laius. King of the Greek city of Thebes, husband of **Jocasta** and father of **Oedipus**. Informed by the **oracle** that his newborn son Oedipus would kill him, Laius gave the child to a herdsman with instructions to put the child to death. However, the man took pity on the baby and left him on a mountain where a shepherd found him and raised him. When full-grown, Oedipus encountered his unknown father on the road, the two began to argue, and Oedipus killed Laius, thus fulfilling the oracle's prophecy.

Lake of fire and brimstone. The name given to Hell by Saint John the Divine (Revelation 21:8). To preach a sermon full of fire and brimstone means to threaten the congregation with damnation in hell for their sins. See also: **John, Saint**.

La Mancha, The Knight of. Cervantes' knight, **Don Quixote**.

A lamb to the slaughter. "He is brought as a lamb to the slaughter" (Isaiah 53:7). In the Acts of the Apostles (8:32): "He was led as a sheep to the slaughter, and like a lamb dumb before his shearer." **Isaiah**'s prophecy alludes to the Suffering Servant, and is understood by Jews to refer to Israel. Philip applies it to Christ (Acts 8). In allusion, signifies the sacrifice of a powerless, innocent soul. See also: **Man of sorrows**, for complete Biblical passage.

Lancelot (or Launcelot or Lancelot of the Lake). One of the greatest knights of Arthurian romance, Lancelot was a member of King **Arthur**'s **Round Table**, the lover of Arthur's queen, **Guinevere**, and the father of Sir **Galahad**. Although he generally represents the very model of knightly chivalry, his adulterous love for Guinevere tarnishes his image somewhat. It contributed to the failure of his quest for the Holy **Grail**, the collapse of the fellowship of the Round Table, and the death of Arthur.

Land flowing with milk and honey. (Bible). "I am come . . . to bring them . . . unto a land flowing with milk and honey; unto the place of Canaanites" (Exodus 3:8; cf. II Esdras 2:19). **Canaan**, a land rich enough to support herds of cattle and swarms of bees, would have seemed like paradise to the desert-dwelling Israelites; now applied to any fertile land.

Land of Goshen.   The fertile land allotted to the Israelites in Egypt. It remained untouched by the plagues (see **Ten Plagues**) God visited on Egypt for its enslavement of the Israelites. Hence, any land of plenty, a place of peace and freedom from fear and evil (Genesis 14:10).

Land of Nod.   The place **East of Eden** where Cain lived after being banished by the Lord, following the murder of his brother Abel. (Genesis 4.) Nod here means "wandering," though most writers mistakenly construe it as the "land of sleepiness." See also: **Cain and Abel**.

Languish, Lydia.   In Sheridan's *The Rivals* (1775), a girl so obsessed with the heroes of fantastic adventure that she cannot marry Captain Jack Absolute, an aristocrat like herself. She relents when Absolute, posing as the destitute Ensign Beverly, plans to fight a duel for her and so please her fancy for romantic heroes.

Laocoön.   Priest of **Apollo** at Troy during the **Trojan War**. Chosen by lot to act as priest of Neptune (**Poseidon**) because the

Trojans had stoned the previous priest for alleged neglect of duty, Laocoön was making a sacrifice to the god at the shore when two immense snakes came out of the sea and strangled his two sons and Laocoön himself. The Trojans believed this was a punishment for his having argued to reject the Wooden Horse left by the Greeks and for having committed prior sacrilege against the temple of Apollo. Part of the story is dramatically told by **Vergil** in Book II of the *Aeneid*. The large statue (made during the Hellenistic period) of Laocoön and his sons, now in the Vatican Museum, is a study in the expression of terror and agony. See also: **Trojan Horse**.

Laodicean. Saint John the Divine (see **John of Patmos**) wrote: "And unto the Angel of the church of the Laodiceans write . . . I know thy works, that thou art neither cold nor hot; I would thou wert cold or hot. So then because thou art lukewarm, and neither cold nor hot, I will spue thee out of my mouth" (Revelation 3:14-16). Hence, any timid or indecisive person.

Laputa. The flying island in Jonathan Swift's *Gulliver's Travels* (1726). Through the Laputans Swift satirizes the absurd preoccupation with abstract philosophy, theoretical matters and innovative technologies. See also: **Gulliver**.

Lares and Penates. The Lares were, at first, spirits who guarded crossroads and then became household gods. The Penates were the old Latin household gods who guarded storerooms. The State, regarded as a great family of citizens, had its own Penates, supposedly brought to Rome from Troy by **Aeneas**. When a Roman family moved, they were supposed to bring their Lares and Penates with them. Hence, the phrase "Lares and Penates" signifies the household, and the possessions uniquely personal and attached to it.

Last Judgment. See **Day of judgment**.

The last shall be first and the first last. "The last shall be first, and the first last, for many be called, but few chosen" (Matthew 20:16). Additionally, "If any man desire to be first, the same shall be last of all" (Mark 9:35). The first quotation is a prophecy of the Kingdom of Heaven; the second is an injunction to humility.

Last Supper. "The Lord Jesus, in the same night in which he was betrayed took bread: And when he had given thanks, he brake it and said, Take, eat: this is my body, which is broken for you: this do in remembrance of me. After the same manner also he took the cup, when he had supped, saying, This cup is the new testament in my blood: this do, as oft as ye drink it, in remembrance of me (I Corinthians 11:23-25; also Matthew 26:26-29; Mark 14:22-25; Luke 22:14-20; John 13:1 ff). Scholars disagree as to what kind of ceremony (in Jewish terms) is here being described. Matthew (26:17), Mark (14:12) and Luke (22:7) state that it was a Passover meal, or seder; John places the meal before the Passover (13:1). Whatever the origin, a reenactment of this meal is the most solemn rite of virtually every branch of Christianity, though again, there is no agreement as to its nature. "Last Supper" is not a liturgical term but a historical one, referring to the meal with the disciples at which Jesus presided before his crucifixion or to its representation in art, most notably in the famous mural (1495-98) by Leonardo da Vinci.

Lazarus. A brother of Mary and Martha, and also a friend of Jesus. He died and lay in the grave four days, and when Jesus came he "cried with a loud voice, Lazarus, come forth," and Lazarus was raised from the dead (John 11:1-44). One of the most important miracles performed by Christ. The name in allusion signifies the miracle of resurrection.

Lazarus and Dives. In this parable of Jesus, Dives (Latin, "rich man") was shown as living sumptuously, while Lazarus the beggar who "laid at his gate," was full of sores and wanted to be fed with the crumbs from Dives' table. When they died, Lazarus was carried to Heaven, while Dives was tortured in Hell (Luke 16:19-31). Today Dives is used to signify a man absorbed by worldliness and materialism.

Leah. See **Jacob**.

Leander. See **Hero and Leander**.

Lear. The old, foolish, raging and tragic protagonist of Shakespeare's tragedy *King Lear* (1605). He gives his kingdom to his two hypocritical and evil daughters, **Goneril** and **Regan**, banishing the youngest, good **Cordelia**, when she refuses to flatter him. He then is cast out by his daughters, and undergoes a tragic transformation, during which he loses his reason and his former kingdom falls apart in warfare. Although some order is restored at the play's end, it comes too late to save the lives of Lear and Cordelia.

Leatherstocking.   See **Bumppo, Natty.**

Leda.   The wife of Tyndareus but loved by **Zeus**, who appeared to her in the form of a swan. The result of their union was **Helen**, who ultimately caused the **Trojan War.** Leda's other children were **Castor and Pollux** and **Agamemnon**'s wife, **Clytemnestra.**

Legree, Simon.   The villainous, brutal slave owner in Harriet Beecher Stowe's *Uncle Tom's Cabin* (1852). A name applied to any merciless master or boss. See also: **Uncle Tom.**

Leopard change his spots.   When the people doubted Jeremiah's prophecies of future destruction, he replied, "Can the Ethiopian change his skin, or the leopard his spots? then may ye also do good, that are accustomed to do evil" (Jeremiah 13:23). In modern idiom, you can't change human nature.

Lesbian.   A person living on the island of Lesbos, one of the Cyclades. In classical literature, the reference is usually to **Sappho**, the Greek poetess born on this island. Because Sappho celebrated female homosexuality in her verse, lesbian has come to denote a female homosexual.

Lester, Jeeter.   A shiftless "poor white" Georgian in Erskine Caldwell's *Tobacco Road* (1932). Ignorant and trapped in brutality, he has had 17 children, is unable to feed himself and his family, and is burned to death in his shack.

Lethe.   The river of forgetfulness, one of the rivers over which the dead shades traveled on their way to **Hades.**

Let my people go.   "And afterward **Moses** and **Aaron** went in, and told Pharaoh, Thus saith the Lord God of Israel, Let my people go . . . And Pharaoh said, Who is the Lord, that I should obey his voice, to let Israel go? I know not the Lord, neither will I let Israel go" (Exodus 5:1-2). Black American slaves in the 19th century incorporated this verse into their spirituals.

Let not thy right hand know.   "But when thou doest alms, let not thy left hand know what thy right hand doeth: That thine alms may be in secret: and thy Father which seeth in secret himself shall reward thee openly" (Matthew 6:3-4). From the **Sermon on the Mount** and now a proverb for any discreetly unostentatious benevolence.

Leto.   Known as Latona to the Romans. A Titaness, daughter of Coeus and **Phoebe** (see **Titans**), mother by **Zeus** of **Artemis** and **Apollo**. Because of **Hera**'s jealousy, no country or land would receive her when she was pregnant until she came to the rocky island of Delos, where Artemis and Apollo were born.

The letter killeth.   "The letter killeth but the spirit giveth life" (II Corinthians 3:6). **Paul** is contrasting the Mosaic law with the "Spirit of the living God," written not on tablets of stone, but in the heart. In the usual modern application, the sense is decidedly weakened. It is common to speak of the "letter of the law" and the "spirit," meaning by spirit no more than the intent of the law, as distinguished from the actual words.

Leviathan.   "Canst thou draw out Leviathan with a hook?" (Job 41:1; see also Psalms 74:14; 104:26; Isaiah 27:1). There are many references in the Bible to a victory of God over a sea monster, variously called Leviathan, Rahab, Tannin, the Serpent, or simply the Sea. These allusions are relics of an ancient and widely diffused myth, found in Canaanite and Babylonian literature, in which the Creator conquers a dragon or monster representing chaos. Modern Biblical scholars have speculated that the Leviathan may have been a whale or crocodile. Now the word is applied to anything immense or monstrous.

Leviticus.   The third book of the **Old Testament**. It contains the fundamentals of Jewish law and religious ceremonial following the rebuilding of the temple about 516 B.C.

Light of the world.   "Ye are the light of the world. A city that is set on a hill cannot be hid. Neither do men light a candle, and put it under a bushel, but on a candlestick; and it giveth light unto all that are in the house. Let your light so shine before men, that they may see your good works, and glorify your Father, which is in heaven" (Matthew 5:14-16). From the **Sermon on the Mount**; Jesus here exhorts his disciples. In general parlance to hide one's light under a bushel (i.e., a bushel basket) is to conceal one's virtues in too modest a fashion. In other contexts the phrase "light of the world" refers to Christ himself (John 8:12).

Lilies of the field.   "And why take thee thought for raimant? Consider the lilies of the field, how they grow; they toil not, neither do they spin; And yet I say unto you, That even Solomon in all his glory was not arrayed like one of these" (Matthew 6:28-29). Christ's words, from the **Sermon on the Mount**, suggest that things of the spirit are superior to any material object of this world.

Lilith.   According to legend, the first wife of **Adam**, created equally with him, and banished from **Eden** after it was impossible for them to live in harmony. She was supposed to have borne him a flock of devils as children, and later was regarded as an evil spirit presiding over desolate places and especially dangerous to women in childbirth. She was associated with the screech owl in Isaiah 34:14. In the Middle Ages, she was one of the devil's temptresses, and these devilish associations cling to her name.

Lilliput.   The country inhabited by the tiny Lilliputian people visited by **Gulliver** in Book I of Swift's *Gulliver's Travels* (1721). Though tiny in stature, the Lilliputians have all the vanities, pretensions and petty strifes of the human race. Today a narrow-minded, petty person might be called a Lilliputian.

Limbo.   The first circle of Dante's hell, in which the virtuous pagans are placed. They do not suffer torture, but have no hope of seeing God; hence, any inconclusive or indefinite condition or place.

Lion in the streets.   "The slothful man saith, There is a lion in the way; a lion is in the streets" (Proverbs 26:13). The lion in this context is simply a far-fetched pretext for not stirring abroad. Thus a lion in the streets is any excuse or fear one contrives to avoid doing an unpleasant task.

Lion lie down with the lamb.   "The wolf also shall dwell with the lamb and the leopard shall lie down with the kid; and the calf and the young lion and the fatling together; and a little child shall lead them" (Isaiah 11:6). A prophecy of the Messianic kingdom under the rule of a descendant of Jesse (the father of King **David**); nature will be so transformed that even wild animals will be friends. Thus the phrase describes a future of ideal peace. In popular allusion, usually only the lion and the lamb, and sometimes the child, are remembered. See also: **Messiah**.

Little child shall lead them.   (See **Lion lie down with the lamb**).

Little Emily.   Daughter of Daniel Peggotty's brother-in-law in Charles Dickens' *David Copperfield* (1850). She is fascinated by the evil **Steerforth**, is seduced by him, and later reclaimed to emigrate to Australia. See also: **Peggotty, Clara**.

Little Eva St. Claire   (Evangeline). In Harriet Beecher Stowe's *Uncle Tom's Cabin* (1852), the saintly daughter of Augustine St. Claire, moved by human love, faith and goodness. Before she dies, she implores her father to free his slaves.

Little John.   The huge, strong, good-humored friend of **Robin Hood**.

Living dog is better than a dead lion.   "To him that is joined to all the living there is hope: for a living dog is better than a dead lion" (Ecclesiastes 9:4). Used to urge one to value the present even if the past seems better.

Loaves and fishes.   When a great multitude followed Jesus into the desert and it came time to eat, Jesus took "five loaves and two fishes," blessed the food and gave it out to be eaten, and miraculously all were filled (Matthew 14:15-21; John 6:5-14).

Lochinvar.   The hero of Sir Walter Scott's ballad *Marmion*. Lochinvar is a young Highlander who goes to the wedding of the woman he loves, abducts her, and rides away before the bridegroom is aware of what has happened.

Lohengrin. The son of **Parsifal**, Lohengrin is Knight of the Swan and arrives at Antwerp in a boat drawn by a swan. Here he champions Else, the Princess of Brabant, who has been dispossessed by Telramud and Ortrud. He then marries her on condition that she never ask his identity; unfortunately Else does so on the wedding night, and Lohengrin is bound by a vow to tell her, but must depart from her nevertheless. Richard Wagner's opera *Lohengrin* (1847) draws on this legend for its subject matter. Lohengrin was a Knight of the Holy **Grail**.

Loki. An evil Norse deity of conflict and discord, father of three monsters. The enemy of the good gods, and responsible for the death of **Balder**, he was eventually chained to a rock and tortured by drops of venom falling on him from a serpent overhead.

Lolita. The "nymphet" loved and abducted by the middle-aged Humbert Humbert in Vladimir Nabokov's novel *Lolita* (1957). By extension, a girl just becoming aware of her sexuality.

Lonelyhearts, Miss. The male reporter who writes the "advice to the lovelorn" column of a New York paper in Nathanael West's novel *Miss Lonelyhearts* (1933). He becomes involved in the genuine suffering of the pitiful people who write to him, and is victimized by those he tries to comfort. He is accidentally shot by one of his correspondents.

Lonigan, Studs. In James T. Farrell's *Young Lonigan* (1932, first part of the *Studs Lonigan Trilogy*), the 15-year-old hero, outwardly tough and determined to prove his manliness to all. He remains nonetheless inwardly sensitive and lonely, yearning after pure love and chivalric honor.

Lord is my shepherd, The. See **Green Pastures**.

Lord's anointed. See **Messiah**.

Lorelei. The name of a rock jutting over the Rhine near Bingen. A folk tradition tells of a **siren** sitting on it, combing her hair and singing sailors to destruction on the rocks. The poem "Die Lorelei," by Heinrich Heine (1797-1856), has made the story famous. The word stands for "siren" today.

Lorry, Mr. Jarvis. A confidential clerk of Tellson's Bank in Dickens' *A Tale of Two Cities* (1859), who helps Dr. Manette, Lucie Manette's father, get to England. See also: **Manette, Dr. Alexandre; Manette, Lucie.**

Lot. The son of Haran and nephew of Abraham. He was one of the inhabitants of the iniquitous city of Sodom, and escaped just before God destroyed it with fire and brimstone. Lot was instructed to take his family and not look back at the burning city; his wife, however, disobeyed, presumably out of a longing for the depravities of Sodom, and was turned into a pillar of salt. Bizarre salt formations in the Dead Sea area are still pointed out to travelers as Lot's wife. Thereafter Lot lived in a cave with his two daughters, who seduced their father because there were no other men on earth (Genesis 19). See also: **Sodom and Gomorrah.**

Lothario. The prototype of the libertine, seducer and debauchee, from Nicholas Rowe's tragedy *The Fair Penitent* (1703).

Lotos-Eaters (Lotophagi). On his homeward journey from Troy to Ithaca, **Odysseus** came to the land of the Lotos-Eaters, a people who ate of the sweet fruit of the lotus, or lotos (*Odyssey,* IX, 82-104). When some of the men whom he had sent to search out the land tasted this, they forgot to come back, lost all desire to return home, and had to be dragged back to the ships by force. The term *lotus-eater* is applied to a daydreamer, to a person who is oblivious of the world about him. Tennyson's poem "The Lotos-Eaters" (1833) is an enchanting study of this theme of detachment and disengagement from the world, based upon the episode in the *Odyssey.*

Lot's wife. See **Lot.**

Love of money. See **Root of all evil.**

Love thy neighbor as thyself. God commanded through **Moses** and Jesus that "Thou shalt love thy neighbor as thyself" (Leviticus 19:18; Matthew 19:19). The phrase is commonly used today as a precept for the brotherhood of man and is an injunction to be charitable. See also : **Sermon on the Mount.**

Love your enemies.   "But I say unto you, Love your enemies, bless them that curse you, do good to them that hate you, and pray for them that despitefully use you, and persecute you; That ye may be the children of your Father which is in heaven: for he maketh his sun rise on the evil and on the good, and sendeth rain on the just and on the unjust: (Matthew 5:44-45). From the **Sermon on the Mount**; Jesus is contrasting the old morality of retaliation with the new morality of forgiveness.

Lucifer.   One of the greatest of the angels. His name means "the maker of light." Rebelling against God, he was hurled from heaven down to hell, where he became **Satan**, the Devil and incarnation of evil. Reference is made to the event in the **Old Testament** *Book of Isaiah*. Milton elaborated the legend in *Paradise Lost*.

Luke, Saint.   One of the four **evangelists**, author of the *Gospel According to Saint Luke* and *Acts of the Apostles*. Thought to have been a doctor, he is often referred to as "the beloved physician." His symbol is the ox.

Lumpkin, Tony.   A character from Oliver Goldsmith's *She Stoops to Conquer* (1773). He is a spoiled, drunken country squire given to practical jokes and bawdy songs.

Lyceum.   The school in Athens on the banks of the river Ilissus where **Aristotle** taught philosophy. Source of the French *lycée*, "school, academy."

M

Mabinogion. A cycle of Welsh stories comprising part of the Arthurian materials. They were first written down in the 14th century, but the material may date to earlier than the 11th century. In addition to the Arthurian tales, the cycle is filled with Celtic and folk motifs. See also: **Arthur.**

Macbeth. Tragic hero of Shakespeare's *Macbeth* (1605), set in medieval Scotland. Spurred by ambiguous prophecies of the **Weird Sisters** about his future grandeur and by Lady Macbeth's and his own obsessive ambition, he embarks on a course of usurpation and murder which leads him to his death. See also: **Macduff.**

Maccabees. See **Judas Maccabaeus.**

Macduff. Thane of Fife in Shakespeare's *Macbeth* (1605). He flees after the murder of King **Duncan** by **Macbeth,** and plots revenge on him after he learns that Macbeth has killed his wife and children. He finally kills Macbeth and gives the realm to young Prince Malcolm.

Macheath, Captain. Leader of a group of robbers and highwaymen in John Gay's drama *The Beggar's Opera* (1728). He courts Polly Peachum, but plays her false, is thrown into jail, pays court to Lucy Lockit, the jailer's daughter, and at the end chooses the devoted Polly. *The Threepenny Opera* (1928), an adaptation of *The Beggar's Opera* by Kurt Weill (music) and Bertolt Brecht (lyrics), has achieved tremendous modern popularity. See also: **Peachum, Polly**.

Mad Hatter, The.   In *Alice's Adventures in Wonderland* (1865) by Lewis Carroll, the two very eccentric hosts of the Mad Tea Party are the **March Hare** and the charming Mad Hatter. The latter asks **Alice** riddles, absurd but delightful.

Maecenas.   The adviser of Augustus, the patron of **Horace** and **Vergil**; now any generous patron of the arts.

Maenads.   In Greek, "the Mad Ones," frenzied female followers of **Dionysos**, or **Bacchus**; another name for the **Bacchantes**.

Magdalene.   Mary Magdalene was the repentant sinner who wept when Jesus was eating in the house of the **Pharisee**. She washed his feet with her tears, drying them with her hair. She appears also at the Crucifixion (Matthew 27; Mark 16; Luke 7). The word "maudlin" derives from her name; in paintings she is frequently depicted weeping.

Magi.   The three Wise Men of the East who journeyed to Bethlehem at the birth of Christ in order to present him with gifts of gold, frankincense and myrrh. A *magus* (pl. *magi*) is literally a wise man or a magician. The identification of the magi as kings has no basis in the **Gospels**; it rests on the prophecy in Isaiah (60:3). Later tradition calls them Gaspar, Melchior and Balthazar.

Magwitch, Abel.   The convict whom Pip helps to escape in Dickens' *Great Expectations* (1860). Magwitch gains a fortune in New South Wales, returns to England, and becomes Pip's secret benefactor. He is eventually caught a second time, his fortune is confiscated and he dies in prison.

Mahabharata.   Indian epic poem dealing with theology and morals.

Maid Marian.   The sweetheart and later the wife of **Robin Hood**. She loved him when he was still Earl of Huntington, then followed him into the forest when he was outlawed, living chastely until her marriage.

Malaprop, Mrs.   A character in Sheridan's *The Rivals* (1775), her name derives from the French *mal à propos*, out of place. She misuses words grotesquely, for instance, "as headstrong as an allegory on the banks of the Nile." Such mistakes are now called malapropisms.

Mammon.   Material wealth. Jesus said, "No man can serve two masters . . .Ye cannot serve God and Mammon" (Matthew 6:24; Luke 16:9,11,13). Thus mammon has come to signify a personification of worldly riches, or an evil god of wealth.

Manette, Dr. Alexandre.   In Dickens' *A Tale of Two Cities* (1859); once a strong, brilliant physician, he is almost destroyed by 18 years in the Bastille until he is released by the French Revolution. See also: **Manette, Lucie.**

Manette, Lucie.   Beautiful daughter of Dr. Manette (see **Manette, Dr. Alexandre**) in Dickens' *A Tale of Two Cities* (1859). She is swept up in the turmoil of the French Revolution, which changes the life of her father, her husband (Charles Darnay) and Sidney Carton, the man who loves her. See also **Carton, Sidney; Darnay, Charles.**

Man Friday.   A devoted, faithful servant, from the character Friday in Defoe's *Robinson Crusoe* (1719). Originally a savage, he is saved from a life of savagery by **Crusoe.**

Manna from heaven.   "And when the dew that lay was gone up, behold, upon the face of the wilderness there lay a small round thing, as small as the hoar frost upon the ground. And when the children of Israel saw it, they said to one another, It is manna: for they wist not what it was" (**Exodus** 16:14-15). The food with which the Israelites were nourished in their wanderings has been identified with the secretion of the tamarisk tree; in the New Testament it becomes a symbol of divine blessing. Today any unexpected and welcome gift or find may be described as manna.

Man of sorrows.   "He is despised and rejected of men; a man of sorrows and acquainted with grief: and we hid as it were our faces from him; he was despised, and we esteemed him not. Surely he hath borne our griefs, and carried our sorrows: yet we did esteem him stricken, smitten of God, and afflicted. But he was wounded for our transgressions, he was bruised for our iniquities; the chastisement of our peace was upon him; and with his stripes we are healed. All we like sheep have gone astray; we have turned every one to his own way; and the Lord hath laid on him the iniquity of us all. He was oppressed, and he was afflicted, yet he opened not his mouth; he is brought as a lamb to the slaughter, and as a sheep before her shearers is dumb, so he opened not his mouth" (Isaiah 53:3-7). Probably every line of this passage is equally as memorable and familiar. It is the prophecy of the Suffering Servant in Isaiah, written not by the eighth century B.C. prophet of that name, but by an anonymous author, probably living in Babylonia in the sixth century. It is understood by Jews to refer to Israel, and by Christians as a prophecy of the coming of Christ, who suffered for the sins of all mankind. These words are used in the liturgy for Good Friday. See also: **Messiah**.

Marathon.   The plain near the sea where a small Athenian force defeated a large invading Persian army in 490 B.C. Tradition has it that news of the victory was brought to Athens by the runner Pheidippides; modern marathon races, run in memory of his feat, cover a distance the same as that between Marathon and Athens.

Marcel.   The narrator of the series of novels known in English as *Remembrance of Things Past*, by the French novelist Marcel Proust. In delicate health and exquisitely refined and sensitive, he records his impressions of his past life in luminous detail, dwelling on his family, his love affairs, and on his obsession with the fine points of class distinction in *fin de siècle* Paris society. The taste of a madeleine (a French cookie) dipped in tea evokes a world of memories for Marcel. See also: **Odette; Swann, M**.

March, Augie.   In Saul Bellow's *The Adventures of Augie March* (1953), the novel's picaresque hero, fiercely dedicated to a free-style pursuit of his fate. Sympathetically open-minded and insatiably curious, he refuses to commit himself to any of the creeds that shape human destiny.

March Hare.   A rabbit who is the rude host, with the **Mad Hatter**, of a "mad" tea party in *Alice's Adventures in Wonderland* (1865) by Lewis Carroll (see **Alice**). The expression "mad as a

March hare" may have originated from the notion that March is their mating season.

Mares   (or Steeds) **of Diomedes**. Diomedes, king of Bistones in Thrace, son of the god **Ares** and the nymph Cyrene, kept a team of ferocious horses whom he fed on human flesh, usually that of innocent travellers who came his way. Bringing these horses back to Argos was Heracles' Eighth Labor (see **Labors of Heracles**). In the process, Diomedes is killed, his horses eat their former master, and become tame. They meekly follow Heracles back to Argos.

Marius.   Hero of Walter Pater's *Marius the Epicurean* (1885). Living during the times of Marcus Aurelius (A.D. 121-180), the idealistic Marius becomes disillusioned and then seeks knowledge through mysticism and epicureanism. He finally converts to Christianity.

Mark, Saint.   One of the four **evangelists**, to whom is attributed the *Gospel According to Saint Mark*. His symbol is the lion; he is the patron saint of Venice.

Mark of Cain.   After God banished Cain for killing his brother Abel (see **Cain and Abel**), Cain cried unto the Lord, "That everyone that findeth me shall slay me." The compassionate Lord said, "Therefore, whosoever slayeth Cain, vengeance shall be taken on him sevenfold. And the Lord set a mark upon Cain lest any finding him should kill him" (Genesis 4:15). Though the mark of Cain, commonly called the curse or brand of Cain, was a mark of protection, it has come to mean a mark of punishment, generally conceived as a crimson brand on Cain's brow.

Mars.   See **Ares**.

Mary, Mother of Jesus.   The pure and virtuous virgin (also known as the Virgin Mary or the Blessed Virgin), who was visited by the Holy Ghost and conceived Jesus (Luke 1:26-38). Subsequently she was married to Joseph (Matthew 1:18-25), with whom she had several other children (Matthew 13:55). She bore the Christchild in a Bethlehem manger (Luke 2:1-20), fled with Joseph to Egypt to escape the **Massacre of the Innocents** (Matthew 2) and sought him when, as a boy, he remained in the temple speaking with the priests (Luke 2:41-51). She was rebuked by her son at the marriage at Cana (John 2:1-5) and was present at his Crucifixion (John 19:25-27). She is foremost of the Christian saints, beloved for her purity, patience and sympathy for human suffering. See also: **Joseph, Saint**.

Massacre of the Innocents.   When **Herod the Great** heard that a child had been born in Judea who would someday be a great king over him, he determined to kill the child. As he could not learn who he was, he ordered his soldiers to massacre all male children below a certain age (Matthew 2:1-16). Mary and **Joseph** saved the infant Jesus by fleeing with him to Egypt. See also: **Mary, Mother of Jesus**.

Matthew, Saint.   One of the twelve **apostles** of Christ and by tradition the author of the *Gospel According to Saint Matthew* (though this is a matter of dispute).

Maupin, Mlle. de.   In Theophile Gautier's *Mlle. de Maupin* (1835), a 20-year-old **lesbian** disguised as the young Chevalier Théodore de Sérannes. She adopted the disguise to learn the true nature of men. What she discovers leaves her bitterly disillusioned.

McTeague.   Hero of Frank Norris' *McTeague* (1899). An enormously strong and stupid man, McTeague goes from feats of strength to sadistic mutilations and murder before he is finally killed.

Mecca.   The birthplace of **Mohammed**; Holy City of the Mohammedans and the goal of the pilgrimages that are a required rite in the Moslem religion. By extension, any goal for pilgrims.

Medea.   Enchantress, daughter of Aeëtes, king of Colchis; niece of **Circe**, she fell in love with **Jason** when he and the **Argonauts** came to Colchis in quest of the **Golden Fleece**. By her magical arts she helped him attain it. She fled with the Argonauts, and while they were being pursued by her father, she cut up her brother Absyrtus, whom she had abducted, and threw his parts into the sea to delay her father's pursuit. When they reached Iolcos in Greece, she killed Pelias, Jason's uncle, who had sent him in search of the Fleece. Driven out of Iolcos, Jason and Medea took refuge in Corinth. When

Jason decided to abandon Medea and to marry Glauce, daughter of **Creon**, king of Corinth, Medea sent the princess a poisoned robe which brought about the death of Glauce and her father. Medea also slew the children that she had borne Jason and escaped to Athens under the protection of King Aegeus, father of **Theseus**. She tried to poison the latter but her scheme was thwarted and she fled to Colchis. Today Medea is most often associated with vengefulness, jealousy and sorcery.

Medusa.   One of the three **Gorgons**, the only one who was mortal, with appearance so terrible that everyone who looked upon her was turned to stone. In one version, **Athena** punished her for lying with **Poseidon** in Athena's temple by turning her hair into snakes. Medusa's head was cut off by **Perseus**, who presented it to Athena, and the goddess placed it in the center of her aegis (protective device) which she wore as a shield on her breastplate.

Meister, Wilhelm.   Hero of Goethe's *Wilhelm Meister's Apprenticeship* (1796) and *Years of Wandering* (1821-29). Meister, the son of a wealthy German merchant, has an abiding passion for the theater and for acquiring experience in life. The first novel begins in his early manhood, and continues through a series of experiences involving art and love, to the first stages of maturity. In the second novel, he wanders over the world seeking purification through art and science.

Melisande.   The dreamy and innocent wife of the dull and uncomprehending Golaud in Maeterlinck's play *Pelleas and Melisande* (1892). His half brother Pelleas becomes her lover, and Melisande dies in childbirth after their love is discovered.

Melpomene.   Muse of tragedy. See **Muses**.

Menelaus.   King of Sparta. The abduction of his wife, Helen (see **Helen of Troy**), provoked the **Trojan War**. Menelaus, who is mentioned frequently in the *Iliad* and the *Odyssey*, fought in the war and eventually recovered Helen when the Greeks won.

Mene, mene, tekel, upharsin.   The "handwriting on the wall" at Belshazzar's lavish feast, meaning literally "numbered, numbered, weighed, divisions," which Daniel interpreted to mean

"God hath numbered thy kingdom, and finished it; thou art weighed in the balance, and found wanting" (Daniel 5:25-31). Today "handwriting on the wall" refers to any ominous portent or unmistakable sign of future disaster.

Mentor.   Friend and adviser of **Odysseus** and teacher of his son **Telemachus**. A "mentor" has since come to mean teacher or wise counselor, usually an older and more experienced person.

Mephistopheles.   In medieval demonology, one of the seven chief devils. In Goethe's *Faust*, the devil-figure who tempts Faust into concluding a pact with the forces of evil, then tries to lead him into perdition. He is famous for his wit, rationality, cynicism and earthly wisdom.

Mercury.   See **Hermes**.

Mercutio.   The friend of Romeo and kinsman of the Prince of Verona in Shakespeare's ***Romeo and Juliet***, one of the wittiest characters in all the plays. Mercutio is accidentally killed by **Tybalt**, Juliet's cousin, when he attempts to intervene in a street duel between Tybalt and Romeo. He is remembered for the line, "A plague o' both your houses!"—often applied today by an innocent bystander when injured, literally or metaphorically, in a dispute between others.

Merlin.   Legendary magician, enchanter and wise man in Arthurian legend and romance of the Middle Ages. Some legends depict him as demonic; others as a wise and good counselor. He is currently associated primarily with magic. See also: **Arthur**.

Messiah.   From the Hebrew *mashiah*, meaning anointed. The ancients used anointing with oil as a sign that priests, prophets and kings were chosen by God for their office; thus **Samuel** anointed **Saul** and **David** as kings over Israel. This custom still survives in the chrism used in coronations and at baptisms and confirmations in certain Christian sects. After the extinction of the kingdom of Judah, the term came to be applied to the hoped-for prince who would restore the Davidic kingdom. At first, the messiah was conceived as an ordinary ruler, and **Isaiah** even applied the term to Cyrus of Persia (Isaiah 45:1). When the political leader did not appear, the messiah was conceived more and more in transcendent, supernatural terms, as a heavenly savior. In the **Gospels**, the messiah is commonly called the Son of Man, and the distinctive claim of Christianity is that the messianic expectation was fulfilled in Jesus of Nazareth. The name Christ is simply "messiah" translated into Greek; it is a past participle derived from *chrisma*, meaning "oil." Jesus is therefore commonly called "*the* Christ," and the form "Jesus Christ" (as if Christ were a proper name) is a later development. The messianic hope continued to flourish in Judaism, producing self-proclaimed messiahs from the time of Bar Kochba (second century A.D.) to Shabbetai Zevi (17th century) and Jacob Frank (18th century). Certain Moslem sects also believe in a messiah, called the *mahdi*.

Methuselah.   The oldest of the Biblical patriarchs, who lived 969 years (Genesis 5:27). Now proverbial for longevity.

Micah.   One of the minor prophets in the **Old Testament**. His prophecy, that Israel and **Judah** would fall, is set down in *The Book of Micah*.

Micawber.   Mr. Wilkins Micawber, one of the famous characters in Dickens' ***David Copperfield*** (1850). He constantly projects schemes that lead to wealth, and they constantly fail, although Micawber remains undaunted, always hoping for something to turn up.

Midas.   A legendary monarch of Phrygia in Asia Minor, who, in return for his hospitality to **Silenus**, was granted a wish. He wished that everything that he touched would turn to gold. However, when even his food turned to gold, he begged to have the gift withdrawn. He had to bathe in the Pactolus River, in which gold was found thereafter. A person who is very successful in business, with whose involvement "everything turns to gold," is said to have the "Midas touch."

Minerva.   See **Athena**.

Minotaur.   A fabulous monster (literally, Minos' Bull), half-man and half-bull, the Minotaur was the offspring of **Pasiphaë**, the wife of Minos, the king of Crete. When Minos refused to sacrifice a bull the god **Poseidon** had given him, Poseidon punished him by making Pasiphaë fall in love with it. The Minotaur was shut up in the **Labyrinth** built for Minos by **Daedalus**. In revenge for their killing one of his sons, Minos demanded that the Athenians send seven boys and seven girls every nine years (or, in some versions, every year) to be devoured by the Minotaur. On the third occasion, the Athenian hero, **Theseus**, volunteered to go and he succeeded in killing the monster.

Miranda.   In Shakespeare's *The Tempest* (1611), the lovely and innocent daughter of **Prospero**, deposed Duke of Milan and now a powerful magician. Brought by her father to a deserted island when she was still an infant, Miranda (whose name derives from the Latin *miror*, to wonder at, to admire) has never seen the "outside" world of treachery and deceit that cast her father out. Miranda, a wonder and a wonderer, speaks the famous line, "O brave new world that has such people in't" upon first seeing the very party of Italians who had deposed her father years before. She represents human virtue untouched by the corruptions of society.

Miriam.   The elder sister of **Moses** and **Aaron** and prophetess of the people. After the Israelites passed through the Red Sea, she led them in music and dance to celebrate the event (**Exodus** 15:20-21).

Mnemosyne.   Goddess of memory, a Titaness (see **Titans**), daughter of **Uranus** and **Gaea**, loved by **Zeus** to whom she bore the nine **Muses**.

Moby Dick.   The huge white whale which is the object of Captain **Ahab**'s obsessive hatred in Herman Melville's novel *Moby Dick* (1851). Moby Dick has been variously interpreted as the embodiment of evil, the urge to destruction at the center of creation, and even as the symbolic victim of modern man's need to dominate nature.

Mock turtle.   In Lewis Carroll's *Alice in Wonderland* (1865); an odd, doleful creature, always weeping and bemoaning his fate. "It's the things," one character says, "Mock Turtle Soup is made from." See also: **Alice**.

Mohammed   (or Muhammad, Mahomet, Mahmud, Mehmed). Founder and prophet of the religion of Islam. The central profession of the Islamic faith is "There is no God but God, and Mohammed is the prophet of God." The revelations which Mohammed (c. 570-632 A.D.) believed he received directly from God were subsequently collected in the *Koran* (or *Qur'an*), the sacred scriptures of Islam.

Moll Flanders.   A novel by Daniel Defoe, published in 1721 and cast in autobiographical form. Moll becomes a harlot, a wife, a thief and a convict, but eventually succeeds in acquiring riches and living honestly.

Molly Bloom.   The unfaithful wife of Leopold Bloom (see **Bloom, Leopold**) in James Joyce's *Ulysses*. Joyce sees her as the embodiment of the "eternal feminine." Molly is a lush, sensual creature who escapes from the boredom of her life in Dublin by affairs with other men. The final section of *Ulysses* is a stream-of-consciousness rendering of Molly's thoughts and reveries. She is sardonically portrayed as **Penelope** to Bloom's Ulysses (see **Odysseus**).

Moloch.   The brutal god to whom parents sacrificed their children in the Valley of Hinnom near Jerusalem. In the Bible, the Jews are expressly forbidden to offer any sacrifices to Moloch (Leviticus 18:21). By extension, any power to whom awful sacrifice is rendered.

Mona Lisa.   The name of the famous painting (early 16th century) by Leonardo da Vinci, also called *La Belle Gioconde*, or La Gioconda. The subject of the painting was the wife of Francesco de Giocondo. Her enigmatic smile is popularly supposed to conceal some secret misery.

Montague.   Romeo's father in Shakespeare's ***Romeo and Juliet*** (1594), who is feuding with old **Capulet**. The feud has tragic consequences for the lovers.

Monte Cristo, Count of.   The hero of a series of romantic adventures in the novel by Alexandre Dumas (1845); the assumed title of Edmond Dantes (see **Dantes, Edmond**), imprisoned by his enemies in the Chateau d'If on the false charge of aiding a Bonapartist plot against the state. After his escape from the island prison and his acquisition of enornmous wealth and power as the Count of Monte Cristo, he seeks and obtains revenge against those who were responsible for his imprisonment, and succeeds in destroying them one by one.

Mordred. In Arthurian legend, the mean-tempered and evil knight, son of King **Arthur** by his sister; instrumental in destroying the unity of the **Round Table**.

Morgan le Fay. A mysterious figure in Arthurian legend, usually represented as a sorceress or siren in command of supernatural power. She plots against **Arthur**, and once steals from him his sword **Excalibur**. Despite the enmity between them, it is Morgan who transports Arthur to **Avalon** after he sustains mortal wounds in his last battle. See also: **Fata Morgana**.

Morpheus. The god of sleep and dreams. The word morphine (a narcotic painkiller made from opium) derives from the god's name.

Moses. The principal **Old Testament** prophet; liberator of the Israelites from captivity in Egypt. Because Pharaoh had ordered all Jewish male children to be killed, Moses' mother placed him in a basket of rushes beside the river, where Pharaoh's daughter found and adopted him. As a grown man, he killed an Egyptian overseer for beating a Hebrew and was obliged to flee to Midian, where he married the daughter of Jethro, a local priest. In Midian, the god of his fathers revealed himself to Moses, commanding him to liberate the Jews. Accompanied by his brother **Aaron**, and strengthened with miraculous powers, he confronted Pharaoh, caused ten plagues to descend on Egypt (see **Plagues of Egypt**), organized his people, and led them out of Egypt through the Red Sea, which the Lord opened, for the Jews, and closed on the pursuing Egyptians. For 40 years the Israelites wandered under Moses' leadership through the Sinai desert. Here the Lord delivered through Moses the **Ten Commandments** and the extensive system of law and ritual observances, recorded in the **Pentateuch** (the first five books of the Old Testament), which is still the foundation of traditional Judaism. Moses never accompanied his people into **Canaan**, the land which God had promised them, but was allowed a glimpse of it from **Mount Pisgah** shortly before his death. See also: **Exodus; Promised Land**.

Mote in thy brother's eye.   See **Judge not**.

Mount of Olives.   Just east of the old city of Jerusalem, this hill or ridge is an important holy place in the Bible. In Jewish tradition the messianic era (see **Messiah**) will commence there. In Christian tradition it was the site of the **Sermon on the Mount** and of the garden of **Gethsemane** where Jesus prayed just before he was betrayed by **Judas Iscariot**.

Mount Olympus.   The dwelling place of the Greek gods, in Thessaly, in northern Greece. Olympian in current usage means majestic and superior, with a suggestion of remoteness, serenely aloof and indifferent to man's fate.

Mount Pisgah   (or Nebo). **Moses** climbed to the top of Mount Pisgah, northeast of the Red Sea, to see the **Promised Land** of **Canaan**, which he was forbidden by God to enter (Deuteronomy 34:1). He died shortly thereafter. A reference to Mount Pisgah suggests hope for, or insight into, the future.

Mount Sinai   (or Horeb). Renowned as the site where God gave **Moses** the **Ten Commandments** and the covenant between God and the Hebrews was forged.

Mowgli.   Boy hero of Rudyard Kipling's *The Jungle Book* (1894). Reared by animals in the wild, Mowgli undergoes numerous adventures with man and beast before realizing his place is with the human community.

Münchausen, Baron.   The hero of a series of burlesque, satirical, highly improbable stories by Rodolf Erich Raspe, published in England in 1785. The Baron meets with a number of miraculous adventures in the course of his travels. Some were based on the accounts of an actual Baron Karl Friedrich Hieronymus von Münchausen (1720-1797), a German soldier and adventurer.

Murdstone, Edward.   In Dickens' *David Copperfield* (1850), David's cruel and ill-tempered stepfather, who with his sister, Miss Murdstone, treated him meanly. One of literature's more hateful characters, Murdstone represents human nature at its meanest and most oppressive.

Muses. The nine muses, the patron goddesses of man's intellectual and creative endeavors, were the daughters of **Zeus** and the goddess of memory, **Mnemosyne.** They were: Clio, history; Calliope, epic poetry; Erato, love poetry; Euterpe, lyric poetry; Melpomene, tragedy; Polyhymnia, songs to the gods; Thalia, comedy; Terpsichore, the dance; Urania, astronomy. It was traditional for poets to invoke the muse or muses at the beginning of their works and either ask them for inspiration or attribute the creation of the work to them. The mountains of **Helicon,** Pierus and **Parnassus** are associated with the muses. See also: **Pierian spring.**

Music of the spheres. Pythagoras, in his search for universal harmonies, established that all solids in motion emit musical tones, and applying this law to the planets, stated that their collective tones constituted the "music of the spheres." The phrase suggests a harmony inherent in the heavens, but imperceptible to man.

My God, why hast thou forsaken me? "And about the ninth hour Jesus cried with a loud voice, saying Eli, Eli, lama sabachtani? That is to say, My God, my God, why hast thou forsaken me?" (Matthew 27:46; also Mark 15:34). These words of Jesus on the cross are a quotation from Psalms (22), and although they appear to be a cry of despair, they should be read in the context of the entire psalm, which ends on a note of praise and confidence. See also: **Seven Last Words.**

My name is legion. "And he asked him, What is thy name? And he answered, saying, My name is Legion: for we are many " (Mark 5:9). Jesus, on a preaching tour of the territory of the Gadarenes, encountered a man possessed by a demon. When Jesus adjured the demon to leave, and asked his name, the demon replied through the lips of the man in the words quoted above: My name is Legion. Since a Roman legion consisted of four to six thousand men, a very large number is implied. After leaving their victim, the demons entered a herd of swine, who thereupon rushed madly into the water and were drowned. In modern allusion, "Their name is legion" means simply, "They are many"; it is generally used in an unfavorable sense.

Myrmidons.   The warlike Thessalian tribe who were followers of **Achilles** during the siege of Troy. They were noted for their brutality. Hence, by extension, faithful followers, or underlings who execute commands without question or scruple. See also: **Trojan War**.

N

Naboth's vineyard. A vineyad in Jezreel near the palace of **Ahab**, king of Samaria, who vainly coveted it. **Jezebel**, wife of Ahab, brought about the death of Naboth, the vineyard's owner, on a false charge. **Elijah** punished Ahab for the crime; Jezebel was later devoured by dogs (I Kings 21). A "Naboth's vineyard" is any object coveted by another, or a possession to be secured at any cost.

Nana. The streetwalker and later successful demimondaine in Emile Zola's *Nana* (1880). She has beauty and great sexual prowess, and in her climb to the lavish life, she ruins many men. She dies disfigured by smallpox.

Nanki-Poo. Son of the emperor in W.S. Gilbert's and Arthur Sullivan's *The Mikado* (1885). He loves **Yum-Yum**, and flees from his aged and ugly fiancee Katisha. He is declared dead, Katisha marries **Ko-Ko**, and the lovers are free to marry.

Naomi. The mother-in-law of **Ruth**. See **Whither thou goest, I will go**.

Narcissus. A beautiful youth who spurned the love of all others and became enamoured of his own reflection in a pool of water. As he bent forward, fascinated by his own image and trying to embrace it, he fell and drowned in the pool. Hence "narcissism" has come to mean excessive self-love.

Nausicaä. In Homer's *Odyssey*, the daughter of Alcinous and Arete, who with the connivance of **Athena** greets **Odysseus** after he is shipwrecked and guides him to her father's palace.

Nazarene. One of Christ's appellations; he came from Nazareth.

Nebuchadnezzar (or Nabuchadrezzar). The king of **Babylon** from 605 to 562 B.C.; he destroyed the temple at Jerusalem and brought the Jewish people to Babylon and into captivity (see **Babylonian captivity**). Notorious for his wickedness, he set up a huge "image of gold" in Babylon and commanded all to worship it or be thrown into a fiery furnace (see **Shadrach, Meshach and Abednego**). Insanity was the king's punishment for his arrogance. He lived out his life grazing in the field like an animal. Nebuchadnezzar's name suggests the humiliation that comes to the mighty when they overreach themselves in their wickedness.

Nemean lion. The first **labor of Heracles** was to kill the Nemean lion. When he found that the lion's skin could not be penetrated by arrows or hurt by his club, Heracles seized him and squeezed him to death.

Nemesis. The daughter of **Erebus** (hell) and Nyx (night) and the goddess of vengeance. A synonym for retribution. Commonly used today to refer to a persistent and unconquerable rival, enemy or stumbling block.

Nepenthe. From Greek *nepenthes*, "driving away pain and sorrow." A drug described in the fourth book of the *Odyssey* as one that brings forgetfulness of every sorrow; hence, any agent that induces euphoric states and enables people to forget their pains and miseries.

Neptune. Roman god of the sea. See **Poseidon**.

Nereids. Fifty sea nymphs, daughters of **Nereus** and Doris, who became the attendants of the sea god **Poseidon**.

Nereus. The son of **Titans Oceanus** and **Gaea** and father of the **Nereids**, nymphs of the Mediterranean. The epithet of Nereus is "old man of the sea," and he is renowned for his wisdom and his powers of prophecy.

Nestor.   A wise and venerable old man in **Homer's Iliad** and **Odyssey**. He was famous for his eloquence, justice and prudence.

Never-Never Land.   The fairyland in James M. Barrie's *Peter Pan* (see **Pan, Peter**) (1904). By extension, any fantasy land.

New Jerusalem.   "And I John saw the holy city, new Jerusalem, coming down from God out of heaven, prepared as a bride adorned for her husband" (Revelation 21:2). Thus Saint John (see **John, Saint**) describes his vision of the Christian **paradise**. New Jerusalem is the equivalent of heaven, the **Celestial City**, where God resides with the Christian saints.

Newspeak.   In George Orwell's *1984* (1949), the reduced and "simplified" language of the society—designed to impoverish thought and ultimately to cripple the mind.

New Testament.   The second part of the Christian Bible. It deals with the embodiment of God's covenant with man and the dispensation of grace revealed through Jesus Christ. There are 27 short books which contain: the four **Gospels** which tell of the life of Jesus; an early history of the Church; and letters of Church Fathers to several congregations. These letters have become the foundation of Christian ethics.

New wine into old bottles.   "No man putteth a piece of new cloth unto an old garment . . . . Neither do men put new wine into old bottles; else the bottles break, and the wine runneth out, and the bottles perish: but they put new wine into new bottles, and both are preserved" (Matthew 9:16-17; Mark 3:21-22; Luke 5:36-37). Jesus is advising his followers that the new spiritual order he is teaching requires new practices. The wine and the bottles metaphorically represent the content and form of institutions or doctrines.

Nibelungenlied.   A 13th-century German epic largely derived from the Norse ***Volsunga Saga***. It tells of the adventures of **Siegfried**, his love for **Brunhild** and the treachery that led to his death. The Nibelungs are a race of dwarves and Siegfried's stealing of their treasure is one of the central events in the epic. Richard Wagner drew on this material for his cycle of four operas known as *The Ring of the Nibelungs*.

Nickleby, Nicholas. Hero of Dickens' *Nicholas Nickleby* (1839). An impoverished widow's son, he slowly betters his financial status to be able to provide for his mother and sister and to marry Madeline Bray.

Nike. In Greek, "victory." Statues of the goddess, Victory, were set up by the ancient Greeks to commemorate military victories. Two examples are especially noteworthy today: the Nike, or Winged Victory, of Samothrace, now in the Louvre; and a set of statues of Nike in various poses in the temple of **Athena** Nike on the Acropolis of Athens.

1984. A dystopian novel by George Orwell (1949), depicting the character of a debased, mechanized and regimented society of the year 1984. Some of the phrases that Orwell used in the novel to characterize totalitarian concepts, such as "**Big Brother** is watching you" and "Doublethink," have become part of the language. See also: **Newspeak.**

Nine Worthies, The. Listing of heroes mentioned together in literature of the early medieval and Renaissance periods; 15th-century English printer and writer William Caxton lists them in the conventional three groups: **Hector**, Alexander, Julius Caesar (pre-Christian pagans); **Joshua, David, Judas Maccabaeus** (pre-Christian Jews); **Arthur**, Charlemagne, Godfrey of Boulogne (Christians). They are represented in a burlesque pageant in the final act of Shakespeare's *Love's Labour's Lost* (1594).

Niobe. Daughter of **Tantalus** and Dione, wife of Amphion (a son of **Zeus**), who boasted of her numerous offspring (varying in number from five to twenty according to legend). Niobe held herself superior to **Leto**, who had only two, **Apollo** and **Artemis**. The goddess Leto heard her and called upon her two children for vengeance. Apollo killed all of Niobe's sons, Artemis all her daughters. Niobe fled to Mt. Sipylos in the land of her father in Asia Minor, where she was transformed into a rock. The most famous literary allusion to Niobe occurs in Shakespeare's **Hamlet** (I,ii,149): "Like Niobe, all tears," which is Hamlet's description of his mother's behavior at his father's funeral.

Nirvana.   In the Buddhist religion, the state in which the drives toward material wealth, earthly fame, and immortality are destroyed and the soul is released from the cycles of reincarnation; hence a state of blissfulness and enlightenment.

Noah.   The Biblical patriarch who was warned by God of the coming flood and who built the ark which was to carry male and female of every species until the waters receded and they could replenish the earth (Genesis 6). Similar stories were told in Babylonia of Utnapishtim, in Greece of **Deucalion** and in India of Manu.

Noah's ark.   See **Noah**.

Noble Savage.   The idea, derived from Jean Jacques Rousseau (1712-78) and incorporated into the thought of the Romantics, that man in his primitive or original condition is good and noble, and that he is corrupted by his flawed and over-sophisticated social institutions.

Nora.   Wife of Torvald Helmer in Ibsen's play *A Doll's House* (1879). Helmer is a shallow and hypocritical model of convention-al morality who has no conception of Nora's humanity and the dignity of her sacrifices for his well-being. She rebels against being stereotyped as a "little squirrel" of a wife, and at the end of the play she forsakes the "Doll's House" that her home has become for her.

Norns.   Norse goddesses who spun the threads of destiny for mankind and from whose decrees not even the gods could escape. There were generally considered to be three Norns: Urd, the oldest, or the Past; Verdandi, the Present; and Skuld, the Future. Compare the Moirai, or **Fates**, of Greek and Roman mythology. See **Yggdrasil.**

Not by bread alone.   "It is written, Man shall not live by bread alone, but by every word that proceedeth out of the mouth of God"

(Matthew 4:4; Luke 4:4; cf. Deuteronomy 8:3). The phrase "not by bread alone" is still used as a rebuke against materialistic values.

Not peace but a sword.   "Think not that I am come to send peace on earth: I came not to send peace on earth; but a sword. For I am come to set a man at variance against his father, and the daughter against her mother, and the daughter in law against her mother in law" (Matthew 10:34-35; cf. Luke 12:51-53). These uncompromising words of Jesus are some source of embarrassment to pacifists; read in context, however, they suggest that Jesus was referring to the conflict between loyalty to the messianic kingdom and loyalty to the family. The sword should probably be understood metaphorically.

Numbers.   A book of the **Old Testament**. It is a record of the wanderings of the Israelites through the desert wilderness and to the entrance of the **Promised Land**. In this book, **Moses** appears as a prophet who speaks directly to God.

Nymph.   Any of a large number of minor female deities associated with trees or water and represented as beautiful, eternally young maidens; generally they were attendants of the more powerful gods. They were not immortal, but were usually sprightly and friendly to human beings. Oceanids were associated with the sea; **Nereids** with salt and fresh water; Naiads with springs, rivers and lakes; Oreads with mountains; Napaiae with glens and dells; Alseids with groves; **Dryads** with forests and trees. Many nymphs became famous in their own right as, for example, Thetis, mother of **Achilles**.

O

Oberon. King of the fairies in Shakespeare's *A Midsummer Night's Dream* (1595). His plot to avenge himself on his wife **Titania** over a quarrel of theirs works all too well: Titania is humiliated by falling in love with an ass and the mortal characters of the play become entangled in absurdly comic romances. In the end, the fairy king and queen are reconciled and all is set right with the mortal lovers.

Oblomov. The satirical novel *Oblomov* (1859), a classic study of indolence, by the Russian Ivan Goncharov, presents that extraordinarily lazy landowner, Oblomov, who is usually in bed or dressed to go to bed. Hence his name is synonymous with irresponsible, pathological laziness.

Oceanus. The son of **Uranus** and Gaea and one of the **Titans**, Oceanus was the god of the great ocean that encompasses the world. He married **Tethys** and the two produced the 3,000 oceanic nymphs known as the Oceanids.

Odette. A courtesan who assumes the aristocratic name Odette de Crecy and becomes the wife of M. Swann (see **Swann, M.**) in the series of novels known in English as *Remembrance of Things Past*, by the French novelist Marcel Proust. Odette's ethereal beauty is by no means equalled by her intellect, which is vulgar and petty compared to that of her aesthete husband and his circle. She bears Swann a daughter, Gilberte, with whom the narrator **Marcel** becomes obsessed for a time.

Odin.   The greatest of the Scandinavian gods (called Woden or Wotan by the Anglo-Saxons); god of wisdom, poetry, war and agriculture.

Odor of sanctity.   The sweet odor which was believed in the Middle Ages to be given off by the bodies of saintly persons when they died.

Odysseus.   Hero of the *Odyssey*; son of Laertes, king of Ithaca. Also known as Ulysses, or by his Latin name, Ulixes. It was he who proposed that the unsuccessful suitors of Helen (see **Helen of Troy**) among whom were the most powerful men in Greece, should vow to protect Helen, whom he himself had wanted to marry before he married **Penelope**. This decision led to the **Trojan War**. Although he was involved in some of the battles of the Trojan War, he was noted more for his strategy and counsel. He was one of the three legates sent by **Agamemnon** to **Achilles** to settle the quarrel between that hero and the leader. He was also concealed in the **Trojan Horse**. For his adventures after the fall of Troy, see the *Odyssey*. After his return home to his wife Penelope and son **Telemachus**, who had waited for him for 10 years, Odysseus resumed his wanderings. To **Homer**, Odysseus was the "man of many wiles"; to some he was a schemer and a trickster; to others (like Robert and John Fitzgerald Kennedy in our time, whose favorite poem was Tennyson's "Ulysses"), he is the embodiment of the human mind at its best: courageous, able to overcome obstacles, inquiring, indomitable—"to strive, to seek, to find and not to yield." See also: *Iliad*.

Odyssey.   The great classical Greek epic poem by **Homer** which charts the wanderings of the Greek hero **Odysseus** from the Greek victory in the *Trojan War* to his ultimate return to his home in Ithaca, where his faithful wife **Penelope** and son **Telemachus** had been waiting for him for 10 years. In the course of his adventures through the Aegean and Mediterranean Seas, Odysseus encountered the Cyclops **Polyphemus**, the cannibal **Laestrygonians**, and the enchantress **Circe**. He descended into the underworld, avoided succumbing to the spell of the **Sirens**, and passed through **Scylla and Charybdis**. At the end of the epic, Odysseus returns to his own home unrecognized; he slays Penelope's suitors, purifies his defiled hall and becomes reconciled with his wife. Today a long and perilous wandering journey or a quest that involves extraordinary discoveries is often called an odyssey.

Oedipus. "Swell-foot" in Greek. **Laius** and **Jocasta**, king and queen of Thebes, were warned by an **oracle** that their son would kill his father. Therefore, at birth he was given to a shepherd to be left to die on Mt. Cithaeron; his hands and feet were bound and a nail driven into his feet. A shepherd of King Polybus of Corinth found the child and brought him to the king and his wife, Merope. Oedipus grew up thinking they were his real parents. When he heard one day that they were not, he went to Delphi to consult the oracle, where he was told that he was destined to kill his father and marry his mother. Persisting in his belief that the rulers of Corinth were his parents, he left that city. At the meeting of three roads near Delphi, he met Laius and, unaware of his identity, killed him in a quarrel. As a reward for solving the **riddle of the Sphinx**, he was made king of Thebes. Oedipus married Jocasta and fathered four children by her: **Antigone**, Ismene, Eteocles and Polynices. A plague struck Thebes; to lift it, the oracle ordered that the murderer of Laius be discovered and driven out. After Oedipus called in **Teiresias**, the blind seer, to help, the evidence clearly pointed to Oedipus. Jocasta committed suicide; Oedipus put out his eyes and wandered from Thebes until he died in Colonus. His tragic story and the stories of some of his children are told in *Oedipus the King, Antigone, Oedipus at Colonus*, by **Sophocles**, and *Seven Against Thebes*, by **Aeschylus**. See also: **Oedipus Complex.**

Oedipus at Colonus.   Colonus, a small locality near Athens, was the birthplace of **Sophocles** and the scene of his last play, *Oedipus at Colonus* (produced posthumously in 401 B.C.). After years of wandering, the blind **Oedipus** attended by his daughter **Antigone**, has arrived in Colonus and refuses to leave it, for he has been told by an **oracle** that he will die here. Protected by **Theseus**, who is now the king of Athens, he learns about the conflict between his two sons whom he curses, then overcomes his own fate, dies at peace with himself and is mysteriously carried away to the gods.

Oedipus Complex.   A psychological condition in which the son feels excessive erotic love for his mother and a corresponding desire to kill the father who frustrates the son's desire for the mother. The condition was analyzed by Sigmund Freud, and it is one of the central themes of Freudian psychology. Freud chose this name because the complex corresponds to aspects of the myth of **Oedipus**.

Oenone.   A **nymph** who dwelt on Mount Ida (see **Ida, Mount**) and the wife (in some versions, the beloved) of the Trojan prince **Paris**. Paris abandoned her for Helen (see **Helen of Troy**), the most beautiful woman in the world, and thus set off the **Trojan War**.

Ogygia.   The island where the nymph **Calypso** lived and where **Odysseus** was detained seven years on his voyage home.

O'Hara, Scarlett.   The beautiful heroine of Margaret Mitchell's novel *Gone With the Wind* (1936). Through her willpower, skill and opportunism, she manages to survive the misfortunes of the Civil War.

Old Man of the Sea.   (1) In **Homer's** *Odyssey*, **Proteus**, capable of assuming any form, but obliged to tell the truth if he can be caught and held. (2) **Nereus**, a sea god. (3) In the *Arabian Nights*, the Old Man of the Sea is a frightful old man who fixes himself tightly on **Sinbad's** shoulders and will not let go, obliging Sinbad to carry the burden for many days before he gets the old man drunk and shakes him off.

Old men dream dreams.   "Your sons and your daughters shall prophesy, your old men shall dream dreams, your young men shall see visions" (Joel 2:28; quoted in Acts 2:17). Joel is prophesying the Day of the Lord; Peter in the book of Acts applies the prophecy to the day of Pentecost.

Old Testament.   The first part of the Christian Bible, covering the history of Israel, its God-given laws, its vicissitudes as a nation. The Old Testament is divided into: (1) the **Torah** or Law: the first five books of the Bible, known as the **Pentateuch**; (2) Eight books of the prophets; (3) the Hagiographs or Writings, including the books of **Job, Ruth, Proverbs, Psalms, Ecclesiastes**.

Olive branch.   "And he [Noah] stayed yet the other seven days; and again he sent forth the dove out of the ark; and the dove came in to him in the evening; and lo, in her mouth was an olive leaf plucked off: so **Noah** knew that the waters were abated from the earth" (Genesis 8:10-11). In Genesis, the olive leaf is an indication of the extent to which the flood waters have receded, for the olive does not grow at high altitudes. The abating of the flood was a sign of the abating of God's wrath (8: 21-22), and so the dove was the herald of reconciliation between God and man. Although the later association of the dove and olive branch with peace is not fully supported by the text, this is the most common significance now. In modern usage, a dove is one who advocates a non-belligerent foreign policy, and to extend the olive branch is to make an offer of peace. See also: **Dove of Noah**.

Olympians, the Twelve.   The twelve major divinities whose principal dwelling place was on the summit of **Mount Olympus**, although they had temples and habitations in other parts of the ancient world. Their Greek names (and Roman equivalents): **Zeus**, Jupiter; **Hera**, Juno; **Apollo**; **Artemis**, Diana; **Poseidon**, Neptune; **Athena** (or Athene), Minerva; **Demeter**, Ceres; **Aphrodite**, Venus; **Hephaestus**, Vulcan; **Hermes**, Mercury; **Ares**, Mars; **Hestia**, Vesta—replaced later by **Dionysus, Bacchus**. Although god of the sea, Poseidon was also an Olympian.

Olympic Games.   One of the four sacred festivals (the other three were the **Pythian Games** at Delphi, the Isthmian games at Corinth and the Nemean games at Nemea) of the ancient Greeks, held every fourth year in July on the plain of Olympia in Elis in honor of **Zeus**, and consisting of all types of sporting and athletic contests, beginning and ending with sacrifices to the gods. In modern times the tradition was reestablished in 1896, with Games held every four years since then, excepting the years of the World Wars.

Olympus.   See **Mount Olympus**.

Omphalos.   Literally "navel." In the mythology of ancient Greece, the oval-shaped stone in the temple of **Apollo** at Delphi marking the exact center of the world. Hence, source, mystical center. See also: **Delphic Oracle**.

Onan. When Onan was forced to go in to the wife of his dead brother, Er, and "raise up seed" to him, he "knew that the seed should not be his . . . and he spilled it on the ground, lest that he should give seed to his brother" (Genesis 38:1-10). The modern usage of the word "onanism" includes masturbation as well as a means to frustrate conception.

Open sesame. In the story "Ali Baba and the Forty Thieves" in the , the magic words that **Ali Baba** overhears that enable him to enter the treasure vault. Hence, any secret or opportunity that permits entry or achievement.

Ophelia. The beautiful daughter of **Polonius** and sister of Laertes in Shakespeare's . In love with Hamlet, she is the victim of conflicts in the play. After her father's death at Hamlet's hands, she goes insane and drowns.

Oracles. In ancient Greece, the pronouncements made by a priest or priestess and supposed to be the reply of a god to some inquiry made by a mortal; or the sacred shrine where such a pronouncement was made. The oracle of **Apollo** at Delphi (see **Delphic Oracle**), of **Zeus** at Dodona and of **Asclepius** at Epidaurus were the most renowned. Today, oracle signifies an authoritative or infallible utterance, with the suggestion of divine inspiration.

Orestes. The son of **Agamemnon** and **Clytemnestra**, and brother of **Iphigenia** and **Electra**. After Agamemnon's departure for Troy, his mother took Aegisthus as her lover and sent Orestes into exile. On reaching manhood, Orestes returned and killed the adulterers to avenge his father's murder. Pursued then by the Furies (see **Erinyes**) as a murderer, he was eventually exonerated by the gods and ascended his father's throne. Subsequently, as one legend reports, he married Hermione, daughter of **Menelaus** and **Helen**, and lived to a very old age.

Orion. The hunter of Greek mythology, in some legends the companion of **Artemis** and in others slain by her. After his death he took his place in heaven as one of the constellations.

Orlando. See **Roland.**

Orpheus.   The master musician and lyre-player, son of **Apollo** and **Calliope**, whose music had almost magical properties, able to tame wild beasts and reconcile contending parties. His wife **Eurydice** was killed by a snake and Orpheus resolved to journey into **Hades** and convince the King of the Dead to allow her to go back with him to the upper earth. Hades consented on condition that Orpheus not look at her while he led the ascent; Orpheus violated the condition as he was emerging into the light and Eurydice fell back into Hades. Orpheus was subsequently dismembered by the Furies (see **Erinyes**), and ascended the heavens as a god, his lyre becoming the constellation Lyra. Today orphic signifies occult, oracular. See also: **Orphic Mysteries.**

Orphic Mysteries.   A celebration of the cult of Orphism, which received its name from the mythical **Orpheus**, who supposedly wrote sacred poems that formed the foundation of this belief. The devotees of Orphism centered their beliefs on the myth of Dionysus Zagreus (see **Dionysos**) and explained the conflict between good and evil in human beings through the story of his birth. In this myth Dionysus was the son of **Zeus** and **Persephone**. He was destroyed and eaten by the **Titans**, but **Athena** rescued his heart, which she delivered to Zeus. In punishment, Zeus burned the Titans with lightning and created a race of men from their ashes. According to the Orphists, man therefore has some divine essence in him. Zeus ate the heart and from it was born the son of Semele, the second Dionysus. The Orphic Mysteries mark a shift in Greek religion toward a more mystical contemplation of the good and evil in human nature.

Osiris.   One of the chief gods of ancient Egypt, forming a trinity with his wife-sister **Isis** and son **Horus**; originally a wise king who spread civilization throughout Egypt and other parts of the world. He married his sister, Isis, who ruled in his place while he traveled over the world. Upon his return, **Set**, his evil brother, had him murdered but Isis restored him to life through magic arts. Osiris, "The Good One," and Set represent the forces of good and evil, night and day, in conflict.

Ossa.   See **Pelion**.

Othello.   Protagonist of Shakespeare's tragedy (1604) of the same name, Othello is a black man, a Moor in the military service of Venice. He marries **Desdemona**, the daughter of a Venetian senator, and his treacherous ensign **Iago**, the archetypal villain, goads him into a jealous rage. At the tragedy's end, Othello kills Desdemona and then himself.

Out of the depths.   "Out of the depths have I cried unto thee, O Lord" (Psalms 130:1). The opening verse of one of the seven Penitential Psalms, also familiar in the Latin as *De profundis clamavi*.

P

Palladium. A statue of **Pallas Athena** that had the power to protect the city that housed it. It was supposed to have been thrown from heaven by **Zeus** and to have come to earth on the site of Troy. During the **Trojan War, Odysseus** and Diomedes stole into the city at night to remove the statue so that Troy would lose the protection of the goddess. Today the word *palladium* means a safeguard.

Pallas Athena (Athene). **Pallas** is part of the full, formal name of Athena. See **Athena**.

Pan. Called Faunus by the Romans; the Greek god of nature, fertility, forests, wild animals, and of shepherds and their flocks. He invented the syrinx, a flute of seven reeds. Depicted as half-man and half-goat, he was very playful and lecherous.

Pan, Peter. The hero of James M. Barrie's *Peter Pan* (1904). An eternal little boy who inhabits a **Never-Never Land**, Peter takes the Darling children along on his adventures against Captain Hook and his pirate gang. By extension, the symbol of every "eternal little boy."

Pandarus. (1) A Lycian warrior fighting on the Trojan side who fires the arrow that breaks the truce between Greeks and Trojans in Book IV of the , where Homer describes him as "noble, stalwart, glorious." (2) In medieval stories and in Shakespeare's

Troilus and Cressida (1609), a corrupt, scurrilous go-between in the love affair of **Troilus and Cressida**; hence, our word *pander*, a person who caters to vice; a procurer.

Pandora.   According to **Hesiod**, the first mortal woman, created out of clay by **Hephaestus** at **Zeus**' order to punish **Prometheus** for creating and helping man. The punishment was to be the releasing of all manner of evil into man's world. All the gods participated in clothing and adorning her and giving her charms and skills, both for good and evil practices. Hence, her name, Pandora, from Greek *pan*, "all," and *dora*, "gifts." She was sent down to Epimetheus, who readily accepted and married her, in spite of the warning of his brother Prometheus, who had advised him not to accept any gift from the gods. Pandora carried with her a jar (or box) containing all types of illness and evil but also Hope, which alone was tightly sealed at the bottom. She opened the jar allowing all the troubles that have plagued mankind ever since to escape. Only Hope remains. Today a Pandora's box is a source of unexpected and ever-increasing trouble.

Pangloss, Dr.   Literally "Dr. All-Tongues," he is the absurd, pedantic teacher of Candide in Voltaire's *Candide* who propounds the nonsensically optimistic philosophy that "All is for the best in this best of all possible worlds."

Pan's Pipe.   Syrinx was a **nymph** pursued by **Pan**. Spurning him, she sank into the earth and was transformed into reeds, from which Pan formed the musical instrument known as a Pan's pipe, or syrinx.

Pantagruel.   In Rabelais' satirical *Gargantua and Pantagruel* (1533) the son of **Gargantua** who travels with his comrade **Panurge**, helping the downtrodden of the earth.

Pantheon.   A temple devoted to all the gods (from Greek, *pan*, "all," *theon*, "of the gods"); specifically, the Roman domed edifice built by Hadrian from 120 to 124 A.D. and incorporating the porch of a structure built by Agrippa in 27 B.C. It became a church in 609 A.D., and is still standing. The word *pantheon* often means a selected group of eminent individuals, such as those honored in a hall of fame.

Panurge.   The beggar comrade of **Pantagruel** in Rabelais' satirical *Gargantua and Pantagruel*; wise in theory but helpless in practice. See also: **Gargantua**.

Panza, Sancho.   The peasant squire of **Don Quixote** in
Cervantes' epic story. He is slightly cowardly, has a great paunch, a
good sense of humor, and endures much. Fundamentally
materialistic, Sancho recites many proverbs, and subscribes to
their good common sense—in marked contrast to the Don, who
believes only in the romantic glory of chivalry as embodied in the
books he reads.

The parable of the sower.   "Another parable put he forth unto
them, saying, The kingdom of heaven is likened unto a man which
sowed good seed in his field: But while men slept, his enemy came
and sowed tares among the wheat, and went his way" . . . (Matthew
13:24ff.). The point of the parable is that God allows good and evil
(wheat and tares) to exist together until the **Last Judgment**.

Parable of the talents.   The parable of the talents (Matthew
25:14-30) tells of a certain man who went on a journey, leaving his
money with his servants. Two of them invested their sums with
bankers, and received interest equal to their deposits. The third
was cautious and hid his sum in the ground, returning it intact. The
master on his return praised the first two with the words, "Well
done, thou good and faithful servant"; he berated the third. A talent
was a measure of weight, differing in amount from place to place. In
Jesus' time a talent of silver would have been worth several
thousand dollars by modern reckoning. The modern meaning of talent, a native ability which should be improved or cultivated,
derives from this parable. The parable illustrates the reckoning
which all men will be called to make at the **Last Judgment**.

Paradise.   From *paradeisos*, a Greed word of Persian origin
meaning a garden or park. In the Septuagint (the oldest Greek version of the **Old Testament**), it is applied to the Garden of Eden
(see **Eden, Garden of**). In the **New Testament** the word is synonymous with "heaven," since in heaven, the second Eden, man is
restored to the state of happiness he forfeited in the first. The final
section of Dante's *Divine Comedy*, in which the poet attains the
realm of heaven, is called "Paradiso." The modern usage of the

word has weakened to mean any extremely pleasant place. See also: **Earthly paradise**.

Parcae.   See the **Fates**.

Paris.   Son of **Priam** and **Hecuba**, also known as Alexandros. Because of a prophecy that he would be the cause of Troy's ruin, he was exposed to the elements but was found by a shepherd. While taking care of sheep on Mt. Ida, he was approached by **Hera, Aphrodite** and **Athena** to render a decision in the famous **Judgment of Paris**. For choosing Aphrodite, he was rewarded with the most beautiful woman in the world—Helen (see **Helen of Troy**). Although he was in love with a nymph named **Oenone**, he went off to Sparta to take **Helen** away with him to Troy. In the **Trojan War** Paris was rather lackadaisical, priding himself more on his beauty than on his valor, and angering both Helen and Priam by his irresponsibility. However, he is supposed to have shot the arrow that killed **Achilles**. He himself was wounded by Philoctetes with one of the arrows that had once belonged to **Heracles**. Paris returned to Oenone begging her to heal his wound but she refused and then took her own life. See also: **Apple of discord**.

Parnassus.   The mountain in Greece consecrated to **Apollo** and the nine **Muses**; hence the home of poetry and music.

Parsifal.   A hero of Arthurian legend. Amfortas, the keeper of the Holy **Grail**, has been wounded by Klingsor, the evil magician; his spear has been stolen. The wound of Amfortas, who is associated with the Fisher King, will not heal, and only a "pure fool," some guileless and innocent knight, can regain the spear and with its healing touch restore Amfortas to health. This Parsifal does, redeeming the temptress Kundry in the process. The medieval tale has Parsifal growing to manhood in the isolation of the forests, joining **Arthur**'s **Round Table**, and maintaining his innocence even after many adventures. He eventually becomes guardian of the Grail itself. Wagner used the legend in his opera *Parsifal* (1882).

Parthenon.   The great temple, constructed in the Doric manner, which crowns the Acropolis over Athens consecrated to the virgin goddess **Athena** (*parthenos*, "virgin"). Built under the direction of the sculptor Phidias, it is one of the finest examples of

Greek architecture, famous for the sculpture of its two pediments, the continuous frieze of its walls, and the huge 42-foot statue of Athena inside, with face, throat, arms and feet of ivory, and clothing of gold.

Pasiphaë.   The wife of Minos, legendary ruler of Crete. As punishment for Minos' refusal to sacrifice a white bull, the god **Poseidon** made Pasiphaë fall in love with the bull. Their union produced the **Minotaur**, a monster half-man and half-bull. The Minotaur was confined in the **Labyrinth** at Knossos on Crete.

Pater noster.   In Latin, "Our Father," the opening words of the Lord's Prayer (Matthew 6:9); also written as one word when it refers to that passage.

Patience of Job.   "Ye have heard of the patience of Job" (James 5:11). **Job**'s proverbial patience appears only in chapters one and two of the *Book of Job*; elsewhere he appears angry and rebellious.

Patroclus.   Bosom friend of **Achilles**, beside whom he fought in the **Trojan War**. When the Trojan hero **Hector** killed Patroclus, Achilles left off sulking in his tent and returned to battle in order to avenge his beloved friend by slaying Hector. The friendship of Achilles and Patroclus is proverbial.

Paul, Saint.   Early Christian missionary and theologian, known as "Apostle of the Gentiles" (see **Apostle**), perhaps the most important figure in spreading the message of Christ to the world. Born to Jewish parents in Tarsus, Paul (his Hebrew name was Saul) was a prominent **Pharisee** who converted to Christianity after a vision of Christ risen came to him on the road to Damascus. Paul traveled through the Roman world preaching and converting people to the new Word of Christ. His letters (gathered in the **New Testament** as the Epistles of Paul) are the earliest New Testament writings. Allusions to Saul on the road to Damascus refer to a sudden revelation or conversion.

Peachum, Polly.   Peachum's merry, buxom daughter in John Gay's drama *The Beggar's Opera* (1728). She becomes **Macheath**'s wife.

Pearl of great price. "Again, the kingdom of heaven is like unto a merchant man, seeking goodly pearls: Who, when he had found one pearl of great price, went and sold all that he had, and bought it" (Matthew 13:45-46). A metaphor for the ultimate value of the spiritual realm, its meaning has been diluted to mean almost anything or anyone of great importance.

Pearls before swine. "Give not that which is holy unto the dogs, neither cast ye your *pearls before swine*, lest they trample them under their feet, and turn again and rend you" (Matthew 7:6). Cast pearls before swine thus means to lavish good things on those who cannot appreciate them.

Pearly gates. "And the twelve gates were twelve pearls; every single gate was of one pearl: and the street of the city was pure gold, as it were transparent glass. And I saw no temple therein: for the Lord God Almighty and the Lamb are the temple of it" (Revelation 21:21-22). John's picture of the **New Jerusalem** has passed into the popular imagination, so that any allusion to pearly gates or streets of gold is understood as referring to Heaven.

Pecksniff. Mr. Pecksniff in Charles Dickens' *Martin Chuzzlewit* (1843) is a canting, unctuous hypocrite who propounds an outrageously false morality and is eventually denounced by Chuzzlewit, Sr. Hence "Pecksniffian", hypocritical.

Peeping Tom. The one citizen of Coventry who (legend says) looked upon the naked **Godiva** during her ride through the town. Hence, a voyeur.

Pegasus. The winged horse that arose from the blood of **Medusa** when **Perseus** cut her head off. Helped by **Athena, Bellerophon** caught Pegasus, mounted him, and thus killed the **Chimaera**. Trying to ascend to heaven on Pegasus, Bellerophon fell to earth and was lamed, but the horse continued to rise and became a constellation. Because of the association of the winged horse with the **Muses** (supposedly the Hippocrene spring arose on Mt. **Helicon**, where the Muses dwelled, at the touch of Pegasus' hoof), "to mount Pegasus" means to do creative or inspired work.

Peggotty, Clara.   In Dickens' ***David Copperfield*** (1850), the loyal servant of Mrs. Copperfield. She becomes David's nurse and friend, and eventually marries **Barkis**.

Pelion.   A Greek myth tells of how the **giants** attempted to scale the heavens by piling the mountains of Pelion on top of Mount Ossa, in eastern Thessaly. Hence the expression "pile Pelion on Ossa," which means to heap difficulty on difficulty.

Pelops.   Son of **Tantalus**, king of Lydia. To test the gods, Tantalus killed his son Pelops, carved him up and served him at a banquet to which the gods were invited. The gods were not fooled: Pelops was restored to life (missing his shoulder, replaced with ivory, that **Demeter** consumed) and Tantalus punished with a horrid torture in hell. Pelops lived on to become king in Elis and to father **Atreus** and Thyestes. The "ivory shoulder of Pelops" is a person's distinguishing characteristic.

Penates.   See **Lares and Penates**.

Pendragon.   In Welsh, "head of a dragon"; this title was given to British chieftains at times of crisis to confer on them great power. In the Arthurian legends, Uther Pendragon is the father of King **Arthur**.

Penelope.   The wife of **Odysseus** and mother of **Telemachus**, who waited for her husband ten years while he fought in the **Trojan War** and ten more while he journeyed home. She resisted the amorous overtures of over 100 suitors. When the suitors became insistent, she agreed to marry one once she had finished weaving a shroud for Odysseus' father. Each day she wove, and each night unwove that day's work. Penelope is the prototype of faithfulness, loyalty and steadfastness. Penelope's weaving is a metaphor for an endless task.

Pentateuch.   From the Greek *penta*, "five," and *teuchos*, "book." The first five books of the **Torah** or **Old Testament: Genesis, Exodus, Leviticus, Numbers** and **Deuteronomy**. These are the books traditionally ascribed to **Moses**, the recipient of God's first revelation to the Jews on **Mount Sinai**.

Persephone.   Also known as Kore, "The Maiden," and called Proserpina (Proserpine) by the Romans. Daughter of **Zeus** and **Demeter**, abducted by **Hades** to be his queen in the Lower World; Demeter wandered grief-stricken over the earth in search of her daughter until Zeus made an effort to have Persephone restored to her. However, while in the Lower World, Persephone had eaten some seeds of a pomegranate, which bound her there forever. Nevertheless, a compromise was worked out by which Persephone had to remain in the Lower World part of the year but could go back to the earth the rest of the year. This alternation of dwelling below the earth and upon it is a form of nature myth symbolizing the cycle of seasons.

Perseus.   The son of **Zeus**; a model Greek hero. He killed the **Gorgon, Medusa,** punished **Atlas** by transforming him into a mountain, rescued **Andromeda,** won her for his wife and remained faithful to her. He rescued his mother from the base desires of Polydectes, whom he also transformed into stone, conferring his throne on the fisherman Dictys. Perseus ruled well on the throne of Argos and Tiryns, and founded Mycenae.

Peter, Saint.   One of the twelve **apostles** of Christ (variously referred to as Simon, Simon Peter or Cephas), he was their acknowledged leader. Christ gave Peter his name (meaning rock), as told in the Biblical passage: "Thou art Peter; and upon this rock I will build my church; and the gates of hell shall not prevail against it. And I will give unto thee the keys of the kingdom of heaven" (Matthew 16:18-19). Catholics interpret this passage as meaning that Peter was given actual jurisdiction over Church affairs, an office that in their doctrine has passed down from him to the popes.

Petruchio.   Masterful and clever, he tames the shrew Katherine in Shakespeare's *The Taming of the Shrew* (1593).

Phaedra.   Daughter of Minos and **Pasiphaë,** rulers of Crete, and **Ariadne**'s younger sister, she married **Theseus** after he had abandoned her sister. Phaedra fell passionately in love with **Hippolytus,** the son of Theseus by the Amazon queen **Hippolyta.** When the chaste young man spurned her advances, Phaedra hanged herself, leaving behind a suicide note claiming that Hippolytus had seduced her. The French dramatist Jean Baptiste Racine used her story as the subject of his tragedy *Phèdre* (1677).

Phaeton.   Son of **Apollo** and Clymene. His reckless driving of the chariot of the sun posed a threat to heaven and earth. **Zeus** killed him with a thunderbolt.

Pharisees.   An ancient Jewish sect composed of students, teachers and scholars who advocated strict observance of the forms of religion, and who were accused by Christ of emphasizing outer forms over the true and inner religious reality. Hence they are associated with hidebound traditionalism, hypocrisy and fulsome self-righteousness. See Matthew 3, 23; Luke 18. They were opposed by the **Sadducee** sect.

Phidias.   One of the great sculptors of ancient Greece, who died around 432 B.C. He is said to have sculpted a 40-foot-high statue of **Zeus** at Elis, and the 42-foot-high statue of **Athena** inside the **Parthenon**, in addition to countless other works.

Philemon and Baucis.   A poor, aged couple living in Phrygia, Asia Minor. When **Zeus** and **Hermes** came to their land in disguise, the rich turned the gods away but Philemon and Baucis received them with kindness and hospitality. As a reward the gods saved them from a flood, turned their poor habitation into a temple, and granted their wish that they be allowed to die at the same time.

Philippic.   Demosthenes often orated against Philip of Macedon in order to incite the Athenians against him. These speeches were full of acrimony, accusation and invective; hence the modern meaning of the word, a speech of bitter denunciation.

Philistine.   An uncultured, narrow person capable only of hackneyed ideas and materialistic values, usually associated with the bourgeois of the 19th century. Matthew Arnold established this connotation of the term, adapting it from the Biblical context in which the Philistines were the traditional enemies of the Jews against whom David, Samson and other Jewish heroes waged war (Genesis 21, 34; Judges 16).

Phoebe.   A female **Titan**, the mother of **Leto**, with whom **Zeus** fathered **Apollo** and **Artemis**. The first moon goddess, her name passed on to Artemis and, in the form *phoebus* (meaning "shining one"), became one of the epithets of Apollo. In literary allusion, Phoebe signifies the moon.

Phoebus.   Literally, "bright." Another name for **Apollo**, the sun god.

Phoenix.   (1) The great bird of myth, said to consume itself in flames every 500 years and rise to another life out of its own ashes. The mythical bird is thus a symbol of resurrection. (2) The old man who serves as mentor to **Achilles** in Homer's *Iliad*.

Pickwick.   Mr. Pickwick is the hero of Charles Dickens' novel *The Pickwick Papers* (1837). The unsophisticated, innocent founder of the Pickwick Club, Mr. Pickwick embarks on a series of delightful excursions with his friends, meeting all sorts and conditions of men in 19th-century England. He loses a breach of promise suit brought against him by Mrs. Bardell, and goes to prison, with his friend and valet, Sam Weller (see **Weller, Sam**), because he refuses to pay damages. Mr. Pickwick was in the habit of using highly insulting language in a completely unmeaning and harmless way—hence the phrase "in a Pickwickian sense" is descriptive of word usage that departs from the sense commonly understood.

Pierian spring.   A spring in Pieria, a district on the slopes of **Mount Olympus** associated in early times with the worship of the **Muses**; hence, inspiration, learning, as in Alexander Pope's famous couplet from *Essay on Criticism* (Part II, lines 15-16): A little learning is a dangerous thing;/Drink deep, or taste not the Pierian spring.

Pilate, Pontius.   The Roman governor in Jerusalem at the time of the crucifixion of Christ. He is said to have found Christ innocent of the charges brought against him by the Jews, but bowed to their desire to crucify him, and symbolically "washed his hands" of Christ's blood. Pilate is an archetypal self-deceiver and hypocrite, and to "wash one's hands" of a matter means to refuse to take responsibility for one's own actions, especially wrongful actions.

Pile Pelion on Ossa. See **Pelion**.

Pilgrim's Progress, The. The 1678 work by John Bunyan which recounts in the form of a religious allegory the pilgrimage of the hero, **Christian**, through danger and distraction to the **Celestial City**. It is generally recognized as the greatest literary expression of the Puritan sensibility and a masterpiece in its own right. The title suggests today the simple person's pious struggle to reach heaven.

Pillar of Salt. See **Lot**.

Pisgah. See **Mount Pisgah**.

Pistol. A bombastic soldier, married to Mistress Quickly, and denizen of Sir John Falstaff's (see **Falstaff, Sir John**) low world in Shakespeare's *Henry IV, Parts One and Two* (1597) and *Henry V* (1598).

Plagues of Egypt. The ten plagues that afflicted the Egyptians (Exodus 7-12) were acts in a mighty struggle between God and Pharaoh, culminating in the Passover, the Exodus of the Jews from Egypt, and destruction of Pharaoh's army. The plagues were: (1) the turning of the Nile to blood; (2) frogs; (3) lice; (4) flies; (5) death of cattle; (6) boils; (7) hail; (8) locusts; (9) darkness; and (10) the death of the Egyptian firstborn. As a result of these plagues, Pharaoh, whose heart had been "hardened—and he refuseth to let the people [Israelites] go," freed the Israelites from bondage (Exodus 7-12). See also: **Moses**.

Plato. The second (424/427-348/347 B.C.) of the triumvirate of classical Greek philosophers, following **Socrates** and preceding **Aristotle**, and the founder of the Academy in Athens. His system of philosophy was based on the theory of pure and eternal Forms or Ideas, entities existing outside the mind and accessible to the mind alone. In Plato's philosophy, particular and material objects are only an imitation of these eternal types. Plato's preferred method of discourse was the dialogue, in which form he wrote nearly all his works. These include *Phaedo*, the *Symposium* and perhaps his most influential work, the *Republic*. Plato has had a profound effect on the course of Western thought and philosophy down through

the ages. In the *Symposium*, Plato discourses on Socrates' definition of the nature of love, which places spiritual union on a higher
plane than physical love. From this derives the concept of "Platonic
love," meaning a nonsexual or nonphysical relationship between
members of the opposite sex.

Pleiades.   The seven daughters of **Atlas** and Pleione. When they
were pursued by **Orion, Zeus** decided to help them outrun him,
since three had been his mistresses. They became a constellation
fixed in the heavens, although only six stars are visible because one
would not show herself for shame at having married a mortal man.

Pluto.   Another name for **Hades**.

Polly, Aunt.   Tom Sawyer's (see **Sawyer, Tom**) kindhearted,
devout and fussy aunt and guardian in Mark Twain's *Tom Sawyer*
(1876).

Pollyanna.   The child heroine of a series of novels by Eleanor H.
Porter; she always looks on the brighter side of things. A "Pollyanna
attitude" now denotes a rather foolish, saccharine optimism.

Polonius.   In Shakespeare's *Hamlet*, the officious and garrulous
old counselor to King **Claudius**, and father of **Ophelia** and Laertes.
Famous for his pompous maxims (the most celebrated being "To
thine own self be true"), Polonius becomes a key figure in the play's
plot when he agrees to spy on Hamlet. The death of Polonius (Hamlet runs his sword through the tapestry behind which the old man is
hiding and eavesdropping) triggers Ophelia's madness and suicide
and the climactic duel between Hamlet and Laertes.

Polyhymnia.   Muse of sacred hymns and songs. See the **Muses**.

Polyphemus.   The cyclops (see **Cyclopes**) who imprisoned
Odysseus and his men in his cave and devoured two at each meal.
Odysseus blinded him, and escaped with his remaining men tied
beneath the bellies of Polyphemus' sheep.

Pomona.   The goddess of fruit trees and bride of **Vertumnus**,
the god of seasons.

Pontifex, Ernest. Hero of Samuel Butler's single novel, *The Way of All Flesh* (1903). Brought up in a strict religious household, Ernest struggles against Victorian repression, hypocrisy and narrow-mindedness to find and assert his own identity.

Pooh-Bah. The haughty Lord High Everything Else in W.S. Gilbert and Arthur Sullivan's *The Mikado* (1885). See also: **Nanki-Poo; Yum-Yum**.

Portia. The intelligent young heroine of Shakespeare's *The Merchant of Venice* (1596). Disguised as a young lawyer, she successfully defends **Antonio** against **Shylock**'s suit for a pound of his flesh in default of payment of his loan. Also, the name of Brutus' noble wife in *Julius Caesar* (1599).

Poseidon. The god of the sea, one of Greece's Twelve Olympian gods (see **Olympians, The Twelve**), son of **Cronos** and **Rhea**, and brother of **Zeus** and **Hades**. His symbol was the trident, his gift to man was the horse. In **Homer** he is given the epithet "earthshaker," as god of earthquakes. He competed unsuccessfully with **Athena** for dominion of Attica, and with **Hera** for Argos.

Potiphar's wife. See **Joseph and Potiphar's wife**.

Potter's field. There are two accounts of the potter's field. In the *Acts of the Apostles* it is stated that Judas bought a field with the reward for his betrayal of Jesus. Falling into it, he burst and died, turning it into an "**Aceldama**," or "field of blood." Thus "Aceldama" now means a battlefield, or any place where blood is shed (Acts 1:18-19). Matthew records that Judas, before hanging himself, returned the 30 pieces of silver to the priests who had paid him for betraying Jesus. Since the money, being polluted, could not be put into the Temple treasury, the priests bought with it a potter's field, to be used as a cemetery for foreigners. This came to be known as the Field of Blood in allusion to the bloodmoney (Matthew 27:3-10). Today a potter's field is a burial place for the poor.

Pound of flesh. **Shylock**, the Jewish moneylender and villain of Shakespeare's *Merchant of Venice* (1596), guarantees a loan to **Antonio** with a pound of Antonio's flesh. When he will show no mercy, Portia, disguised as a young lawyer, defeats his suit by insisting he cut no more than one pound and not spill any blood in the process. To exact "a pound of flesh" today means to enforce a highly unequal bargain with severe penalties.

Powers that be.   "Let every soul be subject unto the higher powers. For there is no power but of God: the powers that be are ordained of God" (Romans 13:1). The "powers that be" are the existing governing authorities. Paul's acceptance of civil authority is often cited to show that Christianity tends to perpetuate the status quo, socially and politically. In 20th-century America, the phrase "powers that be" always carries a hint of sarcasm.

Praxiteles.   Sculptor, born in Athens c. 390 B.C. and considered by ancient authorities to be the greatest Greek sculptor. Some of his works in their original form have survived, among them the statue of **Hermes** carrying the infant **Dionysos**, discovered in 1877 in Olympia and now in the museum there. Among other famous works of Praxiteles are the statues of **Eros**, of the **Aphrodite** of Cnidos, and the **Satyr**, or Faun—now known only through copies or representations on coins.

Preacher, The.   In Hebrew, *koheleth*. The speaker of the book of **Ecclesiastes** in the **Old Testament**.

Priam.   The king of **Troy**, husband of **Hecuba** and father of **Hector, Paris**, Troilus (see **Troilus and Cressida**), Helenus, Deiphobus, Polydorus, Polyxena, **Cassandra** and others. In one of the greatest scenes in ancient literature, near the end of **Homer**'s *Iliad*, he went to **Achilles** to ask for the body of his dead son Hector. He was slain by Pyrrhus, the son of Achilles, during the sack of Troy.

Priapus.   The son of **Dionysos** and **Aphrodite**, and god of the fertility of nature and the reproductive forces of man. In modern usage, a reference to the libido or sexual urge.

The price of wisdom is above rubies.   "Where shall wisdom be found? and where is the place of understanding? Man knoweth not the price thereof; neither is it found in the land of the living. The depth saith, It is not in me: and the sea saith. It is not with me. It cannot be gotten for gold, neither shall silver be weighed for the price thereof. It cannot be valued with the gold of Ophir, with the precious onyx, or the sapphire . . . No mention shall be made of coral, or of pearls: for the price of wisdom is above rubies" (Job 28:12-18). The phrase is now proverbial for the immeasurable value of wisdom.

Pride goeth before a fall.   "Pride goeth before destruction, and a haughty spirit before a fall" (Proverbs 16:18). In popular quotation, the proverb is always abbreviated. The notion that God punishes men for their pride is common in the Bible, and appears in such stories as the Tower of **Babel**, the **Plagues of Egypt**, and **Nebuchadnezzar**.

Primrose path.   The path to iniquity and destruction, from two lines in Shakespeare: the "primrose path of dalliance" (*Hamlet*, I, iii, 47); and the "primrose way to the everlasting bonfire" (*Macbeth*, II, iii, 22).

Prince of Darkness.   See **Satan**.

Priscilla.   In the narrative poem, *The Courtship of Miles Standish* (1858), by Henry Wadsworth Longfellow, the Pilgrim captain Miles Standish (see **Standish, Miles**) enlists the young scholar John Alden to press his suit to marry the orphaned Priscilla. Priscilla refuses Standish and tells Alden to "Speak for yourself, John." He does and the two are married.

Procrustes.   He made travelers fit the size of his bed; if they were short he stretched them, if too long he cut them down to size. He was killed by **Theseus**. Thus, "Procrustean" signifies an arbitrary enforcement of conformity, or the harsh enforcement of preestablished norms.

Prodigal son.   In this parable of Jesus, a young man took the goods that his father had set aside for him, traveled "into a far country, and there wasted his substance with riotous living . . . And when he came to himself, he said . . . I will arise and go to my father, and will say unto him, Father, I have sinned against heaven, and before thee, And am no more worthy to be called thy son: make me as one of thy hired servants. And he arose, and came to his father . . . But the father said to his servants . . . Bring hither the fatted calf, and kill it; and let us eat, and be merry: For this my son was dead, and is alive again; he was lost, and is found" (Luke 15:17-24). "Prodigal" means "lavish, spendthrift." "A prodigal," a wayward child who repents and returns to his family, takes its meaning from this parable. "To kill the fatted calf" is now a proverbial expression for any lavish welcome. See also: **Fatted calf, kill the**.

Prometheus. The son of the **Titans** Iapetus and Clymene; his name means "forethought." He is the brother of **Atlas**, Menoetius and Epimetheus ("afterthought"). Superior to all the gods in guile and fraud, he is famous for having stolen fire from the heavens and given it to man. He was punished by **Zeus** by being chained to a rock and having his liver chewed daily by a vulture for 30 years until he was freed by **Heracles**. He refused Zeus' gift of a bride, Pandora. In addition to giving man fire, Prometheus reportedly fashioned the first mortals from clay, and taught them to raise plants and use them for medicines, to cultivate the land, and to tame horses. He also invented numbers. Prometheus is cited in allusions for his inventiveness, his shrewdness, and for the sufferings his genius brought him. "Promethean" means daringly creative and original.

Promised Land. "And the Lord appeared unto Abram and said, Unto thy seed will I give this land" (Genesis 12:7). God's promise of **Canaan** to Abraham (later extended to include everything between the Nile and the Euphrates, cf. Genesis 15:18) is renewed when the land is reconquered by **Joshua** and again in the restoration after the **Babylonian captivity**; it is one of the most persistent themes in the **Old Testament**. In Protestant hymns, the promised land sometimes means heaven.

A prophet is not without honor. "And they were offended in him. But Jesus said unto them, A prophet is not without honour, save in his own country, and in his own house" (Matthew 13:57; see also Mark 6:3-4; Luke 4:24; John 4:44). Jesus' comment after being unfavorably received in his home village of Nazareth. Modern usage applies to anyone not respected or honored in his own country.

Proserpina. Roman name for Greece's **Persephone**, goddess of the underworld. Called Proserpine in English.

Prospero. Deposed duke of Milan, magician and hero of Shakespeare's last play, **The Tempest** (1611). Alone on an enchanted island for years with his daughter, **Miranda**, the evil monster, **Caliban**, and the airy sprite **Ariel** who does his bidding, Prospero contrives the shipwreck of his brother (who had usurped his dukedom) and his party. With wisdom, patience and the art of magic, Prospero effects the reconciliation of all parties, and demonstrates the power of goodness and justice.

Pross, Miss. The brusque servant and devoted companion to Lucie Manette in Dickens' *A Tale of Two Cities* (1859). See also: **Manette, Lucie**.

Proteus. A lesser sea god, son of **Oceanus** and **Tethys**, to whom **Poseidon** gave the power to utter the truth and the ability to change his form. "Protean" means changeable, versatile, able to assume many roles.

Proudie, Bishop. The proud, pompous, dictatorial new bishop of Barchester in Anthony Trollope's *Barchester Towers* (1857). He is dominated by his strong-minded wife, Mrs. Proudie.

Proverbs. A collection of sententious, wise sayings appearing in the 20th book of the **Old Testament**. In secular usage, a proverb is a pithy saying that expresses some commonplace or accepted truth.

Prynne, Hester. The adulterous heroine of Hawthorne's *The Scarlet Letter* (1850). Her partner in adultery is Arthur Dimmesdale and their daughter is Pearl. See also: **Dimmesdale, Arthur**.

Psalms. The 19th book of the **Old Testament**. It contains 150 hymns (songs to God). **David**, called the "sweet psalmist of Israel" (II Samuel 23:1), is said to have written many of them.

Psyche. A mortal girl loved by **Eros**, the god of love, who visited her each night on condition that she not ask his name or look on his face. One night Psyche lit a lamp and saw the god asleep; he awoke and fled, leaving Psyche at the mercy of his mother, **Aphrodite**, the goddess of love. Psyche wandered long in search of Eros and eventually she was united with him and made immortal. She has since come to symbolize the human soul.

Puck.   The mischievous, humorous elf, a type of **Robin Goodfellow**, who carries out the orders of **Oberon**, king of the Fairies, in Shakespeare's **A Midsummer Night's Dream** (1595). Together they plot and enjoy the confusion of the other characters in the play.

Pygmalion.   A youthful sculptor who spurned the love of all women, thereby incurring the wrath of **Aphrodite**. To satisfy his own demand for ideal beauty, he created a perfect woman in marble, naming her **Galatea**. Then Aphrodite had her revenge, making Pygmalion fall in love with the statue which could not return his love. In this one instance, however, Aphrodite relented, and transformed the statue into a woman of flesh and blood. Bernard Shaw's play *Pygmalion*, and the popular musical comedy based on it, *My Fair Lady*, are modern adaptations of the legend. Pygmalion's myth is a cautionary tale about how the pursuit of ideal beauty may ultimately destroy all feeling in the artist, enslaving him to an ever colder and more lifeless art.

Pygmies.   A legendary race of dwarfs, said to have lived somewhere in Central Asia. They were attacked by **Heracles** who rolled them up in his lion's skin. In actuality, there are tribes of Pygmies living in equatorial Africa.

The Pyramid of Cheops.   See **Seven wonders of the ancient world**.

Pyramus and Thisbe.   Lovers whose parents opposed their meeting. Consequently they agreed to a tryst in an outlying district. Thisbe, arriving first, was attacked by a lion. She fled and dropped her scarf, which the lion, having just eaten some animal, bloodied with his mouth. When Pyramus arrived and saw the bloody scarf, he thought that Thisbe was dead, and killed himself. Thisbe returned, saw the body of her lover, and killed herself. The most popular version of the story is the hilarious play presented by the artisans in Shakespeare's **A Midsummer Night's Dream** (1595).

Pythias.   See **Damon and Pythias**.

Pythian Games.   One of the four Panhellenic festivals of ancient Greece, convened to commemorate the victory of **Apollo** over the **Python** near **Delphi**. See also: **Olympic Games**.

Python.   The great serpent, born in the mephitic waters left by the great deluge sent by **Zeus**. Python was killed by **Apollo** near **Delphi**. Python was subsequently the name given to a subfamily of snakes.

Quasimodo. The ugly, deaf, deformed bellringer of the Cathedral of Notre Dame in Victor Hugo's *Notre Dame de Paris* (1831). He becomes devoted to Esmeralda, a gypsy dancer on trial for witchcraft and saves her from the scheming Archdeacon Frollo. Esmeralda is finally hanged through Frollo's machinations. At her death, Quasimodo throws Frollo from the bell tower. Years later, the skeletons of a woman and a misshapen man are found together in Montfaucon, the criminals' burial vault.

Quick and the dead.   "From thence he shall come to judge the quick and the dead" (Apostles' Creed; also Acts 10:42; II Timothy 4:1; I Peter 4:5). "Quick" is here used in the archaic sense of "living."

Quilp, Daniel.   The ugly, cunning and malevolent dwarf in Dickens' *Old Curiosity Shop* (1841).

Quince, Peter.   The carpenter and member of the group of artisans in Shakespeare's *A Midsummer Night's Dream* (1595). He stages and directs the "Pyramus and Thisbe" interlude.

Quo vadis?   In Latin, "Whither goest thou?" According to legend, when Peter was fleeing Rome to escape martyrdom, he encountered Christ. Peter asked him this question, to which Christ replied, "To Rome to be crucified again," whereupon Peter turned about and returned to Rome. The title of a historical novel by the Polish writer Henry Sienkiewicz, which was adapted several times for the screen.

R

Ra. Originally the supreme deity of Egypt, god of the sun, creator of the first universe. When he grew old, men rebelled against him with the result that he became bitter at their ingratitude and retired to the heavens. He was represented in many forms, notably with the head of a hawk above which there was a disk. After about 2750 B.C., Ra was especially worshiped by the Pharaohs, who called themselves, "Sons of Ra."

Race is not to the swift, nor the battle to the strong. "The race is not to the swift, nor the battle to the strong, neither yet bread to the wise, nor yet riches to men of understanding, nor yet favour to men of skill; but time and chance happeneth to them all" (Ecclesiastes 9:11). A biblical reminder that human events do not always turn out in the way men expect them to.

Rachel. The daughter of **Laban** and second wife of **Jacob**, who bore him two sons, **Joseph** and **Benjamin**, dying in childbirth with Benjamin.

Rackstraw, Ralph. The most intelligent man in the fleet in W.S. Gilbert and Arthur Sullivan's *H.M.S. Pinafore* (1878). Because of the difference in their social positions, he cannot marry the captain's daughter, Josephine. When his identity as the true captain is revealed, the lovers are united.

Raffles. Archetype of the "gentleman burglar" type of criminal. He appeared originally in the short story collection, *The Amateur*

Cracksman, a bestseller of 1899, and in other collections and a novel by E.W. Hornung, brother-in-law of Sherlock Holmes's creator, Arthur Conan Doyle. Synonymous with the elegant crook.

Ragueneau.   In Edmond Rostand's play, *Cyrano de Bergerac* (1897), the cook-poet and friend of Cyrano. He provides refuge for poor artists, drinks a good deal, and tolerates his shrewish wife.

Rain on the just and the unjust.   See **Love your enemies**.

Ramayana.   "Adventures of Rama"—one of the two great epics of India, the other being **Mahabharata**. It contains about 24,000 couplets and is primarily the work of Valmiki. The hero, Rama, an avatar, or incarnation of **Vishnu**, is considered a perfect model of humanity: loyal, devoted, pious. His wife, Sita, is a model of wifely devotion, and his brother, Laksama, or Lakshman, a true type of brotherly loyalty. The story is concerned with the exile of Rama from his kingdom through the machinations of a stepmother, the devotion of his wife who follows him, her abduction by a monster named Ravana, the battle in which the two brothers, aided by an army of monkeys headed by Hanuman, a favorite of Indian folklore, defeat the forces of Ravana. The latter has ten heads and as fast as one is cut off another springs up (compare with the **Hydra**). But Rama despatches the monster at last with a special weapon. After an ordeal by fire to prove the chastity of Sita, Rama returns to his kingdom, mission accomplished.

Regan.   The hateful second daughter of **Lear** in Shakespeare's *King Lear* (1605). She joins her evil older sister **Goneril** in humiliating Lear, but the two sisters become deadly rivals for the affection of Edmund. At the play's end, Goneril poisons her and then commits suicide. Both sisters are archetypes of ungrateful, wicked children.

Render unto Caesar.   "Then saith he unto them, Render therefore unto Caesar the things which are Caesar's; and unto God the things that are God's" (Matthew 22:15-20; also Mark 12:17; Luke 20:21-25). A group of **Pharisees**, attempting to trap Jesus in a damaging statement, ask him if it is lawful to pay tribute money to Rome. If Jesus says it is not lawful, he will offend the Roman rulers, and if he answers to the contrary, he will offend the Jewish patriots.

He evades the dilemma by pointing out that the money bears Caesar's likeness and superscription, and that it is not wrong to pay the state in its own coin. The answer thus distinguishes between the claims of the sacred and the secular spheres, and is still quoted in discussions of the relation of church and state.

Rhea.   One of the 12 **Titans**, goddess of the earth and fertility and wife of **Cronos**, to whom she bore **Zeus, Hera, Demeter, Hades, Poseidon** and **Hestia**. Because of a prophecy that his children would dethrone him, Cronos devoured each of them at birth. Rhea, however, tricked him when Zeus was born, presenting him with a stone swaddled like a baby. Zeus escaped, fulfilled the prophecy, overthrew his father and became the chief deity, head of the Olympian gods. See also: **Olympians, The Twelve.**

Richard II.   Historic king of England (from 1377 to 1399) whose deposition from power and murder Shakespeare portrays in the historical drama *Richard II* (1595). Richard appears as a theatrical and self-obsessed ruler, as effete, self-pitying and poetic. His opponent, Henry Bolingbroke (later Henry IV), is decisive, ambitious and practical.

Richard III.   Historic king of England (from 1483 to 1485) whose rise to power Shakespeare portrays in the historical drama *Richard III* (1592). Shakespeare depicts Richard as almost a stock villain, physically deformed, fiendish in his pursuit of power and gleeful in the defeat of his enemies. It is a role much prized by actors.

The Riddle of the Sphinx.   After unknowingly killing his own father, **Oedipus** encounters the **Sphinx** at the gates of Thebes. She has the city completely cut off, stopping all who would enter and posing a riddle to them; the wrong answer brings their death, while the correct one would break the Sphinx's power. The riddle runs: What creature goes on four legs in the morning, two legs at noon and three in the evening? Oedipus' correct answer: "Man, who as a child crawls on all four, as a man walks on two legs, and as an old man hobbles leaning on a staff." This answer made Oedipus savior of the city and consort of the widowed Queen **Jocasta**, his mother.

Rima. In W.H. Hudson's *Green Mansions* (1904), the mysterious and elusive half-girl and half-bird of the Venezuelan forest, the friend and protectress of all wildlife in the Green Mansions. She is loved and pursued by Abel, a Venezuelan nature-lover in flight from the complexities of civilization.

Rip Van Winkle.   The central character in Washington Irving's most popular story. Rip appears in Irving's *The Sketch Book of Geoffrey Crayon, Gent.* (1819). Sometime before the Revolutionary War, Rip and his dog get lost in the Catskill Mountains. Rip falls asleep and awakens 20 years later, an old man. He returns to his hometown to find his shrewish wife has died, his daughter has married, and other local changes have taken place. He is typical of persons who are out of step with their times.

Rivers of Babylon.   Psalm 137, to commemorate the exile of the Jews in **Babylon**, begins, "By the rivers of Babylon, there we sat down, yea, we wept, when we remembered Zion." The phrase is often alluded to by those mourning for the dead or for the destruction of something passionately valued.

Road to Damascus.   Saul, the Hebrew name of Paul (see **Paul, Saint**), the **Apostle** of the Gentiles, is on the road to Damascus to find followers of Jesus and to return them bound in chains to Jerusalem when ". . . suddenly there shined round about him a light from heaven. And he fell to the earth, and heard a voice saying unto him, Saul, Saul why persecutest thee me? . . . I am Jesus whom thou persecutest." Saul experienced immediate conversion "and straightway he preached Christ in the synagogue, that he is the Son of God" (Acts 9:1-22; 22:1-22; 26:1-23). Thus anyone said to be on the road to Damascus is on the way to conversion of some kind, to some cause or belief.

Robin Goodfellow.   In English folklore, a mischievous fairy on whom were blamed all sorts of domestic mishaps. Also known as **Puck**.

Robin Hood.   A legendary English outlaw and hero of the people, said to be the outlawed earl of Huntington, born around 1160 at Locksley in Nottinghamshire. From his base in Sherwood Forest he is said to have robbed the rich in order to give to the poor, and is noted for his daring, courage, generosity, and skill in archery. Robin Hood's followers were known as the Merry Men. Important members of his band included **Little John, Friar Tuck**, Will Scarlet (see **Scarlet, Will**) and **Maid Marian**. His name is colloquially associated with those who act as benefactors or guardians of the poor.

Rochester, Edward Fairfax.   In Charlotte Brontë's *Jane Eyre* (1847), the brooding master of Thornfield Manor. Trapped in a marriage with an insane woman, Rochester keeps his secret from Jane (see **Eyre, Jane**) as the two fall more and more in love. Tortured, passionate, burdened by past guilt, and seeking love and release, Rochester is a type of the romantic hero.

Rogers, Mildred.   In W. Somerset Maugham's *Of Human Bondage* (1915), an utterly unattractive and self-seeking woman, who is yet able to enslave the infatuated Philip Carey (see **Carey, Philip**).

Roland.   One of the most famous and accomplished knights of Charlemagne, the prototype of the loyal, courageous, self-sacrificing hero of chivalry. The *Song of Roland*, one of the *Chansons de Geste*, recounts an incident following the invasion of Spain by Charlemagne. A treacherous knight takes a bribe from the Saracen leader and betrays Roland, who is protecting the rear guard of the retreating army. Ambushed by a greatly superior Saracen force, the courageous Roland refuses to blow his horn as a signal to Charlemagne until it is too late to save any of his men; Charlemagne returns to defeat the Saracens. Roland is known as Orlando in the Italian works of the 15th and 16th centuries, for example Ariosto's *Orlando Furioso* (1532).

Romeo.   See **Romeo and Juliet**.

Romeo and Juliet.   The doomed lovers in Shakespeare's *Romeo and Juliet* (1594). Romeo, a young member of the **Montague** family of Verona, falls passionately in love with Juliet, the beautiful daughter of the **Capulet** family, despite the blood feud between their elders. Romeo and Juliet are the archetypal star-crossed lovers; their brief, tragic marriage is symbolic of youthful, poetic passion thwarted by the strife of contending families.

Romulus and Remus.   Legendary twins associated with the founding of Rome. In one myth they are the children of **Mars** and Rhea Silvia. Since their mother was a **Vestal virgin**, the twins were supposed to be drowned, but they were rescued by divine intervention and suckled by a she-wolf. Later, Romulus killed Remus and went on to found Rome, name the city after himself and declare himself the first king. According to another myth, they were the offspring of Ilia, the daughter of **Aeneas** and Lavinia, his Latin bride.

Rosalind.   The witty, sensible heroine of Shakespeare's *As You Like It* (1599). Disguised as a boy, she is the "stage director" in the Forest of Arden (see **Arden, Forest of**), falls in love with Orlando almost despite herself, and marries him at the end.

Rosencrantz and Guildenstern.   Courtiers and friends of **Hamlet** in Shakespeare's *Hamlet* who are suborned by **Claudius** and betray their friend. When he discovers their treachery, Hamlet secretly changes their commission to England and sends them to their deaths. Not really important enough to be evil but too foolish to be good, they are pawns caught between the conflicting powers of the tragedy. Tom Stoppard made them the central characters in his play *Rosencrantz and Guildenstern are Dead* (1967).

Rose of Sharon.   In the "Song of Solomon," (see **Song of Songs**) the bride sings of herself as "the rose of Sharon, and the lily of the valleys" (Song of Solomon 2). Sharon was the name of a fertile plain along the coast of ancient Palestine.

Rosinante.   The scrawny, rickety horse of **Don Quixote** in Cervantes' novel (1605 and 1615).

Round Table.   King **Arthur** and his 150 knights sat around a table, supposedly made round by the magician **Merlin** in order to prevent arguments about precedence from breaking out. One of the major symbols of Arthurian legend, the Round Table also refers generally to Arthur and his group of knights.

Roxane.   In Rostand's *Cyrano de Bergerac* (1897), the charming, beautiful woman, beloved by Cyrano and Christian. At first somewhat superficial and flighty, she deepens, as a suffering widow, into warm, mature womanliness.

Ruth.   In the **Old Testament**, she is a Moabite widow. After her husband dies, she refuses to leave her mother-in-law, saying to her: "Entreat me not to leave thee or to return from following after thee; whither thou goest, I will go; and where thou lodgest, I will lodge; thy people shall be my people; and thy God my God" (Ruth 1:15). Ruth is the epitome of devotion and loyalty.

S

Sabine women, Rape of the. Shortly after the founding of Rome (753 B.C.) Romulus, according to the story told by the Roman historian Livy, asked neighboring tribes for wives for his men. When they refused, he inaugurated a festival and spectacle to which he invited many of these tribes. Among them came the Sabines with their wives and children. At a prearranged signal, the Roman young men seized the Sabine girls (*virgines*). War followed but eventually, through the intercession of the women, the two peoples were united. See also: **Romulus and Remus**.

Sackcloth and ashes. "They would have repented long ago in sackcloth and ashes" (Matthew 11:21; Luke 10:13; Jonah 3:6; Esther 4:1, 3). To wear sackcloth and ashes was a traditional sign of grief and repentance; the expression is used literally in the Bible, metaphorically today.

Sacred cow. This expression is one of the very few to come into English from Hinduism. The origins of the cult of the cow are not known for certain; it was not introduced to India by the Aryan invaders, who were beef-eaters, and the edicts of Ashoka (third century B.C.) show that the slaughter of cows was not yet prohibited. Today, however, the Hindu taboo against killing cows or eating beef is even more powerful than the Jewish and Moslem prohibition against eating pork. In American usage a sacred cow is anything—a creed, institution or person—so revered as to be beyond public criticism.

Sadducees. Members of this Jewish sect, which flourished in the centuries before and after the birth of Christ, were mostly priests and aristocrats. They interpreted the Bible literally, rejected the oral laws and traditions and denied the afterlife and the **Messiah**'s coming. They opposed the beliefs and practices of the **Pharisees**.

Saint John the Divine. See **John, Saint**.

Salome. The stepdaughter of **Herod Antipas** and daughter of his wife, Herodias, who in return for dancing before Herod demanded the head of **John the Baptist** (Matthew 14; Mark 6). Synonymous with a treacherous siren.

Salt of the earth. "Ye are the salt of the earth: but if the salt have lost his savour, wherewith shall it be salted? It is thenceforth good for nothing, but to be cast out, and to be trodden under foot of men" (Matthew 5:13). Salt is a preservative of food, and hence a symbol of incorruption. The coarse salt of Jesus' time contained a large proportion of mineral impurities; if exposed to the weather the solutes would leach out, leaving a tasteless residue ("lose its savour"). In modern usage, to call someone the salt of the earth is an ambiguous compliment; it implies that he is eminently virtuous but possibly a bit unexciting.

Samson and Delilah. "And Delilah said to Samson, Tell me, I pray thee, wherein thy great strength lieth, and wherewith thou mightest be bound to afflict thee" (Judges 16:6). Samson, a judge of ancient Israel renowned for his great strength, was the Hebrew counterpart of Hercules (see **Heracles**); as a common noun a Samson now means any strong man. Delilah, who robs Samson of his strength by cutting his hair, has come to typify any seductress who brings ruin upon her lovers.

Samuel. Jewish religious leader of the 11th century B.C. whose life and deeds are told in the two **Old Testament** books of Samuel. He anointed **Saul** and **David**, the first kings of Israel.

Sandals, Winged. In Latin, *talaria*, the "shoes of swiftness," worn by **Iris, Eos, Eros**, the **Erinyes, Perseus**, the **Gorgons** and the **Harpies**. The winged sandals of **Hermes** are perhaps the best known; they symbolized his swiftness as a messenger of **Zeus**.

Sappho.   Greek poetess, born about 600 B.C. in Mytilene on the island of **Lesbos**. Though only fragments of her work remain, her lyrics, along with those of her contemporary Alcaeus, were counted among the greatest in that tradition, earning her the epithet "the tenth muse." She is supposed to have headed a cult to **Aphrodite**, and to have thrown herself into the sea for unrequited love of the boatman Phaon. Many of Sappho's lyrics celebrate her passionate friendships with women, hence Sapphism is synonymous with Lesbianism, female homosexuality (see **Lesbian**).

Sarah   (or Sarai). In the **Old Testament**, Abraham's wife and **Isaac**'s mother. Childless, she prayed to God for a child. God promised her that in her old age she would bear a child to Abraham. The child's name was Isaac.

Satan.   The name of the Devil, meaning the "hater" or the "accuser," often characterized also as "the adversary." The word "devil" is from the Greek "diabolos," which has the same meaning. In the oldest portions of the Bible, Satan is not mentioned. In **Job**, he appears as a tempter and accuser whose powers are strictly limited by God and who functions only with God's permission. In the intertestamental period, under the influence of Jewish apocalypticism, and perhaps also of Persian dualism, Satan is conceived as a major power opposed to God and second only to him. In the **gospel**s, all the kingdoms of the world are in his power (Luke 4:6). In *Revelation*, his eventual overthrow is prophesied (Revelation 20:10).

Saturn.   See **Cronos**.

Saturnalia.   The Roman harvest festival of celebration and debauchery, named after Saturn (**Cronos**), god of agriculture. Unusual liberties were granted during these festivals, and the normal rules of order were suspended. Today any wild, unrestrained festivity may be described as saturnalian.

Satyrs.   Lesser gods of the forest with bodies of men, legs and feet of goats, hair over all their bodies and short horns on their heads.

Attendants of **Dionysos**, they represented the vital forces of nature, and were famous for their lust. Nowadays, satyr is another term for a lecher.

Saul. (1) The son of Kish and first king of the Jews, anointed by **Samuel**, leader of successful wars against the **Philistines**. Saul was a melancholy and jealous man, often in conflict with **David**, Samuel and **Jonathan**, his son. Following a defeat by the Philistines, he committed suicide with his own sword (I Samuel). (2) The Hebrew name of the **Apostle** Paul (see **Paul, Saint**).

Sawyer, Tom. The mischievous, adventure-hungry hero of Mark Twain's novel *The Adventures of Tom Sawyer* (1876). Tom and his friend **Huck Finn** set off on a series of adventures after they accidentally witness a murder by the evil **Injun Joe**. Wily, resourceful and not above lying to get himself out of a scrape, Tom is much cannier about the ways of the world than his friend Huck. Much to Huck's dismay, Tom chooses the pretty Becky Thatcher (see **Thatcher, Becky**) as his sweetheart. Tom has become a symbol for American boyhood as a time of romantic escapades and wild imaginings.

Scarlet, Will. One of **Robin Hood's** trusty Merry Men in Sherwood Forest.

Scarlet woman. See **Babylon, Scarlet whore of**.

Scheherazade. The narrator of the ***Arabian Nights*** tales and the beautiful wife of the Emperor Shahriar. Believing all women to be unfaithful, Shahriar marries a new bride each day and condemns her to death the following morning. When Scheherazade is chosen to be his next wife, she weaves an enchanting tale on her wedding night—so enchanting that Shahriar puts off her execution for a day so he can hear the end. Cleverly, Scheherazade makes the tale last for one thousand and one nights, at the end of which time the emperor lets her live as his consort.

Scrooge, Ebenezer. The repulsive skinflint of Charles Dickens' *A Christmas Carol* (1843). See also: **Ghosts of Christmas Past, Present and Yet to Come**.

Scylla and Charybdis.   Since Scylla was loved by **Poseidon**, Poseidon's jealous wife, **Amphitrite**, transformed her into a monster with dogs' heads. Her fixed habitation was a cave in the Strait of Messina. Opposite her was another monster, Charybdis, who lived on the Sicilian side of the strait. Charybdis, the daughter of Poseidon and **Gaea**, had been thrown into the sea and transformed into a monster by **Zeus**. As a ship passed close to Scylla, she would pull the sailors up to devour them; if the ship avoided her, it would have to pass by Charybdis, which would suck up the sailors. Actually, Scylla was associated with the rocks and Charybdis with a whirlpool. Hence, the expression "between Scylla and Charybdis" means to find oneself between two dangers where escaping from one means falling prey to the other—or "out of the frying pan into the fire"; or "between the devil and the deep blue sea."

Second Coming.   In *Revelation* (see **Apocalypse**), Saint John foresees the return of Christ in his glory. At the Second Coming will occur the Last Judgment (see **Day of Judgment**) in which Christ will resurrect the dead and reward the just with everlasting bliss in heaven and the sinners with eternal damnation in hell. The Second Coming is also associated with the Millennium, the thousand-year period of Christ's kingdom of peace and prosperity on earth. Some believe the Second Coming will occur at the end of the Millennium, others that the Second Coming will begin the Millennium. See also: **John, Saint**.

Seek and ye shall find.   "Ask, and it shall be given you; seek, and ye shall find, knock, and it shall be opened unto you: For everyone that asketh receiveth; and he that seeketh findeth; and to him that knocketh it shall be opened" (Matthew 7:7; cf. Luke 11:9). An encouragement to prayer.

See through a glass darkly.   "Now we see through a glass, darkly; but then face to face" (1 Corinthians 13:12). Through a glass: in a mirror (mirrors then were not well polished, and gave a poor reflection). Paul (see **Paul, Saint**) is contrasting our present imperfect knowledge with the fullness of knowledge which man will ultimately enjoy when God's purpose is revealed. In allusion, the phrase is used to contrast the limitations of the senses with the higher truth of spiritual perception.

Selene. A moon goddess, daughter of **Hyperion**. She fell in love with the beautiful shepherd boy **Endymion**, who was plunged into a perpetual sleep so that she might come to him always in his dreams.

Sermon on the Mount. The Sermon on the Mount (Matthew 5-7) is not a connected discourse so much as an anthology of sayings of Jesus. The Sermon opens with the so-called **Beatitudes**, Jesus' singling out of those who are blessed, beginning with "Blessed are the poor in spirit." A comparison with the **Gospel** of Luke (see **Luke, Saint**) suggests that these were originally delivered on a number of separate occasions. The scene of the sermon is not specified; Matthew may have located it on a mountain to suggest a parallel to the delivery of the old Law on **Mount Sinai**. The Sermon on the Mount sets forth a new law of love, extending even to one's enemies, and thus marks a clear departure from the **Old Testament** law of retribution.

Serve two masters. See **Mammon**.

Set (or Seth). Ancient Egyptian god of fertility, storms and conflict. Usually depicted as a doglike creature sitting on its haunches or as a man with the face of a dog, Set is a villainous god, the eternal opponent of the gods **Horus** and **Osiris** (Set's brothers).

Seven Deadly Sins. Pride, Lust, Avarice, Gluttony, Envy, Wrath and Sloth. The list is not Biblical, but derived from patristic literature.

Seven Last Words. The Seven Last Words of Jesus upon the cross are not single words, but the seven last sentences he uttered, compiled from all the **Gospels**. They are used devotionally in meditations upon the Passion, and have been set to music by Schutz, Haydn and Gounod. The Seven Words are as follows: (1) "Father, forgive them; for they know not what they do" (Luke 23:34); (2) "Verily I say unto thee, today shalt thou be with me in Paradise" (Luke 23:43); (3) "Woman, behold thy son. Behold thy mother" (John 19:26-27); (4) "My God, my God, why hast thou forsaken me?" (Matthew 27:46); (5) "I thirst" (John 14:28); (6) "It is finished" (John 19:30); and (7) "Father, into thy hands I com-

mend my spirit" (Luke 23:46). See also: **Father forgive them** and
My God, why hast thou forsaken me?

Seventh Heaven.   Ptolemaic cosmology divided the space en-
circling the earth into concentric circles or heavens, their number
varying from seven to eleven. The Jews recognized seven heavens,
of which the seventh was the place of God. Hence, the highest bliss.

Seven wonders of the ancient world.   The following are
generally accepted as the seven most remarkable structures of the
ancient world, from the grouping originally made by Antipater of
Sidon in the second century B.C.

1.   The Pyramid of Cheops (Khufu, of the fourth Dynasty, about
     3,000 B.C.). Situated near Memphis, Egypt, this is the largest of
     the Pyramids, supposedly designed as the tomb of Cheops, con-
     taining a complicated inner structure. It is still *in situ*, though
     not of course in its original splendor.
2.   The Pharos (Lighthouse) at Alexandria. Built on an island in the
     harbor of Alexandria, Egypt, during the reign of Ptolemy
     Philadelphus (285-277 B.C.), about 590 feet high, consisting of
     at least four towers; designed by Sostratus, who devised an in-
     genious system of lighting with fires and a huge mirror. It was
     partly destroyed by the Arabs in the ninth century, and the
     remainder was used as a mosque for a time; in 1375 an
     earthquake destroyed it entirely.
3.   Hanging Gardens of Babylon. Not really "hanging" but built on
     terraces or balconies, with arches as supports, to a height of
     about 350 feet, and irrigated by hydraulic pumps. Built by **Neb-
     uchadnezzar** II (605-562 B.C.).
4.   Temple of Artemis at Ephesus. Built on the site of earlier
     shrines, the great temple at Ephesus in Asia Minor was erected
     in the sixth century B.C. with the help of donations from
     Croesus and others. It was so magnificent that Herodotus
     compared it to the Pyramids. Sacked and burned in the third
     century A.D., the temple's marble was later used for building.
     Parts of the columns and sculpture are now in the British
     Museum.
5.   Statue of the Olympian Zeus. Known mainly from descriptions
     by ancient writers, especially Pausanias, from coins, and from

circumstantial evidence of excavators. Situated at Olympia, it was the work of **Phidias**, and was made of gold and ivory. Zeus sat on a throne, carried a **Nike**, or Victory, in his right hand, a sceptre in his left. Elaborately sculptured scenes from mythology adorned the throne. The fate of the statue is unknown.

6. Mausoleum at Halicarnassus. Built in 353-350 B.C. in Halicarnassus, Asia Minor, as a tomb for King Mausolus by order of his widow, Artemisia. It was a tremendous structure, 140 feet high, with different levels. It has, of course, given the English language the word *Mausoleum*. In the 15th and 16th centuries opposing sides in a war between Turks and Christians took turns in occupying and destroying parts of the Mausoleum; parts of it can, however, be seen in the British Museum.

7. Colossus of Rhodes. A gigantic bronze statue, about 105 feet high, of **Helios**, the sun god, set up (292-280 B.C.) at the entrance to the harbor of Rhodes, an island in the Aegean Sea. The belief that the statue stood astride the harbor waters and that ships passed under it is a bit of medieval fancy not authenticated by ancient writers. The statue was erected as an offering of thanksgiving to Helios, protector of Rhodes, to commemorate the successful resistance of the Rhodians to the siege by the forces of Antigonus and Demetrius, successors of Alexander, in 307 B.C. It was toppled by an earthquake in 224 B.C., and its fragments sold as junk in 672 A.D. Our word "colossal" (gigantic, vast) derives from the Greek work *colossus*, meaning gigantic statue.

Seven years of plenty. See **Joseph**.

Shadrach. See **Shadrach, Meshach and Abednego**.

Shadrach, Meshach and Abednego. When Shadrach, Meshach and Abednego refused to worship the golden idol, King **Nebuchadnezzar** had them thrown into a fiery furnace, from which they were rescued by the Lord (Daniel 3). They are remembered in allusion for the miracle of their emerging from the fiery furnace unscathed, while the servants who threw them in perished from the heat. Allusions to the Biblical fiery furnace signify a punishment that harms those who attempt to enforce it instead of its intended victims.

Shandy, Tristram. The hero of *The Life and Opinions of Tristram Shandy, Gentleman* (1759-67) by Laurence Sterne (1713-68). Tristram "tells" his life story as a seemingly endless series of digressions, uninhibited associations of ideas and events and whimsical asides. Shandean describes both the type of character who behaves in this way and this method of narrating a story.

Shangri-La. The **Utopia** of eternal youth and peace, supposedly located in Tibet, in James Hilton's novel *Lost Horizon* (1933). Hence, any ideal retreat from the world.

Sharp, Becky. Young, beautiful, unscrupulous and social-climbing heroine of Thackeray's ***Vanity Fair***. Becky rises from humble origins to a fairly high station in the society of the Napoleonic era, but her egocentricity and double-dealing are exposed and she is eventually ostracized.

Sheba, Queen of. The "queen of the South," the kingdom of Saba in southwestern Arabia, who came to King **Solomon** in order to challenge his wisdom, and found him more than equal to her own abilities (I Kings 10; II Chronicles 9).

Shibboleth. A peculiarity (of behavior, dress, speech, etc.) which distinguishes a particular group or class of people. Or a magic charm or a password used to test someone's identity. The victorious Gileadites required those Ephraimites who had escaped battle and tried to cross the Jordan again to pronounce the word "Shibboleth" when they denied their identity; unable to say "sh," the Ephraimites pronounced it incorrectly as "Sibboleth" and were killed. The word literally means "stream in flood" (Judges 12).

Shirt of Nessus. The shirt soaked with the poisonous blood of the **centaur** Nessus that caused the death of the hero **Heracles**. The story goes that when Heracles shot Nessus with a poisoned arrow, the dying centaur told Heracles' wife Deianeira that his blood had the power to summon a husband away from adulterous love affairs. When Deianeira heard that her husband had fallen in love with the beautiful Iole, she saturated a cloak (or shirt) with the centaur's blood and sent it to Heracles. The pain this so-called shirt of Nessus caused him was so excruciating that Heracles had himself burnt on a funeral pyre.

Shiva.   The third member of the Hindu **Trimurti**, along with **Vishnu** and **Brahma**. In this trinity, Shiva is the destroyer, a terrible creature depicted with numerous arms and three eyes, surrounded by snakes and the skulls of the dead and followed by demons.

Shylock.   The avaricious Jewish moneylender in Shakespeare's *The Merchant of Venice* (1596). He hates **Antonio**, a rival merchant, and lends him money on condition that if it is not repaid in three months, a pound of Antonio's flesh will be forfeited to him. **Portia** thwarts his plan.

Sibylline Books.   Oracular sayings originally transported from Greece to Cumae where they were kept by the **Cumaean Sibyl**. They were carefully kept in a temple of **Jupiter** on the Capitoline Hill in Rome but were destroyed in a fire during the rule of Sulla (83 B.C.). The Sibylline Books were consulted at critical moments to find ways of averting the disfavor of the gods. Under Christian emperors there was no longer any need for them and they were destroyed. See also: **Oracles**.

Sibyls.   Prophetesses whose origin was ascribed to the East. Their number was variously given as from four to ten. Some, like the Delphic (see **Delphic Oracle**) and the **Cumaean Sibyl**, were inspired priestesses of **Apollo**. One of the best-known is the Cumaean Sibyl, who guided **Aeneas** through the Lower World. The **Sibylline Books** played an important role in Roman history. Michelangelo incorporated famous paintings of the Libyan, Delphic, Cumaean, Persian, and Erythraean Sibyls into his magnificent fresco on the ceiling of the Sistine Chapel at the Vatican.

Siege Perilous.   In French, *siège*, "chair," had the early meaning of "seat of a Knight," similar to *chaise*, "chair." Specifically, that seat at the **Round Table** reserved for the knight whose destiny it was to reach the Holy **Grail**. If any other knight happened to sit in it, he would die. Sir **Galahad**, son of **Lancelot** and **Elaine**, proved to be its rightful occupant.

Siegfried.   See **Sigurd**.

Sigurd   (Siegfried). The hero of the ***Volsunga Saga***, he is the slayer of the dragon Fafnir and the beloved of **Brynhild**. In the ***Nibelungenlied***, the Teutonic version of the myth, he is known as Siegfried; he is the hero of Richard Wagner's cycle of operas *The Ring of the Nibelungs*. In the 20th century the Nazis used him as the symbol of Aryan manhood and heroism.

Sikes, Bill.   The violent leader of Fagin's young thieves in Charles Dickens' *Oliver Twist* (1838).

Silas Marner.   The miserly weaver who obsessively hoards gold in the 1861 novel by George Eliot. After it is stolen, he finds new meaning in his love for the abandoned child **Eppie**. A reference both to miserliness and to devotion and love.

Silenus   (plural: Sileni or Silenoi). Minor Greek gods of the forest, the Sileni were often confused with the **Satyrs** but were depicted as older, were shown with horse's ears, sometimes with the tail and legs of a horse. Though they lacked the Satyrs' reputation for lechery, they were almost constantly intoxicated. They had, however, a reputation for wisdom and prophecy.

Silver, Long John.   The mysterious ship's cook in Robert Louis Stevenson's *Treasure Island* (1883). He seems thoroughly evil at times, yet treats Jim Hawkins kindly. Long John plays off the owners of the treasure ship *Hispaniola* against the mutinous pirates he leads, manages to survive (and protect Jim), and disappears when the group returns to England. See also: **Hawkins, Jim.**

Silver, Mattie.   In Edith Wharton's *Ethan Frome* (1911), the graceful, pretty cousin of Zeena, Ethan's nagging wife. Her coming to the farm provides the only bit of brightness in Ethan's existence, but their love for each other ultimately leads them to a dismal fate. See also: **Frome, Ethan.**

Silver cord be loosed.   "Remember now thy Creator in the days of thy youth, while the evil days come not . . . Or ever the silver cord be loosed, or the golden bowl be broken, or the pitcher be broken at the fountain, or the wheel broken at the cistern. Then shall the dust return unto God who gave it" (Ecclesiastes 12:1, 6-7). The destruction of the cord, bowl, pitcher and wheel are all symbols of death. Commentators disagree as to whether this passage contains four images, two, or one. One reading suggests that the bowl and cord are a lamp suspended by a chain; and when the chain is broken, the lamp falls and the light goes out. Similarly, the pitcher and wheel are the bucket and windlass in a well. Thus this passage is organized around two familiar symbols of life: light and water. Henry James used the image of the broken golden bowl as the title and central symbol in his novel *The Golden Bowl* (1904).

Sinbad the Sailor.   The hero of one of the ***Arabian Nights***. Sinbad narrates a series of seven voyages which bring him great wealth mixed with much suffering and misfortune.

Sins be as scarlet, they shall be white as snow.   "Come now, And let us reason together, saith the Lord: Though your sins be as scarlet, they shall be as white as snow; though they be red like crimson, they shall be as wool" (Isaiah 1:18). A promise of God's forgiveness of the errors and crimes of mankind.

Sirens.   In **Homer**'s **Odyssey**, the sea goddesses who lured sailors to destruction on the rocks with their enchanting, irresistible song. **Odysseus** and his men pass them safely because only Odysseus, chained to the mast, can hear them, while his men have their ears plugged. Today a seductive and beguiling woman may be called a siren.

Sir Galahad.   See **Galahad, Sir**.

Sir Kay.   See **Kay, Sir**.

Sisyphus, Burden or labor of.   For a variety of misdeeds on earth Sisyphus, king of Corinth, was punished in **Tartarus** by being compelled to roll a huge stone up a hill. No sooner had he pushed it to the summit than it rolled down again. Thus Sisyphus's labor never ended. Hence, a ceaseless and fruitless task that must be repeated is called a burden or labor of Sisyphus or a Sisyphean task.

Slaughter of the Innocents.   See **Massacre of the Innocents; Herod the Great**.

Sleeping Beauty.   The princess in Charles Perrault's (1628-1703) fairy tale who is charmed into a 100-year-long sleep from which only the kiss of a prince brave enough to penetrate the thick forest around her castle can waken her. Colloquially, a woman whose full potential remains unawakened, unrealized.

Slop, Dr. The incompetent country doctor who delivers Tristram (see **Shandy, Tristram**) and manages, in the process, to distort his nose, in Laurence Sterne's *Tristram Shandy* (1759-67).

Slough of Despond. In John Bunyan's *Pilgrim's Progress* (1678), the first place that **Christian** wanders into after leaving the City of Destruction on his journey to the **Celestial City**. A slough is a swamp or place of soft, muddy ground; today one might describe a mental condition of degradation and helplessness as a slough of despond.

Snodgrass, Augustus. In Charles Dickens' *The Pickwick Papers* (1836), the poetic member of the **Pickwick Club**.

Snopes, The. An amoral, materialistic and completely depraved family who invade **Yoknapatawpha County**, the setting of many of William Faulkner's (1897-1962) novels. Their viciousness and opportunism enable them to take over the county from the older, decadent remnants of the previous generation. They appear principally in *The Hamlet* (1940), *The Town* (1957) and *The Mansion* (1960).

Socrates. Athenian teacher and philosopher (470-399 B.C.), whose ideas and philosophical method have been transmitted chiefly through the writings of his pupil **Plato**. A stonecutter by profession, Socrates wandered about Athens questioning the wisdom of his fellow citizens, seeking exact definitions, rationality of method and clarity of ideas. Professing to know nothing, he eventually revealed the ignorance of his interlocutors. Using a new and extremely rigorous dialectical method, Socrates sought to redefine the old value of virtue (in Greek, *areté*) which had been obscured and corrupted by the Sophists, and to revitalize traditional philosophical and political values which he saw in decay. Unfortunately his ideas were confounded with the very ones he sought to combat, and the irony of his pedagogy and personal style made many enemies. After the collapse of Athens at the end of the Peloponnesian War, he was tried by the Athenians on a charge of impiety and corruption of youth, and forced to kill himself by taking hemlock. The ideas and methods of his teaching, as elaborated in the works of his major disciple Plato, have exerted a great influence on Western philosophy. A teacher who employs the "Socratic method" today pretends ignorance on a given subject (a technique known as "Socratic irony") and asks questions in order to prompt his students to develop their own thoughts and ideas.

Sodom and Gomorrah.   "The men of Sodom were wicked and sinners" (Genesis 13:13). Sodom and Gomorrah were cities, traditionally located near the south end of the Dead Sea (hence the phrase, "cities of the plain"), which God destroyed for the corruption and wickedness of their inhabitants. The full story of Sodom, where Lot and his family lived, is told in Genesis (18:16-29). The cities are repeatedly mentioned in the Bible as a warning against wickedness. The word sodomy (anal intercourse) derives from Sodom, where it was among the sins for which the city was destroyed. Sodom and Gomorrah remain bywords for depravity.

Solomon.   The son of **David** and **Bathsheba**, king of Israel from 960 B.C. to 922 B.C., famous for his many wives, his wealth, and his unsurpassed wisdom. He built the Temple and many splendid palaces (I Kings: 1-11). The wisdom of Solomon is proverbial.

Solomon's judgment.   "There came two women, that were harlots, unto the king, and stood before him. And the one woman said, O my Lord, I and this woman dwell in one house; and I was delivered of a child with her in the house; and it came to pass the third day after that I was delivered, that this woman was delivered also . . . . And this woman's child died in the night; because she overlaid it. And she rose at midnight, and took my son from beside me, while thine handmaid slept, and laid it in her bosom . . . And the other woman said, Nay; but the living is my son, and the dead is thy son . . . . Then said the king, Bring me a sword . . . Divide the living child in two, and give half to the one, and half to the other. Then spake the woman whose living child was unto the king, for her bowels yearned upon her son, and she said, O my Lord, give her the living child, and in no wise slay it, but the other said, Let it be neither mine nor thine, but divide it. Then the king answered and said, Give her the living child, and in no wise slay it: she is the mother thereof. And all Israel heard of the judgment which the king had judged; and they feared the king: for they saw that the wisdom of God was in him, to do judgment" (Kings 3:16-28).

Somnus.   God of sleep; son of Nox.

Song of Roland.   See **Roland**.

Song of Songs.   *The Song of Solomon*, also called *The Song of Songs*, and in Roman Catholic usage, *Canticles*, is a book of the Bible, traditionally ascribed to **Solomon**, but probably of later composition. It is a love idyll, possibly a wedding liturgy, which has been allegorically interpreted by Jews as expressing the love of God for Israel, and by Christians, the love of Christ for the Church.

Sophocles.   Born at Colonus near Attica in 496 B.C., lived until 406 B.C. Writer of 120 to 130 tragedies, he is considered to have brought tragedy to its most perfect and classic style. He introduced the third actor, dwelled on man's will and character, gave to his plays a noble simplicity and economy unburdened by the psychological trappings of Euripides or the primitive and mystic grandeur of **Aeschylus**. **Aristotle** (in his *Poetics*) looked upon Sophocles' *Oedipus Rex* (*Tyrannos*) as the exemplar of tragic style. Six other extant plays by Sophocles are *Ajax*, *Antigone*, *Electra*, *Women of Trachis* (*Trachiniae*), *Philoctetes*, *Oedipus at Colonus*. Aristotle reports that Sophocles said of himself that he portrayed men as they ought to be, whereas Euripides showed them as they were. In "Sonnet 2, To a Friend," Matthew Arnold calls Sophocles an even-balanced soul, "Who saw life steadily and saw it whole." "Sophoclean" means quintessentially Greek: direct, simple, lucid, reasonable. See also: **Oedipus; Oedipus Complex**.

Sop to Cerberus, A.   See **Cerberus, A Sop to**.

Spade, Sam.   Prototype of the tough, handsome, hard-boiled private detective, in Dashiell Hammett's novel *The Maltese Falcon* (1930).

Spartacus.   A Thracian slave who escaped in 73 B.C. from the school for gladiators in Capua, Italy, he stirred up an insurrection of slaves and other desperate men, defeated Roman armies in several battles until his own army was finally crushed by Crasus in 71 B.C. and he himself was killed. Spartacus is the subject of a novel (1951) of the same name by the American writer Howard Fast, and of a ballet (1954), also so named, by the Soviet composer Aram Khachaturian.

Sphinx.   In Greek, "strangler," a monster with the body of a lion, wings, and the breasts and face of a woman. The best-known Sphinx of Greek mythology is the one that beset Thebes and propounded a riddle to all whom she met. Death was the penalty for those who failed to solve it. See: **Riddle of the Sphinx**. After **Oedipus** answered the riddle correctly, the Sphinx, mortified, killed herself. The Egyptian Sphinx, famous in the colossal statue at Gizeh, preceded the Greek version. Egyptian statues show the Sphinx in a recumbent position, wingless, with the face of a man (sometimes the pharaoh) and the body of a lion. Today a person given to enigmatic pronouncements might be called a sphinx.

The spirit is willing.   "The spirit indeed is willing but the flesh is weak" (Matthew 26:41; cf. Mark 14:30). These words of Jesus to his disciples were meant as a warning against succumbing to temptation; today they are commonly quoted as an apology for having yielded.

Square, Mr. Thomas.   In Fielding's *Tom Jones* (1749), a deist who argues with Rev. Thwackum over reason and religion. He does not like Tom, but on his deathbed clears him of certain bad deeds. See also: **Jones, Tom; Thwackum and Square**.

Squeers, Mr. Wackford.   The coarse, ignorant and dishonest headmaster of Dotheboys Hall, in Yorkshire, in Charles Dickens' *Nicholas Nickleby* (1838). He cheats his pupils, feeds them little and teaches them nothing. See also: **Nickleby, Nicholas**.

Standish, Miles.   The Pilgrim captain in Longfellow's poem *The Courtship of Miles Standish* (1858). Because he has no confidence in his ability to court **Priscilla**, he asks John Alden to do the wooing for him. Priscilla refuses Standish, but accepts Alden, saying, "Speak for yourself, John."

Stark, Willie. In Robert Penn Warren's novel, *All the King's Men* (1946), the "Boss," governor of a southern state, a pragmatic despot who tries to shape men and events to his will. The book and this character are loosely based on the career of Louisiana politician Huey Long (1893-1935), a man noted for his demagoguery and tight control over the state's political machine.

Steerforth. The corrupt and vicious seducer of **Little Emily**; childhood friend of David in Charles Dickens' *David Copperfield* (1850).

Stentor. In **Homer**'s *Iliad* one of the Greek warriors with a powerful "voice of bronze," like that of 50 men. Hence, "stentorian," very loud.

Still small voice. "And he said, Go forth, and stand upon the mount before the Lord. And behold, the Lord passed by, and a great and strong wind rent the mountains, and brake in pieces the rocks before the Lord; but the Lord was not in the wind: and after the wind an earthquake: And after the earthquake a fire, but the Lord was not in the fire: and after the fire a still small voice . . . and said, What doest thou here, Elijah?" (I Kings 19:11-13). The still small voice came to **Elijah** on Mount Horeb (see **Mount Sinai**), telling him to anoint the kings of Syria and Israel, and to make Elisha his successor. In modern parlance the still small voice usually means the conscience, with the further implication that God speaks to men inwardly, and not by noisy, spectacular convulsions.

Stockmann, Dr. Thomas. The incorruptible doctor and inspector of the baths in Ibsen's play *An Enemy of the People* (1883). At the cost of his being treated as the "enemy" of the town, he maintains his integrity to the end after discovering and declaring that the bath waters are polluted.

Strain at a gnat and swallow a camel. "Ye blind guides, which strain at a gnat, and swallow a camel" (Matthew 23:24). Small insects which had fallen into a drinking cup would have to be strained out. This verse, in which Jesus criticizes the **Pharisees** for their emphasis on outer forms, is an extravagant metaphor meaning, "You quibble about trifles but ignore the really important issues."

Strait is the gate and narrow is the way.   "Enter ye in at the strait gate: for wide is the gate, and broad is the way, that leadeth to destruction, and many there be which go in thereat: Because strait is the gate, and narrow is the way, which leadeth unto life, and few there be that find it" (Matthew 7:13-14). From the **Sermon on the Mount**; strait means "narrow." Straying from the strait and narrow path is now a euphemism for any kind of wrongdoing.

Stymphalian Birds.   See **Labors of Hercules**.

Styx.   The river which flows around **Hades**. The dead are ferried across the river by the boatman **Charon**. "Stygian" thus denotes darkness and dread.

Suffer little children.   "Suffer little children to come unto me, and forbid them not: for of such is the kingdom of heaven" (Matthew 19:14). The disciples reproved the people for bringing their children to Jesus for a blessing, but Jesus insisted that the children be permitted to be brought. Further, Christ identifies the innocence of children with the innocence the soul regains in "the kingdom of heaven."

Sufficient unto the day is the evil thereof.   In the **Sermon on the Mount**, Jesus said, encouraging his followers to trust in divine Providence, "Seek ye first the kingdom of God and his righteousness: and all these things shall be added unto you. Take therefore no thought for the morrow: for the morrow shall take thought for the things of itself. Sufficient unto the day is the evil thereof" (Matthew 6:33-34).

Sulk like Achilles in his tent.   After **Agamemnon** had taken away Briseis, the girl who was **Achilles**' prize, Achilles retired to his tent and did not take part in the war against Troy until after his friend **Patroclus** was killed. The expressions "sulk like Achilles," "a sulking Achilles" or "sulk in his tent" are applied to anybody who withdraws from active participation in an undertaking because of a personal grievance, affront or insult. See also: **Trojan War**.

Superman.   The human type embodied in the person and ideas of Zarathustra, the **Ubermensch**, in Nietzsche's *Thus Spake*

Zarathustra (1883). The Superman idea represents a future state in which man vastly transcends his present abilities and potentialities, realizing his earthly purposes through the free exercise of his natural and intellectual forces. Modern "spirituality" is seen as a symptom of the diseased, decadent and morbid condition of Western man, who can only be sacrificed to this ultimate and transcendent condition.

Surface, Sir Oliver.   The rich old gentleman in Richard Brinsley Sheridan's *The School for Scandal* (1777), who must discover which of his two nephews, the smooth and insincere Joseph Surface or the overgenerous, boisterous Charles Surface, is worthy of inheriting his fortune. By two stratagems he exposes the evil and rewards the good.

Susanna and the Elders.   The beautiful Susanna, virtuous wife of Joakim of Babylon, was lusted after by two Jewish elders while she bathed in her garden. When she refused their advances, they falsely accused her of adultery. She was convicted, but the Lord sent a young man named Daniel to expose the perfidy of the elders, who were then executed (**Apocrypha**: History of Susanna).

Svengali.   A musician in *Trilby* (1894), a novel by George du Maurier. He exercises such a hypnotic influence over the heroine, Trilby, that she learns to sing and becomes a superb artist. Hence, a "Svengali" is one who can exercise an almost magical influence over another through force of will.

Swann, M.   One of the major characters in the series of novels known in English as *Remembrance of Things Past,* by the French novelist Marcel Proust. Swann, the son of a wealthy businessman, devotes his life to his passions for art, women and high society, until he succumbs to the charms of the courtesan known as **Odette** de Crecy and marries her. See also: **Marcel.**

Swan of Avon.   William Shakespeare, born at Stratford-on-Avon in 1564.

Sweat of thy face.   See **In the sweat of thy face.**

Sword of Damocles.   See **Damocles, Sword of.**

Sword into plowshares, and their spears into pruninghooks. "They shall beat their swords into plowshares, and their spears into pruninghooks: nation shall not lift up a sword against a nation, neither shall they learn war any more" (Isaiah 2:4; Micah 4:3). This oracle, predicting a restoration of Zion and a reign of peace is ascribed both to **Isaiah** and his younger contemporary, Micah. It is frequently cited in prayers for peace.

Symplegades. Two dangerous rocks ("clashing rocks, clashing cliffs") guarding the entrance to the Black Sea. They crushed ships passing between them by moving together. The **Argonauts** lost only one rudder when they sailed through these rocks. Legend has it that after the Argonauts' successful pass-through, the Symplegades merged to form a solid rock.

T

Take the sword, perish with the sword. "All they that take the sword shall perish with the sword" (Matthew 26-52). Jesus' words to his disciples when he was arrested; a warning against resorting to violence.

Talmud. The traditional body of Jewish law, consisting of the *Mishnah*, which contains the obligatory precepts of the elders and is a supplement to the ***Pentateuch*** and the *Gemara*, which comments on the contents of the *Mishnah*. Its codification was completed by the end of the fifth century A.D.

Tamburlaine. Also Tamerlane, from Timur i Leng (1336-1405), meaning Timur the Lame, the legendary Mongolian conqueror, and great-great-grandson of Genghis Khan. From his capital at Samarkand, he conquered large portions of India, Persia and Russia, dying during preparations to invade China. The first play of Christopher Marlowe (1564-93), *Tamburlaine the Great* (1587?), was based on his life.

Tantalus. The son of **Zeus** and an Oceanid and later king of Lydia, father of **Pelops** and **Niobe**. He brought about his severe punishment in **Hades** for having stolen a favorite dog of Zeus, for giving **ambrosia** and nectar (the food of the gods) to men, and for killing his son and serving him as a meal for the gods. For these crimes, Tantalus was made to stand chin-deep in water with branches of fruit just overhead: whenever he tried to eat or drink, the water would recede or the fruit rise out of reach. "Tanta-lize"—to torment by offering something only to withdraw it—derives from his punishment.

Tarpeian Rock. Named after Tarpeia, daughter of the command-er of the Roman fortress of the Capitoline Hill during a war with the Sabines (see **Sabine Women, Rape of the**). As Livy tells the story (in I, xi of his history), the Sabines, under their king, Tatius, were storming the hill. Tarpeia, tempted by the gold bracelets the enemy soldiers wore on their left arms, offered to open a gate of the fortress if they would give her what they had on their left arms. The king accepted her terms and as the soldiers entered, they threw upon her the other thing they bore on their left arms, their shields. That part of the hill was named the Tarpeian Rock after her; later, Roman criminals were hurled to their death from it.

Tartarus.   A region of the underworld, where **Zeus** imprisoned the **Titans** and sent the worst of sinners for punishment; a place darker than night, surrounded by three walls and the river of fire, Phlegethon. The name was also used poetically for the Lower World as a whole. See also: **Hades**.

Tartuffe.   An obnoxious, pious hypocrite, the central character in Moliere's comedy, *Tartuffe* (1664).

Tarzan.   The hero of the jungle in a series of stories by Edgar Rice Burroughs. The son of an English noble, he is abandoned in the jungle and reared by apes. He learns the language of the animals, marries an American woman named Jane, and has a son. Burroughs' immensely popular stories were translated into 56 languages, adapted into comic strips, and used in many movies. By extension, any man of superhuman strength.

Tearsheet, Doll.   A slatternly friend of **Falstaff** in Shakespeare's *Henry IV, Parts One and Two* (1597).

Teiresias.   Blind prophet who plays a role in a number of Greek myths, and literary works, most notably in *Oedipus Tyrannos* of **Sophocles**. According to one legend, Teiresias had been both a man and a woman, and because of this **Zeus** and **Hera** called upon him to settle a dispute over whether men or women experience greater pleasure in love-making. Teiresias said that sex is nine times more pleasurable for a woman, an answer that so angered Hera (who had been insisting that men enjoy sex more) that she struck him blind. To make up for this misfortune, Zeus bestowed on Teiresias the gift of prophecy.

Telemachus.   See **Odysseus**.

Tell it not in Gath.   "And **David** lamented with this lamentation over **Saul** and over **Jonathan** his son: . . . The beauty of Israel is slain upon thy high places: **how are the mighty fallen**. Tell it not in Gath, publish it not in the streets of Askelon; lest the daughters of the **Philistines** rejoice . . ." (II Samuel 1:17, 20). Gath was a city of the Philistines; "Tell it not in Gath" means not to allow an enemy to exult in our misfortune.

Tempe.   The beautiful valley in Thessaly, between **Mount Olympus** and Mount Ossa (see **Pelion**), sacred to **Apollo**. Here **Daphne** was loved by the god, pursued and changed into a laurel tree. By extension, "the vale of Tempe" is a reference to an extremely beautiful location.

Ten Commandments, The.   Atop **Mount Sinai** in the Holy Land, God inscribed on two tablets of stone for **Moses** the 120 Hebrew words that are the Ten Commandments.

1. Thou shalt have no other gods before me.
2. Thou shalt not make unto thee any graven image, or any likeness of any thing that is in heaven above, or that is in the earth beneath, or that is in the water under the earth.
3. Thou shalt not take the name of the Lord thy God in vain; for the Lord will not hold him guiltless that taketh his name in vain. Remember the sabbath day, to keep it holy.
4. Honor thy father and thy mother: that thy days may be long upon the land which the Lord thy God giveth thee.
5. Thou shalt not kill.
6. Thou shalt not commit adultery.
7. Thou shalt not steal.
8. Thou shalt not bear false witness against thy neighbor.
9. Thou shalt not covet thy neighbor's house.
10. Thou shalt not covet thy neighbor's wife, nor his manservant,

nor his maidservant, nor his ox, nor his ass, nor any thing that is thy neighbor's.

These commandments, given in **Exodus** (29:3-17), form the basis of Jewish law and morality.

Ten Plagues, The.   See **Plagues of Egypt**.

Terpsichore.   See **Muses**.

Tethys.   One of the 12 **Titans**, Tethys is the daughter of **Uranus** and **Gaea**. She married **Oceanus** and bore him the sea **nymphs** known as Oceanids.

Thaïs.   An Athenian courtesan, mistress of Alexander. She went with him on his Asiatic expedition, and is said to have urged him to burn the palace of Persepolis. "Thaïs" became a common Greek reference to a courtesan. In the novel of Anatole France, *Thaïs* (1890), set in late classical antiquity, the monk Paphnutius, a former Alexandrian voluptuary, deceives himself into thinking his dreams of the actress/courtesan Thaïs require him to convert her to Christianity. After her conversion he cannot conquer his lust for her, and seeks her out in her convent as she dies. Jules Massenet wrote an opera (1894) of the same name based on this novel.

Thalia.   The muse of comedy. See **Muses**.

Thanatos.   Greek personification of death.

Thatcher, Becky.   In Mark Twain's *Tom Sawyer* (1876), the lovely, blonde, blue-eyed little girl whom Tom chooses for his sweetheart. See also: **Sawyer, Tom**.

Thermopylae.   Literally the "hot gates," the pass in Thessaly where Leonidas and a force of 300 Spartans stood off the Persian Army in 480 B.C.; they were finally defeated through treachery. Hence by extension, any heroic, last-ditch defense against an overwhelming opposing force.

Thersites.   A misshapen, vulgar, scurrilous, troublemaking Greek soldier in the second book of **Homer**'s *Iliad*, he is roundly hated by all the heroes. A "Thersites" is one who does nothing but criticize and revile. See also: **Trojan War**.

Theseus.   Son of Aegeus, king of Athens, and Aethra. Aegeus had placed his wife and young son in Troezen in Argolis, the birthplace of Aethra, and had imposed a test of strength on him. Theseus was supposed to lift a great rock, remove from under it a sword and sandals (see **Arthur**) and carry them to Athens. He succeeded. On his way to Athens by land he had many adventures, among them the encounter with **Procrustes**. In Athens he encountered **Medea**, killed the bull that **Heracles** had brought from Crete (see **Cretan Bull**) and that was laying waste to Marathon. He volunteered to go to Crete to kill the **Minotaur** and thus end the yearly tribute of 14 young men and women exacted by King Minos as punishment for the murder of his son Androgeus in Athens. Theseus had promised his father to hoist white sails as a sign of his safe return from Crete, but he forgot and Aegeus drowned himself in grief when he saw the black sails. (The Aegean Sea is named for him.) Theseus then succeeded his father as king of Athens. He fought against the **Amazons**, married **Hippolyta**, who bore him a son, **Hippolytus**, then he sent her away and married **Phaedra**, sister of **Ariadne**. See also: **Daedalus; Labyrinth; Pasiphaë**.

Thespis.   An almost legendary Greek poet who is credited with having introduced the first actor in Greek tragedy (c. 543 B.C.). Up to his time performances had been given by only a chorus. Thespis had a speaker impersonate a character. The word *thespian*, derived from his name, is used as a noun to signify actor or an adjective to describe matters pertaining to the dramatic arts.

They toil not, neither do they spin.   See **Lilies of the field**.

Thief in the night.   Addressing the Thessalonians, Paul (see **Paul, Saint**) said: "But of the times and the seasons, brethren, ye have no need that I write to you. For yourselves know perfectly that the day of the Lord so cometh as a thief in the night" (I Thessalonians 5:1-11). The reference here is to the suddenness and surprise of Jesus' coming, not the time of day or night.

Thirty pieces of silver.   As set forth in the **New Testament, Judas Iscariot**, disciple and betrayer of Jesus, "went unto the chief priests and said unto them, What will ye give me and I will deliver him unto you? And they covenanted with him for thirty pieces of silver." After the betrayal, Judas repented, and "cast down the pieces of silver in the temple, and departed, and went and hanged himself" (Matthew 26:15; 27:3-5). Thirty pieces of silver has become the symbol of the price paid for betrayal.

Thor.   Also known as Donar ("Thunder") in Old German. God of thunder, often considered a god of war. In some areas of the Teutonic world he was held to be a son of **Odin**, in others, Odin's equal or superior. He was more renowned for his physical feats than for his mental dexterity. He often left his large palace on **Asgard** to roam over the world, frequently accompanied by **Loki**, who supplied schemes and advice. Thor possessed a number of magic objects, a hammer, a pair of iron gloves with which to hold the hammer, and a magic girdle that renewed his strength. A long list of exploits was ascribed to him, especially encounters with giants and monsters. Once his hammer was stolen as he slept, Loki discovered that the giant Thrym had stolen it and concealed it, and would return it only if he could have Freya as his wife. Loki persuaded Thor to disguise himself as Freya, go through a long pre-nuptial ceremony, and thus recover the hammer as a customary gift before the wedding. Then Thor killed Thrym and his fellow-giants. On another occasion Thor fought with the huge serpent Midgard and forced the latter to take refuge under the sea. At "The Twilight of the Gods" (Ragnarok), Thor and Midgard, who will come up from the sea for the final battle, will meet in combat again. Thor will kill the serpent but himself will die from breathing the air that has been filled with poisonous fumes emitted by Midgard. Thursday and *Donnerstag* (German for "Thursday") are named after Thor.

Thorn in the flesh.   "And lest I should be exalted above measure through the abundance of revelations, there was given me a thorn in the flesh, the messenger of **Satan** to buffet me" (II Corinthians 12:7). Saint Paul (see **Paul, Saint**) adds that he "besought the Lord thrice" to have his infirmity removed, but was told to rely instead on divine grace to endure it. It is not clear what troubled Paul; various chronic illnesses, both organic and psychosomatic, have been suggested. In common parlance, a thorn in the flesh is any chronic vexation which hampers the sufferer without completely disabling him.

Thoth.   The Egyptian god of wisdom and magic, with a human body and the head of an ibis, who developed the arts, sciences and the hieroglyph alphabet. See also: **Hermes Trismegistus**.

Thou art the man.   After the adultery of **David** with **Bathsheba** (II Samuel 11), the prophet Nathan comes before the king and tells a parable of a rich man who steals the one ewe lamb of his poor neighbor. "And David's anger was greatly kindled against the man; and he said to Nathan, As the Lord liveth, the man that hath done this thing shall surely die . . . And Nathan said to David, Thou art the man." As a punishment, David's child by Bathsheba dies.

The Three Wise Men of the East.   See **Magi**.

Through a glass darkly.   See **See through a glass darkly**.

Thwackum and Square.   The two tutors of Tom Jones (see **Jones, Tom**) and **Blifil** in Fielding's *Tom Jones* (1749). Mr. Roger Thwackum represents traditional high church doctrine regarding the natural depravity of man, and Mr. Thomas Square praises the beauty of virtue. Both are pedantic, ungenerous and hypocritical.

Tilt at windmills.   At one point in Cervantes' *Don Quixote*, the Don mistakes some windmills for evil giants, which as a knight of chivalry he is obliged to fight. He charges them with extended lance and injures himself. The phrase now means to follow an ideal, to fight imaginary foes.

Timeo Danaos et dona ferentes.   From the Latin of **Vergil**'s *Aenid* (II, 49): "I fear the Greeks even when bearing gifts"; originally referring to the **Trojan Horse** and now an expression indicating suspicion of an enemy who suddenly makes a peace offering.

A time to be born, and a time to die.   See **To everything there is a season**.

Tinker Bell.   A tiny fairy girl in James M. Barrie's *Peter Pan* (see **Pan, Peter**) (1904). She is in love with Peter and jealous of Wendy Darling.

Tintagel.   Near a small village on the northern coast of Cornwall, England, rising on cliffs above the sea, are some ruins now called Tintagel Castle. Here, according to legend, King **Arthur** was born, and here too, **Tristram** and **Isolde** (Isevlt, Isold, Isonde) are buried.

Tiny Tim Cratchit.   See **Cratchit, Bob.**

Titania.   The haughty queen of the Fairies, wife of **Oberon**, in Shakespeare's *A Midsummer Night's Dream* (1595).

Titans.   Children of **Uranus** and **Gaea**, the Titans, often called the Elder Gods, were deities of the early Greeks. They represent either primitive forces of nature or abstract qualities. **Hesiod** lists 12 as the original Titans: Six males, **Cronos, Oceanus,** Coeus, Iapetus, **Hyperion,** Crius; and six females, **Rhea,** Themis, **Mnemosyne,** Theia, **Phoebe, Tethys.** Later writers also placed some of the children of Titans among the Titans, e.g., **Prometheus,** son of Iapetus and Clymene, herself the daughter of Oceanus and Tethys. The Titans, with the exception of Oceanus, revolted against Uranus, deposed him, and made Cronos ruler of the world. Cronos married Rhea. Eventually, their children headed by **Zeus** and aided by the **Giants** and other divinities, fought for ten years against Cronos and almost all the Titans. The Titans were defeated and placed in **Tartarus.** Zeus then became ruler in place of Cronos, but by lot his brothers **Poseidon** and **Hades** received the power over the seas and the lower world respectively. The adjective "titanic"—of enormous size and power—is a reminder of the Titans' role in Greek mythology.

Toby, My Uncle.   The uncle of Tristram Shandy (see **Shandy, Tristram**) in Laurence Sterne's novel *Tristram Shandy* (1759-67). He is a kindly old soldier and a gentleman, and he delights in retelling his past military campaigns.

To everything there is a season.   "To every thing there is a season, and a time to every purpose under the heaven. A time to be born, and a time to die; a time to plant, and a time to pluck up that which is planted; a time to kill, and a time to heal; a time to break down, and a time to build up; a time to weep, and a time to laugh; a time to mourn, and a time to dance; . . . A time to get, and a time to lose; a time to keep, and a time to cast away; a time to rend, and a time to sew; a time to keep silence, and a time to speak; a time to love, and a time to hate; a time of war, and a time of peace" (Ecclesiastes 3:1-6). This much-quoted Bible passage instructs man on the harmonious ordering of human affairs.

Tophet.   A valley in southern Jerusalem. Here children were burnt alive as sacrifices to **Moloch**. At all times a flare burned at Tophet to consume the bodies of the children together with garbage and other materials deposited there. Tophet was regarded as "The very gate or pit of Hell," "the abhorrence of Jerusalem" (II Kings 23:10; Isaiah 30:33; Jeremiah 11:13). By extension, a place or condition resembling hell.

Topsy.   The mischievous, impish Negro girl in Harriet Beecher Stowe's *Uncle Tom's Cabin* (1852), who says she "just growed." Hence anything or anyone who flourished and grew without apparent tending could be said to have "grown like Topsy." See also: **Uncle Tom**.

Torah.   The scriptural writings of the Jews containing the word and revelation of God; sometimes, the **Pentateuch** alone, sometimes the entire **Old Testament** and sometimes the Old Testament and the **Talmud**.

To the pure all things are pure.   "Unto the pure all things are pure; but unto them that are defiled and unbelieving is nothing pure; but even their mind and conscience is defiled" (Titus 1:15). From Paul's epistle to Titus. Paul makes faith the crucial determinant in man's perceptions and thoughts. See also: **Paul, Saint**.

Touchstone.   The witty and satirical jester in Shakespeare's comedy *As You Like It* (1599).

Treasure in heaven.   "Lay not up for yourselves treasures upon earth where moth and rust doth corrupt, and where thieves break through and steal: But lay up for yourselves treasures in heaven where neither moth nor rust doth corrupt, and where thieves do not break through nor steal: for where your treasure is, there will your heart be also" (Matthew 6:19-21). From the

Sermon on the Mount. Thus "treasure in heaven," when used as an allusion, refers to the enduring value of spiritual wealth.

Tree of Life, Tree of Knowledge.   "And out of the ground made the Lord God, to grow every tree that is pleasant to the sight, and good for food; the *tree of life* also in the midst of the garden, and the tree of knowledge of good and evil . . ." (Genesis 2:9). The tree of life was believed to confer immortality, and the tree of knowledge, wisdom. Modern allusions to eating from the tree of knowledge usually carry the implication that knowledge can be acquired only at the cost of a tragic loss of innocence.

Trimurti.   Trimurti, which literally means three shapes, refers to the three forms taken by the godhead in Hindu mythology: **Brahma** the creator, **Vishnu** the preserver, and **Shiva** the destroyer.

Tristram   (or Tristan) **and Isolde** (or Iseult or Isoude). Tristram, a knight who lived at the time of the **Round Table**, fell passionately in love with Isolde, the daughter of the king of Ireland, but was bound by oath to obtain her hand for his uncle, King Mark of Cornwall. Mark and Isolde were married, but Tristram and Isolde continued to love one another with a hopeless love. Tristram summoned Isolde to his deathbed, instructing the messenger to hoist white sails if she consented to come and black sails if she refused. Isolde came, but Tristram was lied to and died when he heard the sails were black. Isolde collapsed and died when she saw the dead Tristram, and the lovers were buried side by side. Theirs is one of the great loves of Western literature and the subject of numerous legends and stories.

Triton.   Son of **Poseidon** and **Amphitrite**, a huge sea god in the shape of a merman, a fish below the waist and a man above it. He is usually presented in art as blowing on a shell, or conch—a "wreathed horn," in the words of Wordsworth.

Troilus and Cressida.   In **Homer**'s *Iliad* Troilus is a son of **Priam** and **Hecuba**. He is killed by **Achilles** during the **Trojan War**. The story of Troilus and Cressida stems from Latin works of the fourth and fifth centuries A.D. and from medieval writers. It was developed by many authors, notably by Chaucer in *Troilus and*

Criseyde (c. 1385), a verse romance, and by Shakespeare in the play *Troilus and Cressida* (c. 1609). In the Shakespearean play, Cressida is the daughter of **Calchas**, a Trojan priest who has defected to the Greeks (in mythology, he is a Greek). She and Troilus are in love (the corrupt **Pandarus** acts as their go-between) but are separated when the Trojans agree to give Calchas his daughter in return for three Trojans held as captives by Diomedes. Though they have exchanged pledges and tokens of eternal love and vows of constancy, Cressida soon forgets her promises and falls in love with Diomedes. Her name has become a byword for fickleness.

Trojan Horse. In the tenth year of the **Trojan War**, despairing of taking the city by storm, the Greeks resorted to a stratagem. They had an artisan fashion a huge wooden horse, inside which armed men were concealed. The fleet then sailed away, ostensibly for Greece but actually to an island nearby. As told by **Vergil** (*Aeneid*, II) they left behind a pretended deserter named Sinon who convinced the Trojans that the horse was an offering to the goddess **Athena** to expiate the sins they had committed against her and that, if it were taken into the city, Troy would be safe. The Trojans had to make a breach in the walls to get the huge horse into the city, and at night Sinon released the men, who then sacked and burned the city. In the meantime the fleet had returned. The expression "Trojan horse" means a gift or offering made to worm one's way into the confidence of another and then to harm the recipient. See **Timeo Danaos et dona ferentes.**

Trojan War. The war waged for 10 years by the Greeks against the Trojans in order to regain Helen (see **Helen of Troy**), the wife of the Greek Prince **Menelaus**, who had been abducted by the Trojan Prince **Paris**. See also: **Achilles**; *Aeneid*; **Homer**; *Iliad*; **Judgment of Paris**; *Odyssey*; **Trojan Horse**; **Troy**.

Trotwood, Betsey. The great-aunt of David in Charles Dickens' *David Copperfield* (1850). Beneath her brusque exterior, she is kind and compassionate, keeping David with her after he comes to her from London. She becomes his benefactress and loving guide.

Troy. The rich and powerful ancient city (also called Ilion or Troja) in what is now northwestern Turkey near modern Hissarlik.

It was the site of the **Trojan War**. Heinrich Schliemann (1822-1890) excavated the site, and discovered, in descending strata, six cities, including the Homeric (see **Homer**) Troy.

The truth shall make you free. "Ye shall know the truth, and the truth shall make you free" (John 8:32). Christ's promise to the Jews that they would find freedom and salvation through knowledge of the truth. It continues to be cited in a wide variety of contexts.

Tubalcain. The first smith, and "instructor of every artificer in brass and iron" (Genesis 4:22).

Tulliver, Maggie. Heroine of George Eliot's *The Mill on the Floss* (1860). Wild and impetuous, Maggie is an outsider in a provincial society. After a series of interfamily and personal conflicts, Maggie is suspected of having designs on her cousin's fiancé, whereas she loves the crippled Philip Wakem, son of a rival family. She is reconciled with her harsh brother Tom before they are drowned in a flooding river.

Tupman, Tracy. A well-fed, well-groomed young man in Charles Dickens' *Pickwick Papers* (1837), in constant amorous infatuation and usually in trouble. See also: **Pickwick**.

Turn the other cheek. "I say unto you, That ye resist not evil: but whosoever shall smite thee on thy right cheek, turn to him the other also" (Matthew 5:39; cf. Luke 6:29). One of the proof-texts for Christian pacifism, the expression has come to mean to offer no resistance to or retaliation for violence.

Tweedledum and Tweedledee. John Byrom (1692-1763), poet and deviser of an early shorthand system, invented these names to satirize two schools of music whose differences were so small as to be negligible; the phrase is now used to denote two persons nearly identical in habits, opinions. Lewis Carroll and used them in his *Alice in Wonderland* (1865). See also: **Alice**.

Twilight of the Gods. See **Götterdämmerung**.

Twist, Oliver.   Hero of Charles Dickens' *Oliver Twist* (1839). A maltreated and helpless workhouse foundling, he is exploited and abused until rescued by Mr. Brownlow (see **Brownlow, Mr.**).

Two-edged sword.   "All iniquity is a two edged sword, the wounds whereof cannot be healed" (Ecclesiastes 21:23). The expression is applied to an argument or a policy that cuts both ways, and so may harm either proponent or opponent.

Tybalt.   The hot-headed nephew of Lady **Capulet** and Juliet's cousin, in Shakespeare's ***Romeo and Juliet*** (1594). He kills **Mercutio** and is later killed in turn by Romeo.

U

Ubermensch. In German, "overman," or the **superman.** The term first appears in Goethe's *Faust* (1808, 1833) to characterize the exceptional, highly gifted, dynamic individual. It is a central concept in the philosophy of Nietzsche, embodied in the transcendent man he delineated in *Thus Spake Zarathustra* (1883-91). The term was vulgarized and distorted by Hitler and the Nazis, and now is commonly understood as the "Blond Beast" of Aryan supremacy.

Ultima Thule. In Latin, "farthest Thule" (Vergil's *Georgics*, I, 30). To the Romans Ultima Thule was the name of the northernmost limit of the world, a land reached by sailing north from Britain for six days—possibly to Shetland or the northern coast of Norway. Hence, any faraway place, the ends of the earth, the farthest point in a journey.

Ulysses. See **Odysseus.**

Uncas. The son of **Chingachgook**, the Mohican chief in James Fenimore Cooper's *The Last of the Mohicans* (1826). Literally the last of his kind, he is killed by Magua in defense of his love, Cora.

Uncle Tom. An old Negro slave who is the central figure in Harriet Beecher Stowe's *Uncle Tom's Cabin* (1852). He suffers much under Simon Legree (see **Legree, Simon**), remains devoted to **Little Eva**, and retains his dignity. In contemporary American usage, an "Uncle Tom" is a subservient Negro who gets by in a hostile, racist environment by adopting an abject and servile attitude toward the white man.

Unicorn. In Latin, "one horn," a fabled animal described by medieval writers as having a lion's tail, a stag's legs and a horse's head and body, with one horn growing from the middle of its forehead. It was said to be ferocious, and catchable only by putting before it a young virgin, before whom the unicorn would lie down and allow itself to be taken. The unicorn's horn was much prized for its magical properties.

Upanishads. A section of the Vedas, or sacred scriptures of Hinduism, dating from the 10th century B.C. Of the 118 existing texts, 18 are recognized as authentic. They contain the basic doctrines of the religion: that the Godhead, or Brahma, is without attribute, that although his nature is incommunicable, it may be realized, that the personal self, or *atman*, is originally part of the Godhead, but has been separated from it by imperfect knowledge and experience, that the obligation of each individual is to realize this original oneness by means of extensive and complex spiritual, moral and physical disciplines.

Uranus. Personification of the heavens. **Gaea** (the Earth), emerging from primal chaos, produced Uranus and then coupled with him to produce, among others, the **Titans**. **Cronos**, a Titan, separated heaven from earth. Uranus is also the name given to one of the planets in the solar system.

Utopia. Literally, Greek for "no place." Colloquially, an ideal, perfect human society. Various utopias have been described, by Plato in his *Republic*; by Sir Thomas More (who first used the word) in his *Utopia* (1516); by Francis Bacon in *New Atlantis* (1627); by Samuel Butler in *Erewhon* (1872); by Edward Bellamy in *Looking Backward (2000-1887)*, published in 1897. The "Utopias" of Aldous Huxley's **Brave New World** (1932) and George Orwell's *1984* (1949) are actually "dystopias," or antiutopias.

V

Valentine, Jimmy. The burglar-protagonist of O. Henry's short story "A Retrieved Reformation" (in *Roads of Destiny*, 1909). Hence an ingenious thief.

Valhalla. The banqueting hall of the Norse gods, where fallen warriors went after death. Hence, a kind of heaven.

Valjean, Jean. The hero of Victor Hugo's (1802-85) *Les Misérables* (1862); prototype of the poor man subjected to the injustices of a rigid social system. See also: **Javert, M.**

Vanity Fair. William Makepeace Thackeray's 1848 novel depicts a panorama of manners and mores in early 19th-century England. The "heroine" of the novel (which is subtitled "a novel without a hero") is the opportunistic, shrewd and amoral Becky Sharp (see **Sharp, Becky**), whose attempts to stay at the top of the fashionable world end in frustration. The title is taken from the Fair in John Bunyan's *Pilgrim's Progress* (1678), at which all kinds of worldly possessions and pleasures are sold. Contemporary usage equates "Vanity Fair" with the materialistic world.

Vedas. The most ancient of the Hindu sacred texts. See also: **Upanishads.**

Venus. See **Aphrodite.**

Vergil (or Virgil). Publius Vergilius Maro (70 B.C.-19 B.C.) was the preeminent poet of the Augustan Age in Rome; he is renowned as the author of the *Eclogues*, the *Georgics* and, especially, the *Aeneid*. The *Aeneid*, one of the greatest works of western literature, is an epic poem recounting the mythical founding of Rome by **Aeneas**. Vergil celebrated the simple virtues of honor, courage and piety.

Vertumnus.   Latin rustic god associated with the changes of season and the ripening of fruit and grain. His bride was **Pomona**, goddess of fruit trees.

Vestal virgins.   The virgins chosen to serve in the temple of Vesta (**Hestia**). Their training began before age 10 and lasted 10 years; their actual service in the temple lasted for another 10, and instruction of new vestals for 10 more. The virgins, sworn to purity, had the primary duty of keeping the sacred fire of the goddess burning on the altar. Grave penalties were imposed on the vestals if they broke their vows, and equally grave ones on anyone who insulted them. Today, often used ironically for questionably virtuous female characters.

Via Dolorosa.   The Via Dolorosa (Latin "sad road") is a street in Jerusalem, believed to be the one traversed by Jesus on his way to **Calvary**; sometimes applied by analogy to any painful suffering.

Vials of wrath.   "And one of the four beasts gave unto the seven angels seven golden vials full of the wrath of God . . . and I heard a great voice out of the temple saying to the seven angels, Go your ways and pour out the vials of the wrath of God upon the earth" (Revelation 15:8; 16:1). In the apocalyptic visions of the *Book of Revelation* (see **Apocalypse**), the seven vials of wrath bring plagues and calamity to the earth, recalling the plagues inflicted on Egypt (see **Plagues of Egypt**). The author, writing in a time of persecution, believed that the troubles of his day were the upheavals which would precede the **Last Judgment** and the establishment of the **New Jerusalem**. In modern usage, to empty the vials of one's wrath means simply to discharge one's anger. See also: **John, Saint**.

Viola.   Heroine of Shakespeare's *Twelfth Night* (1600). Shipwrecked on the coast of Ilyria, she disguises herself as a young man and becomes entangled in a web of amorous intrigues. One of the quick-witted, eloquent heroines characteristic of Shakespeare's comedies.

Vishnu.   Of the Hindu "trimurti," or three forms of the godhead, Vishnu is the preserver, in contrast to **Shiva**, the destroyer, and **Brahma**, the creator. He is described as having four arms, carrying in them a club, a lotus, a discus and a shell. In general, he is a kindly, benevolent god.

Voice crying in the wilderness.   "In those days came **John the Baptist**, preaching in the wilderness of Judaea, And saying, Repent ye: for the kingdom of heaven is at hand. For this is he that was spoken of by the prophet Esaias, saying, The voice of one crying in the wilderness. Prepare ye the way of the Lord, make his paths straight" (Matthew 3:3; repeated in Mark 1:3; Luke 3:4; John 1:23; From Isaiah 40:3). An important **New Testament** prophecy about the advent of Christ and how this was prefigured in the **Old Testament**. Today, "a voice crying in the wilderness" generally refers to any prophet who is not listened to.

The voice of the turtle is heard in the land.   "For, lo, the winter is past, the rain is over and gone. The flowers appear on the earth; and time of the singing of birds is come, and the voice of the turtle is heard in our land; the fig tree putteth forth her green figs, and the vines with the tender grape give a good smell" (Song of Songs 2:11-13). Today, a metaphor for the coming of spring. The "turtle" is not the shell-encased reptile but the turtledove, a bird.

Volpone.   "The fox," Italian hero of Ben Jonson's *Volpone* (1605). A master of deception and disguise, he sets out to cheat a crooked lawyer, a merchant and a miser. His ally in deception is his servant Mosca, "the fly." Synonymous today with slyness and ingenious chicanery.

Volsunga Saga.   A major collection of Scandinavian prose legends; it provided much of the source material for the German ***Nibelungenlied***, with some variation in names and plot.

Vronsky, Count Alexey Kirilich.   The polished, wealthy officer in Count Leo Tolstoy's (1828-1910) *Anna Karenina* (1875-76) who loves Anna (see **Karenina, Anna**) and elopes with her.

Generous, brilliant socially, even artistic within the limits of his class, he comports himself according to the accepted social code in his adulterous affair with Anna and wishes, even more than she, to legitimize it. He deteriorates after Anna's suicide. A classic portrait of the passionate, adulterous lover doomed to a tragic end.

Vulcan.   See **Hephaestus**.

Vulgate.   From the Latin, *editio vulgata*, "spread among the people." The Latin translation of the Bible, made chiefly by St. Jerome between 382 and 384, is the authorized version of the Roman Catholic Church; "vulgate" in general today means any accepted text of any work, or any work in common use.

Vye, Eustacia.   In Thomas Hardy's *The Return of the Native* (1878), the selfish and sensual woman who, bored with her home life on a heath, seeks escape by marrying Clym Yeobright (see **Yeobright, Clym**). He refuses to leave the heath. She then approaches an earlier suitor, but cannot be unfaithful, and hence commits suicide. English literature's gallery of "femmes fatales" is richer for her portrait.

W

The wages of sin. "The wages of sin is death; but the gift of God is eternal life through Jesus Christ our Lord" (Romans 6:23). In his epistle to the Romans, **Paul** sets forth this statement concerning sin and redemption. The contemporary use of the first four words is often lightly ironic: the wages of sin may be any twinge of moral or physical discomfort.

Wailing wall. The wall in Jerusalem said to be the only part of the temple of **Solomon** left standing after the destruction of the city by the Romans. At this wall the Jews lamented the fall of their nation. Visitors to Jerusalem today revere this monument as one of the holy places of Judaism; it is customary to slip prayers written on bits of paper into the cracks between the wall's stones.

Walden. The title of Henry David Thoreau's classic account (published in 1854) of his life near Walden Pond, living close to nature. It has become synonymous with the idea of solitary communion with nature in a life free of the values of materialistic civilization.

Walls of Jericho. See **Jericho.**

Walpurgisnacht. In German folklore, the Walpurgisnacht falls between April 30 and May 1, when a host of devils and monsters disport themselves in orgies on the highest peak in the Black Forest. In pagan days these rituals marked the May Day eve, the beginning of summer. In Christian times the day was renamed for the birthday of St. Walpurgis (died 780), which fell on April 30. The Walpurgisnacht has become synonymous with any general revelry, and particularly for the breaking out of demonic lewdness and disorder, as in Part One of Goethe's *Faust*.

Wandering Jew.   The Jew said to have denied Christ any rest on his way to the Cross, and to have taunted him to move more quickly. He was consequently condemned to wander the earth until Christ's second coming. Reappearing in folk legends in various guises, he undergoes changes in character, sometimes appearing as a wise man who urges repentance and righteousness on others. The legend has been the subject of modern literary treatments, the most famous of which is Eugene Sue's *The Wandering Jew* (1845).

Watson, Dr.   The companion of renowned detective Sherlock Holmes (see **Holmes, Sherlock**). Prototype of the "assistant sleuth," what Watson lacks in brilliance, he makes up for in loyalty and readiness to accompany Holmes and face any perils, mental or physical, that will lead to the solution of the "case."

The way of a man with a maid.   "There be three things which are too wonderful for me, yea, four which I know not: The way of an eagle in the air; the way of a serpent upon a rock; the way of a ship in the midst of the sea; and the way of a man with a maid" (Proverbs 30:18-19). In contemporary usage, a reference to the power (and sometimes the mystery) of the relationship between the sexes.

Way of transgressors.   "Good understanding giveth favor: but the way of transgressors is hard" (Proverbs 13:15). In modern usage, one of many Biblical injunctions against sinning.

Weaker vessel.   "Likewise, ye husbands, dwell with them according to knowledge, giving honor unto the wife, as unto the weaker vessel, and as being heirs together of the grace of life . . ." (I Peter 3:7). Peter regards the wife as physically weak and socially subordinate to her husband, though not on that account less holy, or excluded from the "grace of life." The word vessel, as applied to persons, suggests that they are useful instruments and the receptacles of divine grace. "Weaker vessel" is now taken as a less than flattering term for woman and has lost its implication of receptacle for grace. The phrase is not popular with feminists and others who oppose sexism.

Weeping and gnashing of teeth. "Many shall come from the east and the west, and shall sit down with Abraham, and Isaac, and Jacob, in the kingdom of heaven. But the children of the kingdom shall be cast out into outer darkness: there shall be weeping and gnashing of teeth" (Matthew 8:11-12; Last phrase repeated in 13:28). A prophecy of the **Last judgment**; in this passage Jesus contrasts the faith of a Roman centurion with the disbelief of his own countrymen. "Weeping and gnashing of teeth" is used today in any general reference to frustration or grief.

Weird Sisters, The. The three witches in Shakespeare's *Macbeth* (1605) who make prophecies about Macbeth's future.

"Well done, thou good and faithful servant." See **Parable of the talents**.

Weller, Sam. The witty and loyal cockney servant of Mr. **Pickwick** in Charles Dickens' *Pickwick Papers* (1837). He is full of proverbs, aphorisms and anecdotes, and embodies in comic form the cockney life and personality.

Werther. The hero of Johann Wolfgang von Goethe's novel *The Sorrows of Young Werther* (1744), one of the important works of the German *Sturm und Drang* movement. Werther, a prototype of the Romantic hero, is a painter-diplomat; a nature enthusiast, he hates the artificiality and hypocrisy of society. He falls in love with a girl already bethrothed to another; after her marriage he cannot free himself from her and is driven to suicide.

"What hath God wrought." Famous as the first message sent by telegraph, May 28, 1844. In Biblical context (Numbers 23:23), meaning "what deeds has God performed!" "Wrought" is an archaic past participle of "work."

What is man? "What is man, that thou art mindful of him? . . . For thou hast made him a little lower than the angels, and hast crowned him with glory and honor. Thou madest him to have domination over the works of thy hands: thou hast put all things under his feet"

(Psalms 8:4-6; 144:3-4; Hebrews 2:6-8). This psalm (in the King James version) is quoted by those who believe in a hierarchy of beings beginning with God and descending through the angels and man to the beasts, a concept systematized in the 17th and 18th centuries as the Great Chain of Being.

What is truth?   "Jesus answered, . . . To this end was I born, and for this cause came I unto the world, that I should bear witness unto the truth . . . . Pilate saith unto him, What is truth?" (John 18:37-38). This episode perfectly expresses the confrontation of the man of faith and the skeptic. The familiar phrase "jesting Pilate" is from Francis Bacon's *Essays* (1597-1625), in allusion to this passage.

White elephant.   The sacred animal of Thailand, formerly Siam, is the white elephant. When the king wished to cause someone's ruin, he gave him a white elephant, which was very expensive and brought no profit. Hence a "white elephant" is an object, hobby or luxury ruinously expensive to maintain.

White Rabbit.   A character in *Alice in Wonderland* (1865) by Lewis Carroll. **Alice**'s pursuit of the rabbit leads her down the rabbit hole and lands her in Wonderland. The rabbit is always in a hurry, pulling his watch from his waistcoat and saying things like, "Oh my ears and whiskers, how late it's getting!" A comparison to the White Rabbit would suggest a self-important and vaguely ridiculous character, always very busy doing something that is not clear.

Whither thou goest, I will go.   "And Naomi said unto her two daughters in law, Go, return each to her mother's house . . . . Turn again, my daughters, go your way . . . And Orpah kissed her mother in law, but Ruth clave unto her, . . . and said, Intreat me not to leave thee, or to return from following after thee: for whither thou goest, I will go; and where thou lodgest, I will lodge: thy people shall be my people, and thy God my God. Where thou diest, will I die, and there will I be buried: the Lord do so to me, and more also, if ought but death part thee and me . . ." (Ruth 1:1-22). Ruth's devoted following of her mother-in-law to Bethlehem has, by extension, come to stand for all devotion.

Whore of Babylon.   See **Babylon, Scarlet whore of**.

Whoring after other gods. "They went a whoring after other gods, and bowed themselves unto them" (Judges 2:17). A reference to worship of Canaanite gods by the Israelites. Since the other gods in question were worshipped with fertility rites and cult prostitution, this passage was not originally understood metaphorically as at present, when it is applied in the general sense of "selling out." See also: **Canaan**.

Wife, Lot's. See **Lot**.

Wife, Potiphar's. See **Joseph and Potiphar's wife**.

Wife of Bath, The. In *The Canterbury Tales*, the 14th-century masterpiece of Geoffrey Chaucer, the Wife of Bath is an earthy, robust and much-married woman who recounts her own story in a famous prologue that overshadows the tale she tells. Hence any earthy female with an attraction for matrimony.

Wind of Doctrine. "Henceforth be no more children, tossed to and fro, and carried about with every wind of doctrine" (Ephesians 4:14). **Paul** is assuring the Ephesians that belief in Christ anchors one and protects one from changing one's beliefs on a whim or according to the latest fashion.

Witch of Endor. See **Endor, Witch of**.

Wodin. Anglo-Saxon form of the name **Odin**.

Woman taken in adultery. See **Go and sin no more**.

Wooden horse. See **Trojan Horse**.

Wormwood and gall. "I will feed them, even this people, with wormwood, and give them water of gall to drink" (Jeremiah 9:15; 23:15; cf. Deuteronomy 29:18). The secretions of the gall bladder have always been a symbol of bitterness. Wormwood is the bitter herb, *Artemisia absinthium*. God is thus punishing the Jews for their transgressions by making them drink deep of bitterness—a meaning the phrase retains in contemporary allusion.

X & Y

Xantippe. **Socrates'** nagging wife. Hence any shrew.

Yahoo. The tribe of brutes in Jonathan Swift's satire *Gulliver's Travels* (1726); they have human form and embody the vices and most degraded aspects of the human race. They are the subjects of the superior **Houyhnhnms**, a noble race of horses who live by the dictates of reason. Nowadays a yahoo is a ruffian, boor or, in certain American usage, a yokel. See also: **Gulliver**.

Yahweh. The ancient Hebrew name for God.

Yeobright, Clym. The idealistic hero of Thomas Hardy's novel *The Return of the Native* (1878). A successful and educated man, he returns to the bleak English heath where he grew up only to see his life blasted by an unhappy marriage to passionate and difficult Eustacia Vye (see **Vye, Eustacia**).

Yggdrasil. A gigantic ash tree symbolic of the world. Its foliage always remained green, one root reached far down into the nether world, its boughs ascended to heaven. Another underground root was a source of streams, while wisdom flowed from a fountain emanating from still another root. On the topmost branches was a golden rooster that warned the gods of danger, while below the tree was a horn that would announce the final battle. Animals, demons and monsters gnawed away at the tree, but the **Norns**, who lived under the third root, constantly renewed the destroyed parts.

Ymir.   The first of all living things, father of the giants. From under his left arm came man and woman. Then came giants who killed Ymir, and from his body parts came the various parts of the Scandinavian universe, including earth, sky, sea, forests, mountains.

Yoknapatawpha County.   A county in Mississippi invented by William Faulkner. It serves as the locale for the action in some of his novels, including *Sartoris* (1929), *The Sound and the Fury* (1929), *As I Lay Dying* (1930) and *Absalom, Absalom!* (1936). Faulkner describes Yoknapatawpha County in realistic terms: its history, geography, sociology and people. He invests it with much realistic detail, and populates it with a wide spectrum of human types.

Yorick.   (1) In Shakespeare's *Hamlet* (c. 1600), the jester of Hamlet's father; Hamlet knew him as a boy. Hamlet comes upon his skull in the famous gravediggers' scene (V, i), and, holding Yorick's skull in his hand, he utters the famous line, "Alas, poor Yorick!" thus beginning a speech in which he recalls the happy times he spent with Yorick when he was alive. (2) An absurd and fanciful clergyman in Laurence Sterne's *Tristram Shandy* (1759-1767) (see **Shandy, Tristram**).

Young Lochinvar.   See **Lochinvar**.

Yum-Yum.   The ward of **Ko-Ko**, the Lord High Executioner, in W.S. Gilbert and Arthur Sullivan's operetta *The Mikado* (1885). Though she is supposed to marry her protector, she loves **Nanki-Poo**, the emperor's son. Through various comic stratagems, the lovers remove the obstacles in their path and, in the end, marry.

Z

Zephyrus. The god of the west wind; also the wind itself.

Zeus. The most powerful god of the Greeks, ruler of the heavens. Identified with Jupiter (hence **Jove**) by the Romans. Son of **Cronos** and **Rhea**, brother of **Hades, Poseidon, Demeter, Hera** and **Hestia**, and husband of Hera. He and his brothers overthrew their father and divided the world by lot, Zeus gaining the heavens and upper world. With the help of the **Giants** and **Prometheus**, Zeus conquered the **Titans**. Zeus was the supreme ruler of the gods but could not overrule the **Fates** nor could he always dictate to Hades or Poseidon. Within these limits he presided over the destinies of man, was looked upon as the giver of laws, the dispenser of justice, the father of gods and men. He was the wielder of the thunderbolt, the hurler of lightning, wore the aegis (the shield bearing the head of the **Gorgon**), and carried the scepter; his favorite bird was the eagle. Before (and after) he married Hera, Zeus had many amorous adventures. Hence his name stands for a kind of legendary master of amours, as well as the mythological father of gods and men. **Phidias**' statue of Zeus was considered one of the **Seven wonders of the ancient world**.